Strike the Blow
for Freedom

Reverend Jeremiah Asher

Strike the Blow for Freedom

The 6th United States Colored Infantry in the Civil War

By

James M. Paradis

WHITE MANE BOOKS

This White Mane Books publication
was printed by
Beidel Printing House, Inc.
63 West Burd Street
Shippensburg, PA 17257-0152 USA

In respect for the scholarship contained herein, the acid-free paper used in this book meets the guidelines for permanence and durability of the Committee on Production Guidelines for Book Longevity of the Council on Library Resources.

For a complete list of available publications
please write
White Mane Books
Division of White Mane Publishing Company, Inc.
P.O. Box 152
Shippensburg, PA 17257-0152 USA

Library of Congress Cataloging-in-Publication Data

Paradis, James M., 1949-
    Strike the blow for freedom : the 6th United States Colored
Infantry in the Civil War / by James M. Paradis.
        p.   cm.
    Includes bibliographical references (p.   ) and index.
    ISBN 1-57249-136-1 (alk. paper)
    1. United States. Army. Colored Infantry Regiment, 6th
(1863-1865) 2. United States--History--Civil War, 1861-1865-
-Regimental histories. 3. United States--History--Civil War,
1861-1865--Participation, Afro-American. 4. Afro-American soldiers-
-History--19th century. I. Title.
E492.94 6th.P37   1998
973.7'415--dc21   98-20365
                                                                CIP

E492.94
6th
.P37
1998

> **"WHO WOULD BE FREE**
> **THEMSELVES MUST STRIKE THE BLOW"**
>
> Frederick Douglass

CONTENTS

LIST OF ILLUSTRATIONS ix

LIST OF MAPS x

LIST OF TABLES xi

LIST OF GRAPHS xii

INTRODUCTION xiv

ACKNOWLEDGEMENTS xvi

CHAPTER

    1. Background 1

    2. Recruitment 5

    3. Camp William Penn 13

    4. The Men 32

    5. They Also Serve 40

    6. The Assault on Petersburg 48

    7. Dutch Gap 61

    8. New Market Heights 69

    9. The Last Campaigns 80

    10. Closing the Books 90

APPENDIXES

    A. Psychological Wounds 95

    B. Statistical Tables and Graphs 100

    C. Field and Staff Officers: 6th Regiment of United States
       Colored Infantry 137

    D. Muster Roll: 6th Regiment of United States Colored Infantry 138

NOTES 180
BIBLIOGRAPHY 193
INDEX 199

ILLUSTRATIONS

Reverend Jeremiah Asher .... frontispiece

Regimental Flag, 6th USCI, Obverse 24

Regimental Flag, 6th USCI, Reverse 25

Colonel John W. Ames 33

Reverend Jeremiah Asher 35

Dutch Gap — Beginning the Canal 62

Dutch Gap Canal — Fall 1864 68

John McMurray 70

Nathan Edgerton 73

Alexander Kelly 74

Thomas Hawkins 74

MAPS

Philadelphia, October 6, 1863 30

Virginia, 1863–1865 39

Dutch Gap 65

Battle of New Market Heights 78

Fort Fisher Campaign 85

TABLES

1. Numbers of Volunteers, Draftees, and Substitutes 100
2. Percentages of Volunteers, Draftees, and Substitutes 101
3. Distribution of Ages by Number of Men 105
4. Distribution of Ages by Percentage 106
5. Distribution of Heights 109
6. Birthplaces of the Men of 6th USCT 112
7. Birthplaces and Numbers of Men from Each, Reported
   by Company 113
8. Occupations of Men of 6th USCI 120
9. Number of Men per Occupation for 6th USCI 121

GRAPHS

1. Distribution of Ages of Volunteers in 6th USCI 101
2. Distribution of Ages of Draftees in 6th USCI 102
3. Distribution of Ages of Substitutes in 6th USCI 102
4. Cumulative Distribution of Ages of Draftees 103
4a. Cumulative Distribution of Ages of Volunteers 103
4b. Cumulative Distribution of Ages of Substitutes 104
5. Distribution of Ages of Volunteers, Draftees, and Substitutes 104
6. Distribution of Ages of Men in Regiment 108
7. Distribution of Ages of Men in Regiment 108
8. Cumulative Distribution of Ages 109
9. Distribution of Heights 111
10. Cumulative Distribution of Heights 111
11. Birthplaces, 6th USCI 114
12. Birthplaces, Company A 115
13. Birthplaces, Company B 115
14. Birthplaces, Company C 116
15. Birthplaces, Company D 116
16. Birthplaces, Company E 117
17. Birthplaces, Company F 117
18. Birthplaces, Company G 118
19. Birthplaces, Company H 118
20. Birthplaces, Company I 119
21. Birthplaces, Company K 119
22. Occupations, 6th USCI 123
23. Occupations, Company A 124

24. Occupations, Company B 124
25. Occupations, Company C 125
26. Occupations, Company D 125
27. Occupations, Company E 126
28. Occupations, Company F 126
29. Occupations, Company G.. 127
30. Occupations, Company H 127
31. Occupations, Company I 128
32. Occupations, Company K.. 128
33. Cumulative Numbers Mustering In 129
34. Cumulative Numbers of Deserters 129
35. Number of Men Separating from Regiment prior to Muster
    Out Date 130
36. Number of Men Joining, Separating from, and Remaining with
    Regiment 130
37. Fates of Commissioned Officers and Enlisted Men 131
38. Cumulative Losses, Company A 131
39. Cumulative Losses, Company B 132
40. Cumulative Losses, Company C 132
41. Cumulative Losses, Company D 133
42. Cumulative Losses, Company E 133
43. Cumulative Losses, Company F.. 134
44. Cumulative Losses, Company G 134
45. Cumulative Losses, Company H 135
46. Cumulative Losses, Company I 135
47. Cumulative Losses, Company K 136

INTRODUCTION

Strike the Blow for Freedom is a study of a regiment of African American Troops recruited in Philadelphia during the American Civil War, The 6th Regiment of United States Colored Infantry. It follows the recruitment and training of these troops and reveals their contribution to the Union war effort. This book also examines the men who made up the regiment, using the original muster records and Samuel P. Bates' *History of Pennsylvania Volunteers* to present a picture of the individual characteristics of the men in the ranks and of their sacrifices in this conflict.

Regimental Histories of Civil War units are indeed abundant. Few specific studies have been made, however, of African American troops in the war. Until recently, even the most comprehensive general studies of that war tended to ignore the military role of black Americans.

In 1913 Frank H. Taylor published his detailed volume, *Philadelphia in the Civil War, 1861–1865* (Philadelphia: Published by the City, 1913). A major section of that book lists all of the regiments raised in Philadelphia and summarizes their involvement in the war. After the author recounts the exploits of the white units, he then includes a segment dedicated to "Army Bands" from Philadelphia. Following this musical interlude Taylor lists the regiments of "Colored Troops" raised in the city and describes their contributions. Although the long-term white units each receive between one and four pages of description, the black regiments each receive but one paragraph, with the sole exception of the 6th United States Colored Infantry which rates two full paragraphs.

Another glaring inequity occurs when Taylor lists the Medal of Honor winners from Philadelphia units. For the United States Colored Troops, only the white officers are listed. None of the black enlisted men, even noncommissioned officers, who won this honor are mentioned. The lack of recognition given to the contributions of African American troops from Philadelphia motivated the research for *Strike the Blow for Freedom* as a doctoral dissertation at Temple University.

xiv

The 6th USCI faced many hardships common to "colored troops" in the Civil War. Black soldiers in general tended to receive more heavy labor assignments than did white troops. This was true for the 6th, which was assigned to the arduous task of digging the infamous Dutch Gap Canal near Richmond. As the men labored at the grueling task of moving tons of earth by hand, Confederate artillery added to their misery by lobbing shells at them.

A number of black regiments suffered heavy casualties, sometimes in costly frontal assaults. The 6th shared this experience, most notably in their assault through withering rifle fire at New Market Heights, Virginia. Sixteen African Americans were awarded the Congressional Medal of Honor for their actions in the Civil War. Sergeants Alexander Kelly (often misspelled "Kelley") and Thomas R. Hawkins, black noncommissioned officers in the 6th, and Captain Nathan Edgerton, a white officer of the regiment, won this award in the desperate fighting at New Market Heights.

Captain John McMurray, Chaplain Jeremiah Asher, and other members of the regiment put down their thoughts and feelings in letters and diaries, and a few have been preserved for us. Reverend Asher stands as one of only twelve African American clergymen to be appointed regimental chaplain during the war. His writing bears special importance because black soldiers, whether from the North or South, were usually deprived of the opportunity for formal education and of the chance to tell their own story. Through those words that have been passed down to us, as well as official records of the regiment and news reports of the time, you will retrace here the footsteps of the men who marched forth to strike the blow for freedom.

CHAPTER 1

BACKGROUND

Each soldier who goes to war does so ultimately for his own private reasons. When Southern guns opened fire on Fort Sumter, thousands of Northerners rallied to support the nation's war effort. Some of the more idealistic volunteers were driven either by an angry impulse to avenge the assault on their flag or by a fervent resolve to restore their beloved Union. For African Americans, however, even at the war's outset, this conflict had deeper meaning.

Black volunteers stepped forward from many quarters. But they were told that this was to be "a White man's war." It was to be a war to preserve the Union, and not a war against slavery. The government pronounced the preservation of the Union to be the official war aim, and the general populace of the North agreed.

President Abraham Lincoln knew that the Northern public would support a war to save the Union. He also knew that he could not count on that support for a war to end black slavery or for a war that employed black troops. This was especially true in the border regions, those slave states that both remained in the Union and contributed troops to the war effort. In rejecting the use of black troops in the summer of 1862 Lincoln argued that "...the nation could not afford to lose Kentucky at this crisis...," and that arming Blacks "would turn 50,000 bayonets from the loyal Border States against us that were for us."[1]

The black men of Pittsburgh, Pennsylvania who composed the "Hannibal Guards" offered their services on April 17, 1861, with the words:

> ...although deprived of all of our political rights, we yet wish the government of the United States to be sustained against the tyranny of slavery, and are willing to assist in any honorable way or manner to sustain the present Administration.[2]

Blacks organized and drilled as a company in Boston and petitioned the Massachusetts legislature to accept them into the militia. The legislature did not respond.[3] Mob violence was threatened against black citizens of Cincinnati when they sought to organize a militia unit.[4] Enthusiastic Blacks in New York City rented a hall to practice military drill but had to abandon their activity in the face of a police order and a similar threat of mob violence.[5] Not dissuaded by this rebuff, other black New Yorkers offered three entire regiments to the state and promised to provide the arms, clothing, and equipment and even the pay and provisions for these troops from the contributions of that state's black citizens. Even when these troops were offered to fight for the duration of the war, Governor Horatio Seymour, a Democrat unsympathetic to the antislavery movement, did not accept the offer.[6] Offers by Blacks across the nation to defend the government met with indifference at best.[7]

But the militant abolitionist William Lloyd Garrison saw in the nature of this war the force that would change the place of black people in America and the attitudes of government and the general public. Garrison read between the lines for a Quaker friend:

> Technically, the war is to restore the old state of things—fugitive slave law and all; practically, it is a geographical fight between North and South, and between free and slave institutions. Of the great body of soldiers who have enlisted at the North, comparatively few have any intention or wish to break down the Slave System; but God "who is above all and greater than all," and who—"moves in a mysterious way, his wonders to perform;" is making use of them to do "a strange and terrible work" in righteousness! [8]

Frederick Douglass even more emphatically argued that saving the Union and destroying slavery were inexorably linked. He pronounced: "The Republic has put one end of the chain upon the ankle of the bondman, and the other end about its own neck." He contended:

> The American people and the Government at Washington may refuse to recognize it for a time; but the "inexorable logic of events" will force it upon them in the end; that the war now being waged in this land is a war for and against slavery; and that it can never be effectually put down till one or the other of these vital forces is completely destroyed.[9]

As one bloody battle followed another, the thousands of deaths and maimings became tens of thousands, then hundreds of thousands. Hope faded for an early end to the war. As early as December 1861 in an address to Congress, Lincoln showed hints of his frustration with the course of the war and with the failure of the limited policy he had imposed upon himself for executing the war. He told the Congress that he did not want the war to become a "remorseless revolutionary struggle." He did not want to abruptly tear apart the social and economic fibers of the South. That is why, he explained:

I have therefore, in every case, thought it proper to keep the integrity of the Union prominent as the primary object of the contest on our part, leaving all questions which are not of vital military importance to the more deliberate action of the legislature.[10]

But emancipation and employment of black troops soon became a matter of "vital military importance." Lincoln had already resolved: "I shall not surrender this game leaving any available card unplayed."[11] By mid-1862 a frustrated Lincoln admitted: "We had about played our last card, and must change our tactics or lose the war."[12]

Congress, however, acted faster than did Lincoln. On July 17, 1862, Congress replaced the section of the seventy-year-old militia act that barred Blacks from military participation with legislation empowering the president to organize and employ Blacks "for any military or naval service for which they may be found competent."[13]

These developments set the stage for the dramatic cabinet meeting at which Lincoln first presented what would be called the Preliminary Emancipation Proclamation. The wording made it clear that it was a military measure.

> And, *as a fit and necessary military measure* for effecting this purpose, I, *as Commander-in-Chief of the Army and Navy* of the United States, do order and declare that on the first day of January in the year of Our Lord one thousand, eight hundred and sixty-three, all persons held as slaves within any state or states, wherein the constitutional authority of the United States shall not then be practically recognized, submitted to, and maintained, shall then, thenceforward, and forever, be free.[14] (emphasis added)

The cabinet generally supported this proposal. Secretary of State William H. Seward agreed with the substance of the document but questioned the timing of its release. Issued now, in the shadow of major Union military reversals, the declaration might appear to be a desperate act by a government on the verge of defeat. Seward suggested delaying the issuance of the proclamation until after a Union victory. It could then be seen as an act carried out from a position of strength.[15]

Lincoln took this advice and waited for the Union victory at Antietam to issue the proclamation. It was fitting that Lincoln would accept this practical suggestion from Seward. After all, the Emancipation Proclamation was an eminently practical document. By this act Lincoln would declare that the slaves in all of the states still in rebellion would become free. This action would undermine the Southern war effort in many ways by pulling out the very base of support for the Southern economy and social order.

The proclamation specifically exempted, however, the slaveholding states that remained loyal to the Union. It even exempted the Confederate territory already conquered and occupied by the Union military. A cynic might sneer that Lincoln had declared free all of the slaves over whom he had no real control and left in bondage all those slaves who were within his power to free. Such criticism misses the real point of the declaration. This action was taken not by President Abraham Lincoln, but by Commander in Chief Lincoln. It was, from first to last, a measure of military expediency, damaging the Confederacy as much as possible while alienating the loyal border states as little as possible. Lincoln also realized that as Union armies advanced they would carry freedom with them.

A lesser-known provision of the Emancipation Proclamation officially authorized the implementation of the Militia Act of 1862, the raising and using of black troops.[16] This pronouncement sanctioned a practice that a few maverick military leaders had already attempted.

Military commanders away from Washington had not waited for Washington to give approval to enlist black soldiers. One was Major General David Hunter, the Union military commander of the Department of the South, who was in charge of the captured sea islands of South Carolina. On April 3, 1862, Hunter had already asked Secretary of War Edwin M. Stanton for "authority to arm such loyal men as I can find in the country."[17] Officially Lincoln unequivocally disavowed any such action. Quietly, however, uniforms were sent to Hunter. Some of the troops organized there would eventually become part of the First South Carolina Regiment, commanded later by Thomas Wentworth Higginson, whose book *Army Life in a Black Regiment* would become a classic of Civil War literature.[18]

On August 22, 1862, Major General Benjamin F. Butler, in charge of the Union occupation of New Orleans, ordered that free Blacks in that region who had already been enrolled in the Confederate militia be enlisted as soldiers of the United States.[19] And in Kansas, the energetic James E. Lane had already enlisted black troops by the fall of 1862 in spite of specific orders from Secretary Stanton to desist.[20]

CHAPTER 2

RECRUITMENT

The Emancipation Proclamation authorizing the recruitment of black troops officially took effect on January 1, 1863. Massachusetts led all of her sister Northern states to the punch. On January 26, 1863, Secretary of War Edwin M. Stanton granted the request of Massachusetts Governor John A. Andrew to raise units of volunteers that included persons of African descent. Andrew wasted no time in organizing two such units, the 54th and 55th Regiments of Massachusetts Infantry.

The Commonwealth of Massachusetts, however, lacked a black population sufficient to provide the two thousand able-bodied men of military age needed to fill these regiments. It recruited in New Bedford and other promising nearby areas, but eventually it targeted Philadelphia, the city with the largest black community in the free states. Massachusetts soon sent agents to this fertile recruiting ground.

Opposition to arming Blacks still simmered in Philadelphia, and local citizens were known to harass recruiters. Accordingly, the agents executed their mission in a clandestine manner. According to Luis F. Emilio, a veteran officer of the 54th Massachusetts:

> Recruiting there was attended with much annoyance. The gathering-place had to be kept secret, and the men sent to Massachusetts in small parties to avoid molestation or excitement. Mr. Corson [the Massachusetts agent] was obliged to purchase railroad tickets himself, and get the recruits one at a time on the cars or under the cover of darkness.[1]

Philadelphians composed most of the 54th Massachusetts Regiment's Company B.[2] Nearly every one of that regiment's ten companies included Pennsylvania recruits. *The Philadelphia Inquirer* went so far as to estimate on June 26 that "Pennsylvania has already lost fully 1,500 men who have enlisted in Massachusetts."[3] Many Philadelphians, black and white, aided the recruitment drive in the city. Philadelphian

Norwood Penrose Hallowell even became the colonel commanding the 55th Regiment.

Why did Philadelphia lag behind Boston as a recruiter of black troops? After all, Philadelphia's black community stood second in size among nonsecessionist cities only to that of Baltimore. The answer lies in a complex combination of geography, economics, and racial attitudes.

Practically bordering on slave territory, Philadelphia maintained many close ties to the South. Since the city's shipping rates were therefore less than those of manufacturing cities farther north, Philadelphia became the shopping market of choice for many Southerners. Many wealthy Southerners were eager to consume Northern-produced luxuries, and they became some of the city's best customers.

Philadelphia-produced Baldwin locomotives operated on every Southern railway. School books, Bibles, printing type, and household furnishings found in the South were likely to have been produced in Philadelphia.[4]

Many Southerners had graduated from Philadelphia's medical schools. Both their medical books and their medications were likewise produced there.[5]

Many wealthy and influential Philadelphians had close Southern ties. Southerners or Southern sympathizers even filled top local military positions.[6] Josiah Gorgas, a Pennsylvania native, nonetheless resigned as commandant of the Frankford Arsenal at the outbreak of the Civil War in order to offer his services to the Confederacy.[7]

Philadelphia also contained the largest black community of any city in the free states. Many of the city's Whites perceived this reality as a threat. Coupled with Philadelphia's ties to the South, this perceived threat produced a decidedly anti-Black attitude that permeated most of the city's white communities.

Frederick Douglass wrote in February of 1862: "There is not perhaps anywhere to be found a city in which prejudice against color is more rampant than in Philadelphia."[8] Segregation was the rule in schools, churches, concerts, and literary institutions. By 1860 eighteen different chartered street railways coursed through the city. Those streetcars that accepted black riders at all required them to ride on the outside platforms.[9]

In 1838 Pennsylvania Hall, the Philadelphia headquarters of the Pennsylvania Anti-Slavery Society, had been burned down by an anti-Black mob. This antislavery organization had infuriated Whites not only because its members were seen as agitators, but also because its leadership included a number of black Philadelphians such as Robert Purvis, who served as vice-president and president of the society, and William Still, who served as clerk.[10]

The Anti-Slavery Society scheduled a sort of public vigil to observe the hour of execution of abolitionist John Brown. Many unsympathetic citizens showed up to jeer, and many more, perhaps six thousand, held a counter-gathering to renounce John Brown and to show support for the Constitution and Southern rights.[11]

The Commonwealth of Virginia refused to allow John Brown's body to be prepared for burial in the state. Consequently, Brown's widow, taking her husband's body by train back to New York State for burial, planned to stop in Philadelphia for proper preparation of the body. But a threatening crowd at the train station prompted Mayor Alexander Henry to order that Brown's body travel through the city without stopping at any undertaker's establishment. To throw the hostile crowd off track a duplicate coffin was conspicuously transported from the train to draw away any possible mob when Brown's actual coffin was transferred.[12]

Two weeks after this upheaval, George William Curtis, a New York abolitionist, gave an address at National Hall. Rock throwing and fist fights erupted when a crowd of some five thousand swarmed outside the hall in opposition to the speaker.[13]

Even after the Civil War began, opposition to emancipation continued. And to most white Philadelphians the idea of arming black men was completely anathema. As soon as war broke out, black Philadelphians formed three companies of volunteers and offered their services to the Commonwealth, but Harrisburg rejected their offer. Pennsylvania's governor, Andrew G. Curtin, even refused permission for black troops from other states to pass through Pennsylvania on their way to the war.[14]

But as the war continued and as Philadelphians began to read of the exploits of black troops from Louisiana and Massachusetts, some began to reconsider. One was Philadelphian George W. Fahnestock, who confided to his diary in June of 1863: "Negro regiments are mentioned in the engagement at Port Hudson, as having fought desperately. I only wish we had two hundred thousand in our army to save the valuable lives of our white men."[15] This sentiment was echoed by many Whites, including an Ohioan, Sam Evans, who wrote to his father: "My doctrine is that a Negro is no better than a white man and will do as well to receive Reble [sic] bullets and would be likely to save the life of some white men."[16]

By the summer of 1863 a faction of the Union League, a Philadelphia patriotic club, enthusiastically supported the raising of black troops. Some of the more zealous members of the group were able to persuade hundreds of people, both within and beyond its membership to support that effort.[18]

On June 8, 1863, the Union League hosted a meeting to discuss raising black regiments in Philadelphia. Guest speakers included Colonel Lafayette Bingham and Major George L. Stearns, both of whom had been commissioned by Secretary of War Stanton to oversee the recruitment of "colored" troops. Stearns, an ardent abolitionist from Boston, had been a financial backer of John Brown's Raid.[19] Two days after this meeting, 276 supporters petitioned the Secretary of War for permission to raise colored regiments in Philadelphia. Stanton would send this authorization on June 17, but even before it arrived momentous events would dramatically force the issue.[20]

Even before the formation of Philadelphia's black regiments, the Democratic Philadelphia newspaper *The Age* reviled the Union League members who supported arming Blacks.[21] *The Age* was the Philadelphia organ for the forces that opposed the Lincoln administration in general and emancipation in particular. It would ceaselessly refer to the arming of Blacks as "a dangerous experiment" and "a gross outrage upon the white freemen of the country."[22] Strong resistance to arming Blacks would continue in Philadelpha. But the Army of Northern Virginia drove a wedge into this resistance by invading Pennsylvania in June of 1863.

On June 15 Philadelphians heard the disturbing news that Confederate cavalry had captured Chambersburg, Pennsylvania. Governor Curtin pleaded for volunteers to come to Harrisburg to defend the capital. The next day he again called for a militia to defend the state. Philadelphia's mayor, Alexander Henry, called on businessmen to close shop and take up arms. An alarm was even sounded on the bell of Independence Hall.[23]

The black community responded with intense excitement to the governor's call for troops. In his official proclamation of June 15 the governor made no distinction of color in his plea for volunteers. The city's black churches hosted meetings to discuss the response of black Philadelphians to the call. Patriotic speeches and the sound of fife and drum echoed through the streets.[24]

The Institute for Colored Youth on Lombard Street became headquarters for recruiting a company of black volunteers. One of the first to volunteer was a brilliant young black teacher from that institution, Octavius V. Catto. Catto was a dynamic community activist, a natural leader, and was quickly chosen to lead the new company. He would be commanding a large number of his own students who now chose to exchange their books for rifles.[25]

Early in the morning on June 17 Catto led his fellow volunteers to Independence Square, where his company joined the swarming throng gathering there.[26] The company included ninety men who had all enlisted within twelve hours. Now at full company strength of about 100, they were mustered into service. White officers, including Captain William Babe, First Lieutenant William Elliott, and Second Lieutenant Thomas Moore, took charge of them.[27]

That day the city hastily sent out to Harrisburg several regiments and independent companies of Philadelphia militia and home guards. To accommodate the emergency volunteers, the City Arsenal at Broad and Race Streets was opened to distribute rifles, uniforms, and a variety of equipment to any group with proper requisitions.[28] During the rush the company led by Captain Babe presented itself at the arsenal. The men were supplied with uniforms, arms, and equipment without question and were marched to the West Philadelphia train station. Black Philadelphians crowded the station to say, "Good-bye," for what might be the last time.[29]

Upon reaching Harrisburg, however, the black volunteers met with unexpected disappointment. Major General Darius N. Couch, commander of the newly formed Department of the Susquehanna, refused to accept them. Couch explained his actions by claiming that he had no authority to receive colored men into the service except under the act of Congress, which provided for their enlistment for three years. This company was only an emergency militia unit enlisted for limited service of a few months.[30] But the rationale given by Couch for refusing to use armed, healthy, and willing volunteers appears unconvincing. At that time 75,000 veteran Confederates were moving through Pennsylvania and threatening to overrun the capital. Under these circumstances the rejection of any volunteers would be difficult to justify. Couch's reason for this rejection stands as glaringly picayune. Apparently not everyone was prepared for the sight of armed and uniformed Blacks.

The next day the black militia company was sent back to Philadelphia. The decision to spurn these volunteers left Philadelphia's Blacks disheartened and indignant. The rejected company sent a committee to call upon Mayor Alexander Henry. He told them that an application had already been sent to the War Department for authority to recruit three-year regiments of "colored" men in Philadelphia and expected approval in a day or two.[31]

Henry was correct. On June 20 a *Public Ledger* headline read: " A Regiment of Colored Men to be Raised." According to the article:

> Yesterday Col. Ruff [Charles F. Ruff, United States mustering officer] received a notice that he had been instructed to receive and muster into the service a regiment of colored troops. They will be mustered into service and provided for in all respects the same as for white troops.[32]

On June 24, less than a week after the black company returned home from Harrisburg, Franklin Hall "filled to overflowing" with a crowd of black and white Philadelphians.[33] They cheered their support for the new soldiers. A black Philadelphian, David E. Gipson, chaired the assembly. There speakers including Gipson, Major Stearns, who was by that time appointed Recruiting Commissioner for U.S. Colored Troops in Pennsylvania; and Captain Babe delivered rousing addresses. The front seats of the hall were reserved for Babe's ground-breaking Company A.[34] In two days it would make history again and would become the first company of Colored Troops from Philadelphia to be enrolled in the service of the United States.[35]

The assembly passed a resolution that

...we, the colored people of Philadelphia, throwing aside the unpleasant memories of the past, looking only at the future, and asking merely
the same guarantees, the same open field, and fair play that are given
our white fellow countrymen, desire here and now to express our
willingness and readyness to come forward to the defense of our im-
perilled country.[36]

They also called upon their brethren throughout the Free States "to
welcome this opportunity to strike not less for the freedom of themselves
and their race than for the liberty of the human race."[37] They also resolved
that, although despised and mistreated by the people of these states, they
would "show them and the world how unjust has been the estimate of
our character, and that we are not wanting in any element of a vigorous
manhood, least of all in a pure and lofty patriotism."[38]

Enthusiastic members of the Union League helped form the "Supervisory Committee on Enlistment of Colored Troops," and began their or-
ganizational work. Octavius Catto was one of the first to leap into this
work. He and some thirty other influential and articulate members of
Philadelphia's black community organized a mass meeting for July 6 to
launch a recruitment drive.[39]

Within the City of Philadelphia there stood several potential sites for
training black troops, many of which had already served as training cam-
puses for white troops earlier in the war. By 1863 many of these sites were
empty and available again.[40] The site eventually selected, however, was in
Cheltenham Township, Montgomery County, more than eight miles from
Central Philadelphia.[41] Although no documentation confirms it, the selec-
tion of this site has been attributed to prejudice and the desire to keep
black recruits out of the city.[42]

But other reasons could satisfactorily explain this decision. One of
the owners of the property was Edward M. Davis, a member of the Supervisory Committee on Enlistment of Colored Troops and an enthusiastic
supporter of the program. Davis held strong antislavery sentiments that
were characteristic of other members of his family. His mother-in-law was
the well-known Quaker abolitionist Lucretia Coffin Mott, whose home
lay in close proximity to the camp. The North Pennsylvania Railroad provided convenient access to the camp from the city, and the Old York Road,
which passed by the camp, accommodated horse-drawn wagons and car-
riages.[43] Isolated from the city crowds, the camp could avoid potential
friction with neighboring Whites. It was named Camp William Penn. Even
the naming of the camp caused controversy, offending many Quakers who
objected to naming a military camp after one of their pacifist founding
fathers.

Meanwhile, the recruiting and organizing of black troops surged
quickly ahead. On June 30 George Fahnestock recorded in his diary:

Later in the day, I saw several hundred colored men in procession march up Sixth to Chestnut, and up Chestnut St. They were not uniformed nor armed, but were a good looking body of men. They had a drum and fife, and carrying inspiriting banners. At Chelton Hills they have a camp, and are raising a regiment.[44]

Fahnestock viewed this sight with approval, but many others surely did not. Mayor Henry was concerned about a possible violent reaction to this procession and made certain that the recruits did not wear uniforms that would draw attention to themselves nor carry arms that might provoke a violent response.[45]

Pressure mounted to overcome these prejudices. Governor Curtin came to Philadelphia to appeal personally for volunteers. Frederick Douglass also came to the League to urge it to train Blacks for the military. On July 6 National Hall became the scene of a mass rally planned by Octavius Catto, some thirty prominent black Philadelphians, and the Supervisory Committee. A band played patriotic songs and the well-known antislavery speakers, Frederick Douglass, Congressman William D. Kelley, and the prodigious Anna E. Dickinson, only twenty-two years old at the time, all spoke there. They met a most enthusiastic audience, already afire with excitement over news of the Union victory at Gettysburg three days earlier.[46] Douglass gave a long and apparently stirring speech ending by exhorting:

Young men of Philadelphia, you are without excuse. The hour has arrived, and your place is in the Union Army. Remember that the musket — the United States musket with its bayonet of steel — is better than all mere parchment guarantees of liberty.[47]

The Union League also drummed up support by publishing pamphlets extolling the bravery of Blacks in the military, in the current conflict and throughout earlier American wars.[48] The Supervisory Committee eventually raised over $33,000, which paid most of the expenses of raising eleven regiments of United States Colored Troops in Philadelphia.

During the Confederate invasion of Pennsylvania, forty-six prominent black Philadelphians had formed a committee to recruit volunteers of their race to defend the city. William D. Forten, Octavius Catto, the Reverend Jeremiah Asher, and a host of other prominent black Philadelphians signed their names to a circular exhorting their brothers to enlist.[49] They distributed recruiting broadsides listing the names of the committee members. Once such troops had been officially sanctioned by the government, the committee issued a new call for enlistment. An eight-foot-high recruiting broadside now bore the names of fifty-five black sponsors.[50]

As might be expected, Octavius Catto was included in the list on both broadsides. Another name appearing on both broadsides was that of a Philadelphia clergyman of color, the Reverend Jeremiah Asher. Asher would be no bystander in this conflict. He would soon become the chaplain for the 6th Regiment of United States Colored Troops. He would be one of the first fourteen Blacks appointed chaplains in the Union army during the Civil War. Asher also eventually became the first chaplain of his race to give his life in this conflict.[51]

CHAPTER 3

CAMP WILLIAM PENN

Colonel Louis Wagner assumed command of Camp William Penn. Wagner, born in Germany, had achieved an impressive record during his service with the 88th Pennsylvania Infantry, receiving his captain's commission in September of 1861. He fought in the Second Battle of Bull Run in August of 1862, where he was wounded in action and captured by the Confederates. and later exchanged to return to the war. After the Battle of Chancellorsville, however, his wound broke out again, and he was taken from combat duty and transferred to invalid service.[1]

Hundreds of Blacks from Pennsylvania and nearby states traveled to the City of Brotherly Love. They traveled in every conceivable manner, some taking a train from Buffalo, some walking from Lancaster. By July 24 the first regiment had filled its roster and recruiting began for a second regiment.[2] The first regiment was designated the 3rd Regiment of United States Colored Infantry. The second regiment organized at Camp William Penn, was designated the 6th Regiment of United States Colored Infantry.

Wagner proved to be a highly capable commander, with many who served under him holding him in high esteem. On October 12, when the regiment had completed its training and prepared to leave camp for the war, its officers demonstrated their appreciation by presenting to him a "magnificent" sword. In announcing the presentation ceremony *The Inquirer* pronounced: "This is another proof that the Colonel's popularity does not extend alone to the men of the regiments organized at this Camp, by whom he is universally beloved but that he also has the confidence of the officers."[3]

Not all of the officers of the regiment, however, shared these positive feelings. Captain John McMurray, who would eventually become a major, would insist: "I never had an overflowing feeling of admiration for him."[4] Wagner gave McMurray good cause to resent him as soon as the young officer arrived at camp. Only twenty-four hours after receiving his captain's commission and assignment in Washington City, McMurray reported to Camp William Penn. He presented himself to Wagner at the headquarters tent and introduced himself by handing his appointment orders to him. According to McMurray, Wagner read the appointment letter very deliberately, then slowly looked the new captain over from head to toe. He quizzed the young man about his previous service, who had commanded his regiment, to what corps, division, and brigade the regiment belonged, and in what battles he had fought. When he had completed his interrogation Wagner disputed McMurray's statements as to who had commanded his division and brigade.[5]

This unpleasant interview continued for over fifteen minutes. Through the entire time McMurray stood with his cap in one hand and his gripsack in the other with an audience of three or four other officers. Wagner finally ordered his adjutant to take the captain to his assigned Company D.[6]

When he arrived at Camp William Penn, McMurray found it to be "pleasantly and beautifully located," and he pointed out that good order and good discipline were maintained under Colonel Wagner's administration.[7] Another visitor found that the camp "presents a neat and orderly appearance, which will at once attract the attention of any one who may visit it."[8]

Enlisted men slept in simple "shelter tents." Officers enjoyed more spacious wall tents. A Headquarters tent accommodated Wagner and his staff. The tents were arranged along intersecting "company streets."[9] The day that Captain McMurray first arrived to assume command of Company D, his regimental commander Colonel John W. Ames asked him why his company street and quarters were not in better condition. McMurray replied that he did not know and explained that he had only just arrived that moment at company headquarters and had been in camp for only an hour.[10]

One of the recruits, by some means, had obtained a large flag pole for the camp. A campwide celebration accompanied the erection of the pole on July 15, with troops marching on the parade ground behind the encampment to mark the event.[11]

A large tent was erected in the camp "for the use of persons who may wish to avail themselves of instruction in the branches of an English education."[12] This was probably the same tent that was elsewhere described as "a very large tent" donated by the Young Men's Christian Association of Philadelphia, a tent so large that it had been used for a revival in 1858. It was intended to be used for school and for "other purposes of a useful character."[13] The teachers, who were from "a religious society," took a great deal of interest in their soldier pupils.[14]

Eventually more permanent wooden barracks replaced the shelter tents, but the 6th Regiment never benefitted from this upgrade of facilities.

They left in mid-fall, leaving the 8th Regiment of U.S. Colored Troops with the pleasure of moving into the new quarters on December 8.[15]

The recruits quickly learned the reality of training camp, an unexciting succession of endless drills. The routine for a typical day in camp can be imagined with a glance at the regiment's official schedule.

Head Quarters 6th Reg't US Colored Troops Camp Wm. Penn Chelten Hills Pa, Sept. 8, 1863

Special Order #7

In accordance with General Order No. 5 Revised Regulations for Camp William Penn the following Calls and Regulations will be strictly adhered to

Reveille and Roll Call	6	o'clock	AM
Surgeon's Call	6 $^1/_2$	"	"
Breakfast "	7	"	"
Sergeant's " (For Morning Report)	7 $^1/_2$	"	"
Drill "	8	"	"
Adjutants "	9	"	"
Guard Mounting	10 $^1/_2$	"	"
Sergeant's Call (To get Morning Reports)	11	"	"
Dinner "	12	"	M
Drill Battalion Call	3	"	PM
Dress Parade	5 $^1/_2$	"	"
Supper	6	"	"
Tattoo and Roll	8 $^1/_2$	"	"
Taps	9	"	"

On Saturdays there will be no Battalion Drill but companies will form at 1 $^1/_2$ o'clock PM to clean camp. Sunday inspection at 8 $^1/_2$ o'clock AM. Church call at 4 o'clock PM.[16]

If anything was as certain to provoke complaints from a soldier as the monotony of drill, it would be the quality of army chow. Recruits at Camp William Penn harbored a particular grievance about their bread, or "hardtack." By August the complaints had become serious enough to merit an investigation by the Visiting Committee of the Supervisory Committee on Colored Camps. The Committee resolved in a meeting at their Chestnut Street headquarters to pay a visit to the manufacturer of the bread.

Their visit confirmed the validity of the complaints. Some of the bread that they inspected was only a few days old and yet "it was found to be so hard that a hatchet would scarcely break it." The Committee discovered some unidentified substance mixed with the dough that they judged to be "not very pleasant to the sight or taste." They also found that some of the bread that they inspected "looked as though coal dust had been mixed in the flour."[17]

The soldiers at Camp William Penn, and particularly those of the 6th U.S. Colored Troops, seem to have been generally of high moral character. The chaplain of the regiment, Jeremiah Asher, noted a year after training camp that the men of the regiment were remarkably free of the vices of profanity and drinking and that they sent a large portion of their pay home.[18] Obedience to camp rules and to the orders of officers was also characteristic of the men. An observer of the troops of Camp William Penn noted that "Subordination has been a marked characteristic of the colored troops."[19]

Camp William Penn maintained records of the conduct of troops stationed there. As might be anticipated, however, camp records tend to barely mention the hundreds of troops who reported to camp, followed camp rules, obeyed orders, and conducted themselves honorably. But the records do document in some detail the infractions of the rules and the disciplinary processes that resulted. Although this selective reporting tends to skew the official records, presenting predominantly the negative conduct, an examination of the documents will give some useful insights into camp life.

Discipline was strictly enforced at Camp William Penn, for, as in any army camp, the potential for disruption lay just below the surface. Private Robert Clark of Company D was court-martialed on the charge that he "did fight with private Jesse P. Foster, Co.D [6th] USCT and attempted to use a drawn bayonet upon said private Jesse P. Foster."[20] These charges may leave the impression that the man Clark attacked was only a helpless victim, but Foster was himself arrested. The court-martial charged that Foster "did when ordered by his commanding officer to desist from fighting or striking Private Robert Clark—violently push aside his commanding officer—saying that he would kill the son of a bitch—at the same time striking at said Robert Clark."[21]

Clark pleaded guilty and was sentenced to be confined on bread and water for twenty-four hours in the Guard House. Foster pleaded not guilty, but was found guilty anyway. He was sentenced to the more conspicuous punishment that he "should carry his knapsack on every drill, for two weeks and stand on a barrel at the Guard House between Morning and Afternoon Drill—during that time—his meals at noon to consist of bread and water."[22]

Clark and Foster had both been mustered into service on the same day, July 17, 1863. They would serve together in Company D throughout the war and would both be in active service when mustered out in September 1865.[23]

Private Eli Sheperd on or about September 6, 1863, "having been duly posted as a sentinal [*sic*] did leave his post—without being properly relieved." He pleaded guilty and suffered forty-eight hours in the Guard House on bread and water.[24] Sheperd had enlisted as a paid substitute for another man who had been drafted. On December 19, 1864, Sheperd deserted.[25]

The regiment also had problems with some of its noncommissioned officers while at Camp William Penn. Two sergeants in Company H were absent without leave on the same day, October 9, 1863, just five days before the regiment would move out to Virginia. Both men pleaded not guilty but were judged to be guilty. One of the two offenders, Sergeant Charles M. Taylor, was sentenced to be shot to death, but his sentence was later commuted to imprisonment at hard labor for the remainder of his term of enlistment.[26] This sentence was apparently further reduced; records indicate that a Private Charles Taylor of Company H was killed in action at Petersburg, Virginia on June 9, 1864.[27]

Taylor's co-offender, Sergeant John H. Clark, was sentenced to a reduction in rank, forfeiture of two months' pay, and one month of confinement to the regimental Guard House, except to be present at all company and regimental drills and the usual fatigue duty required of the men in the regiment. Clark's confinement was remitted, but the reduction in rank and the loss of pay stood. Clark served with his regiment throughout the war and was mustered out as a corporal in September 1865.[28]

In spite of announcements assuring Blacks of pay equal to that of the white soldier, actual practice belied this promise.[29] White enlisted men received thirteen dollars per month with a clothing allowance of an additional three dollars and fifty cents. Black soldiers, however, were paid only ten dollars per month, three dollars of which might be deducted for clothing.[30]

Blacks were also generally denied bounties. Bounties were cash bonuses paid to volunteers by federal, state, or local authorities as an incentive to enlist. These bounties often totaled five hundred dollars or more, a generous amount exceeding the average annual wages for a Northern worker.[31] The Commonwealth of Pennsylvania eventually contributed a token bounty of ten dollars to each black recruit. By the end of 1863, through the efforts of the Union League, the City of Philadelphia began contributing an additional 250 dollars per recruit.[32]

The War Department had also refused to commission black officers. A manyfold rationale stood behind this decision. First, the concept of black troops would be more acceptable if white men exclusively were permitted to become officers in such units. Organizing "colored" regiments would create thousands of new positions for regimental officers. The awarding of these commissions to Whites could create more support for the program and could reward those who had already shown support.

Widely held negative stereotypes of Blacks prompted many Whites to believe in the necessity of their taking control of those regiments. Blacks were seen, on the one hand, as needing to be reined in by responsible white leaders to prevent savagery on the battlefield. On the other hand, they were seen as childlike incompetents who badly needed strong leadership and direction.

Finally, the image of black officers was a repulsive one to most Whites. Would white enlisted men be required to salute a dark-skinned man, call him "Sir," and obey his orders? This was unthinkable to most.

The men of Camp William Penn constantly experienced another reminder of their inferior status through the discriminatory policy of the streetcar companies of Philadelphia. Of the nineteen streetcar and suburban railroad companies that operated in and around Philadelphia, eleven refused outright to permit Blacks to ride. The other eight tolerated black riders but required them to stand on the front platform with the driver.[33] On those streetcars that did accept black riders, the humiliation of being forced to stand facing the rumps of the draft horses would have been injurious enough. To this was added the physical discomfort of standing for the entire ride when seating was available and of being exposed to the wind, the cold, and the rain.

This discrimination paid no heed to the wealth or position that a black man may have achieved. Even William N. Still, one of Philadelphia's most prosperous merchants and a prominent agent of the underground railroad, could not escape this treatment. Still wrote to *The Press* in December of 1863 to recount his own humiliating experience. Still had ridden on the North Pennsylvania Railroad to Camp William Penn in the morning but was forced to resort to a city streetcar for the return trip. He stepped aboard a car carrying only a few passengers and gave the conductor his fare. Before the conductor even handed Still the change he directed Still to "step out on the platform." Still protested that no one was complaining, but the conductor insisted that "It is against the rules." The Negro was forced to accept this indignity. It began to snow on the return trip, and the bitter cold weather was matched by his bitter resentment of receiving discriminatory treatment after paying the same fare as white customers.[34]

Still's angry letter to the newspaper was widely reproduced. It was even printed in *The Times* of London. An American correspondent in London pronounced that the news of this incident did "more harm to the Union cause in England than a military defeat."[35]

The crusade to end discrimination on Philadelphia's streetcar lines would be a long and frustrating struggle. In 1864 two railway lines did agree to admit Blacks on a basis of equality, but more than a dozen lines continued to discriminate. Not until after the Civil War would any significant progress take place.[36]

Just as the men of Camp William Penn were aware of the goings-on in their neighboring community, so too their curious neighbors made efforts to find out more about this nearby camp as many visited the camp daily.[37] According to *The Inquirer*, the camp presented "a neat and orderly appearance, which will at once attract the attention of anyone who may visit it."[38] Unfortunately, the soldiers often exhibited a reciprocal interest in the outside world by going absent without leave. Those offenders, when captured, were brought back to camp and were compelled to stand on barrel heads at the entrance to camp.[39] A noncommissioned officer might expect more severe punishment.

Desertion was a common problem in Civil War training camps. Camp William Penn was no exception. Desertions presented a constant annoyance to Colonel Wagner, and he apparently had little patience with offenders in this area. Upon apprehending a man who had deserted some six times, Wagner wrote to Major Charles W. Foster, head of the Bureau of Colored Troops: "He is a bad man and ought to be shot. How am I to dispose of him?"[40] On many occasions soldiers slipped out of camp at night. This situation drove Wagner to redouble his efforts to secure the camp perimeter. At one of the most popular points of surreptitious departure from camp, the desertion problem had become so serious that sentries patrolling that area carried loaded muskets.[41]

This action set the stage for perhaps the most controversial incident in the short history of Camp William Penn. It involved Private Charles Ridley of Company B of the 6th. Ridley had enlisted on July 30 and a mere eight days later was given first assignment of guard duty, patrolling the camp boundary at that often-breached border.

On the evening of Friday, August 7, several white civilians, men and boys who lived in the neighborhood, passed by the camp near Ridley's post. Returning from the nearby swimming hole, Sharpless Pond, they stopped at the fence and asked Ridley if any companies of soldiers had been sent out of camp that day.[42] He told the group to move on. They all moved away except for William Fox, who remained at the fence insisting that he had a perfect right to be there and that Ridley had no right to force him to go.[43]

Ridley, serving his first guard duty, apparently did not know what to do. In the next few moments he called out twice for the Corporal of the Guard. The brother-in-law of Fox, also in the group, grew concerned. He returned to his defiant relative and urged him to leave, but Fox refused.[44]

The Corporal of the Guard did not come, but a number of enlisted men overheard his call. Some of them were getting water at a nearby spring and asked what the problem was. When Ridley replied that there were some civilians at the fence who would not go away, someone shouted: "Shoot them."[45] The sentry then raised his gun and said: "Are you going to leave? If you don't I'll shoot."

"I guess not," Fox replied according to one account.[46] In another version of the story Fox answered Ridley's threat to shoot with: "I guess you won't," and Ridley gave one more warning.[47] At this point Ridley squeezed the trigger, and the report of a musket rang through the camp.

Colonel Wagner stood in front of his tent synchronizing his watch with the camp clock. At that moment, twenty-seven minutes after nine o'clock, the distant sound of a musket blast reached his ears. Someone told him that a man had been shot, and the colonel headed in that direction, quickly crossing a creek and passing through the challenge of an unseen sentry. Finally bounding over the wall of the camp, he found a man in the road in great pain. The bullet had passed through his wrist and had torn into his abdomen. The wounded man recognized him and said: "Colonel is that you?"[48]

Colonel Wagner gave testimony under oath three months later offering a detailed account of the events from that point onward. "The Post surgeon came and examined his wound," Wagner testified:

> while he examined, I had asked how it happened; he said that he heard that a certain number of men had come to the camp that day, and he had stopped to ask the sentry if that was so; I asked whether he did not know it was against the rules to stop and talk to the sentry, and whether the sentry had not told him to go on? he said the sentry had told him to go; I said, 'why didn't you go? What did you say?' he said he knew it was against the rules, but he told the sentry that he would go when he got ready; I asked him whether the sentry had not told him that he would shoot if he did not go? he said he had; I asked him why he did not take the warning? he said he did not think he would shoot; said he never would have any luck; ought not to have shot him.[49]

Dr. J. F. Holt, the post surgeon, extracted the musket ball. Fox was then carried to his residence where he died an hour later.[50] He left a wife and four children.[51]

The reaction of the local press to this incident varied considerably. *The Philadelphia Inquirer* headline announced a "Startling Affair at Chelton Hill." The article gave an objective account of the events. It concluded with a seeming defense of the sentry's actions: "In his defense, CHARLES RIDLEY, the sentinel, stated that he imagined Fox pointed a pistol at him and attempted to climb over the fence. It was Ridley's first time on guard."[52]

The *Public Ledger* gave an apparently unbiased account of the incident. It ended the narration of the event by reporting, "Reilly [sic] gave as an excuse for the shooting that he thought the man was getting over the fence. Coroner Conrad [no first name given] will investigate the matter today, and the investigation should be a thorough one." The article concluded, however, with the commentary: "The shooting, as it now appears, was wholly unjustifiable. There was no attempt to get within the camp ground, nor was anything done to call for interference on the part of the sentry. The deceased was there as a mere spectator, and it is not pretended that he did not conduct himself properly."[53]

The Age, as might be expected, took this opportunity to denounce not only this incident, but the entire concept of Blacks in the military. Its headline announced: "The Outrage at Chelton Hills." It began by declaring that the shooting "demands the most prompt and searching investigation." It went on to declare "It is generally believed that the act was wholly unjustifiable," and a "cold blooded assault of the negro."

The paper went on to revile Colonel Wagner, who, it seemed to the writer, had acquitted Ridley of all blame. "It is very clear that the negro committed a heinous crime, and that to justify himself he willfully perverted the truth; and yet *upon his statement alone* he is to be exonerated from all wrong, and permitted further to disgrace the uniform which temporarily covers his back."

The Age then condemned placing guns in the hands of Blacks as a "dangerous experiment" and a "gross outrage upon the white freemen of the country," and predicted a time when those who supported Negro enlistments would "hang their heads in shame." The article concluded that the incident required an investigation of the charge of murder against Ridley. If he was found guilty, "the fate of HAMAN should be his, and the outraged majesty of the law should be promptly vindicated."[54]

On August 11 *The Philadelphia Inquirer* carried a statement by Fox's brother-in-law, who attempted to refute the suggestion that Fox had a pistol in his possession at the time of the shooting. The article indicated that "four negroes" were examined at the hearing after the shooting. Their testimony was inconsistent. One witness indicated that two dozen men were present at the time of the shooting, and another stated that there were only six.[55]

The same day the *Public Ledger* reported that an inquest was held on Fox's body by Coroner Jacobus, no first name given. The newspaper stated: "After the verdict had been rendered the coroner then demanded that the soldier be given up. To this Col. Wagner refused to give his consent unless commanded to do so by order of the War Department. The case now waits decision from Washington."[56]

Wagner stood in a politically sensitive position. Many in the white community demanded punishment for Ridley, or demanded at least a civilian tribunal. But Wagner needed to demonstrate to his own men and to the local community that he was in charge at the camp and that he was in no way accountable to citizens with grievances about the camp, his administration, or the concept of black troops.

The story of this shooting incident disappeared from local newspapers for the next three months, giving the impression that "Wagner nevertheless refused to deliver Ridley to the county officials. Eventually the excitability subsided, the shooting of a white man by a black forgotten."[57]

This conclusion is supported by the fact that Ridley is listed as being mustered out of service with his comrades on September 20, 1865.[58]

But *The Philadelphia Inquirer* on November 19, 1863, re-reported on the trial of Charles Ridley before Montgomery County Court. Ridley was charged with murder, and the trial lasted from Thursday morning through Saturday, November 12–14.

Two men who had examined the body, Coroner Jacobus and Dr. J. B. Dunlap, testified. Colonel Wagner and other witnesses were examined. *The Inquirer* printed a portion of Wagner's testimony. Charles Hunsicker appeared as counsel for the prosecution, while James Boyd represented the defense. District Attorney Enoch A. Banks[59] delivered the Commonwealth's closing address, and Benjamin Brewster closed for the defense.

Judge Henry Chapman[60] charged the jury and they retired to deliberate. After several hours the jury returned a verdict of guilty of voluntary manslaughter.[61]

A search of Montgomery County court records has revealed that no cases of that date are preserved. No documentation exists that indicated what sentence Private Ridley received.[62] Apparently Ridley was detained in some manner by civil authorities for at least six months. Company muster rolls for November of 1863 through June of 1864 list him as "Detained by Civil Authority on Charge of Manslaughter at Norristown, Pa. since Aug. 7, 1863." He returned to the regiment on August 14, 1864.[63]

The Ridley incident did not, however, distract the regiment from its task of preparing itself for combat. Nearly every Union regiment carried two flags with it into battle. One flag was the "Stars and Stripes," the other was either a special regimental flag or a state flag. The flags of a regiment, its "colors," were a regiment's most precious possessions. They were far more than guides in battle for advancing or retreating. They were even more than symbols. The colors became the embodiment of the spirit of the regiment. In the course of the Civil War thousands of soldiers would give up their lives defending or rescuing their flags, including members of the 6th Regiment.

The ceremony in which the colors were formally presented to the unit was often an elaborate affair. That day was certainly one of the most memorable for the 6th. In addition to the national colors, the unit proudly accepted their regimental flag, "represented to be a splendid affair." The banner had been "gotten up by a committee of colored citizens" and was presented by a deputation from the black community. For this special occasion a large number of spectators flocked to the camp. Special trains leaving Berks Street Station at two o'clock and three thirty were arranged to help accommodate the throng.[64] As a preliminary to the ceremony the troops paraded smartly before the impressed observers: "Their muscular frames elicited the admiration of those who witnessed the drill."[65]

At five o'clock the regiment drew up in line in the center of the camp. They faced to the south, toward Philadelphia where so much activity had helped bring about the formation of this regiment. They now also faced their ultimate destination, the battlefields of Virginia and Carolina.

The regimental flag to be presented this day was the creation of the talented black artist David Bustill Bowser. He had created a six-foot square work of art on the finest of silk.[66] On the obverse of the flag two figures stand in the foreground. A woman representing Liberty holds a flag and exhorts a black soldier armed with a rifle to do his duty. In the background a young Black applauds the soldier. Ornate designs surround the painting, and two scrolls, one above, one below, proclaim "Freedom for All" and "6th United States Colored Troops."

An eagle dominates the reverse of the flag, the national symbol clutching an olive branch and arrows. The lower scroll on the reverse identifies the regiment, and the upper scroll announces: "Presented by the Colored Citizens of Philadelphia, Aug. 31, 1863."[67]

The ceremony was ready to begin. Jacob White, one of the most active members of the Supervisory Committee, spoke first to the assembled spectators. He spoke of the history that black soldiers were making for themselves, writing their names "high upon the scroll of fame." He concluded: "The colored man's time is now, and by striking with a firm, strong hand for the privileges offered in the present hour the black man's nation will be secured for all coming time."[68]

Prominent black Philadelphian John Bowers also spoke. Bowers, an active churchman and antislavery leader,[69] paid tribute to the troops and expressed appreciation for the way that they "had left friends, kindred and home and volunteered when the bounties and pay of the whites were denied."[70]

But the two men who raised the ceremony to its highest emotional point were Robert E. Purvis, another leader of Philadelphia's black community, who formally presented the flag, and Colonel Wagner, who accepted the banner on behalf of the regiment. At the time, Purvis served as president of the Pennsylvania Anti-Slavery Society and as aide-de-camp to Major Stearns. The soldiers of the camp received his speech "with marked deference." Purvis expressed his confidence that the troops would prove themselves to be worthy bearers of these colors and that "you will see that the flag of your country suffers no dishonor at your hands." He went on to recount the heroic deeds already performed by Blacks earlier that year at Fort Wagner, Milliken's Bend, and Port Hudson and expressed certainty that the men of the 6th would display the same "loyalty, prowess and devotion."[71]

Finally, taking the flag in his hands, he extended the banner to Colonel Wagner with the words: "Receive this standard." Then, turning to face the troops, he charged them: "Soldiers, under this flag let your rallying cry be 'for God, for freedom, and our country.' If for this you must fall you fall the country's patriots, heroes and martyrs."[72]

Regimental Flag, 6th USCI, Obverse

University of Maryland, Baltimore County

Regimental Flag, 6th USCI, Reverse

University of Maryland, Baltimore County

Wagner received the flag reflecting:

It affords me pleasure, indeed, to receive this magnificent standard this day presented to the Sixth Regiment of the United States
Colored Infantry. It will never be disgraced. Wherever the soldiers of
the Sixth Infantry go they will with honor uphold and defend this
banner. There are two regiments of colored troops now at Charleston
[the 54th and 55th Massachusetts Infantry], who left this city, and they
have sustained the reputation of their race by the conduct displayed
before Fort Wagner. The soldiers to whom this flag is committed will
be found true as they were true. They will follow it to victory, or,
falling, they will fall only when the flag falls with them. We will uphold it and preserve it; protect its honor and maintain its supremacy
against all who would injure its folds.[73]

Following the ceremony, the Supervisory Committee placed the flag
on display at their headquarters on Chestnut Street. A reporter for *The
Inquirer* declared it to be "a most beautiful specimen of workmanship, and
reflects great credit upon the donors and artist."[74]

This ceremony added to the *esprit de corps* of the men of the 6th Regiment. A brotherly bond developed among the men who shared the feeling
of fighting together to end slavery. Before the month of September was
over, a threat from outside the camp would compel the men to demonstrate this bond.

A soldier from Company I named John Price, who had enlisted in
Delaware, visited home on furlough during the week of September 6, 1863.
When he returned to camp he was followed by a George Biddle of Cecil
County, Maryland. Biddle rode out to Camp William Penn in a carriage
with the intention of seizing Price, whom he claimed as his slave.

When the purpose of Biddle's visit became known excitement shot
through the camp. The thought of being carried away into slavery loomed
as the ultimate nightmare for any Black. Agitated soldiers surrounded
Biddle in a threatening manner, and he wisely "beat a hasty retreat." Biddle
then sought out Colonel Wagner and found him in a neighboring house.
Wagner dismissed his claim and told him that he could not take Price.
When Biddle returned to his carriage he was again surrounded by an angry group and "would have met with rough treatment but for the timely
arrival of Colonel Wagner." The colonel assured the soldiers that even if
Price was alleged to be a slave he would not be taken back. Wagner's
support apparently put them more at ease, and they became "pacified" at
that point.[75]

By around this time the men of the 6th Regiment seemed to become
restless. They had now received their colors, and their numbers had increased to nearly the full complement of one thousand needed to leave
camp and march off to war. A visiting reporter observed on September 12:

There appears to be a growing anxiety among the men to leave for the more active duties of the battleground. The number at present in the camp is seven hundred and ten, and it is thought that during the coming week the regiment will be full and leave for their future place of destination.[76]

This reporter was correct. That very day new recruits had arrived at the Chestnut Street headquarters and were to leave for camp the next morning.[77] This addition filled its ranks completely.[78]

The anticipation must have been contagious. Fine weather on Friday, September 11, drew a large number of visitors to the camp. The 6th Regiment regaled the visitors with a battalion drill under the direction of Colonel Wagner and received rave reviews. "The men went through with all the field manoeuvres such as forming squares, charging bayonets and loading and firing. All the manoeuvres were done with great precision, and equal to those of the white troops."[79]

They attended a religious service on Sunday afternoon, September 13, in the huge tent donated by the YMCA. The hundreds of people drawn to the service included nearly all of the soldiers in camp. The announcement of the service attracted many interested people from outside the camp also, including Governor John A. Andrew of Massachusetts. At the end of the sermon Andrew addressed the assembly. A trailblazer himself in raising black troops, he took this occasion to pay high compliments to the new soldiers and to urge them on in their crusade.[80] The 6th Regiment was now ready to finally go forth and strike the blow.

On September 24 the announced "Grand Review" of the 6th U.S. Colored Troops drew a huge crowd of spectators of all races. Vehicles crowded the road leading to the camp for a long distance. Trains leading to and from Chelten Hills were "densely packed."[81]

The field chosen for the review was a hollow a short distance from the North Pennsylvania Railroad. The surrounding hills provided a natural amphitheater for the spectators to witness the 6th's snappy drill. By all accounts it presented an impressive spectacle. "The soldiers presented a very neat appearance. The manner in which they went through the evolutions of drill created quite a sensation. Their marching around the brow of the hills and forming into divisions, was a splendid sight."[82]

Contributing to the smartness of their appearance was the new style of knapsacks that adorned their backs. The 6th USCT had been issued "patent slinging knapsacks" that rested higher on the back than the previous model. They were improvements both aesthetically and practically over the older style, since they provided "more ease in marching" and helped project a "more soldierly appearance."[83]

Major General George Cadwalader, commander of the Department of Pennsylvania, and his staff reviewed the troops. A band embellished the event. After the review Colonel Wagner escorted the general and his staff on a tour of the camp and provided refreshments. The Supervisory Committee also attended the affair.

General Cadwalader gave a long oration complimenting the troops on their proficiency in the drill and applauding them for their patriotism and for "offering their services to the country in this hour of her greatest need."[84] He had no doubt that when the war finally ended, the "colored" soldier would be able to look back with satisfaction at his role in history.

Other speakers included Ex-Governor William F. Johnston and Miss Anna E. Dickinson, the youthful recruiting speaker. Evidently all were inspiring speakers, as the audience frequently interrupted them with enthusiastic applause.

The "Grand Review" and battalion drills had all been executed in the friendly confines of the training camp itself. Colonel Wagner and the other commanders of black troops recognized the risks they would face when their units left their camp. Earlier in the year, on September 18, the 3rd Regiment of U.S. Colored Infantry marched through Philadelphia on its way to war. At that time the mayor and concerned officials compelled them to march unarmed and in civilian clothes.

Now it was time for the 6th USCT to march out through Philadelphia to Virginia, but this time they would take a bold new step. Wagner and Regimental Colonel John W. Ames would lead the regiment marching through the streets of Philadelphia as complete soldiers, fully uniformed and fully armed.

Finally the date had arrived, October 3, 1863. Nature had set a perfect stage for the occasion, a clear, cloudless Saturday with the sun shining "as if smiling an approval."[85] The regiment boarded a train at Chelten Hills and detrained at the station at Fourth and Masters Streets. They formed into a line of march with the 6th leading the way, followed by four companies of the newly formed 8th Regiment of U.S. Colored Infantry led by Captain Charles W. Fribley. At the head of the troops rode Colonel Wagner and, according to one spectator, Senator Henry Wilson of Massachusetts.[86] All were uniformed, but the partially formed Eighth was not armed.

The black soldiers manifested a striking visual image with their muskets and bayonets flashing in the bright sunlight, and there was "nothing white about them, save their dress-parade gloves."[87]

They marched "in admirable order, the muskets of the 6th Regiment, of course, giving greater steadiness and precision to their marching."[88] Others agreed that "the appearance of the men was good and they marched and went through evolutions in a manner that showed considerable proficiency."[89]

The parade route seems to have been consciously planned to give optimum opportunity to show marching precision. They marched in a convoluted route requiring more than a dozen ninety-degree turns. The route covered a large part of the city, showing their marching precision to as many citizens as possible.[90] General Cadwalader reviewed the troops from the steps of the Union League house on Chestnut Street and was "highly pleased" with what he saw.[91]

The people of Philadelphia well realized the significance of the event. One newspaper proclaimed Saturday, October 3, 1863, as a "remarkable one in the epoch of the military history of the City of Brotherly Love; the parade of the black regiment made its mark upon the page."[92]

Nevertheless, an underlying tension still simmered because of the many residents who harbored deep prejudices. This threatening situation had caused the mayor to delay an earlier planned parade of the 3rd U.S. Colored Troops even after it had been publicly advertised. When finally permitted to march, they were not allowed to bear arms.

During the 6th's parade the fear of violence prompted marching officers to carry loaded revolvers to be used in an emergency. The enlisted men, carrying musket and bayonet, "were not trusted with any ammunition." No outbreak of violence occurred, however. An observer believed that "the determined appearance of the colonel at the head of the negro soldiers, ...had a good deal to do with overawing the mob, which had threatened attack."[93] This "determined" colonel could have been either Colonel Wagner or Colonel Ames, both of whom were capable of presenting a stern appearance.

They approached the intersection of 9th and Chestnut Streets. This location had been the site of a confrontation earlier that year. In July of 1863, a group of uniformed Blacks marched through the streets of Philadelphia on a recruiting mission. One of the men in the group carried a flag. As they passed the Continental Hotel, a man from the crowd moved out in front of the regiment and snatched the flag out of the hands of the color-bearer. The color-bearer responded by knocking the intruder to the ground. The soldier's actions drew three cheers from the spectators.[94] Reflecting on this incident a year later, a Philadelphian noted that this event

> ...was the first giving way of prejudice in this community. From that day the colored soldiers tramped through this city by day and by night bringing in recruits for the army, successfully overcoming by their good conduct and steady bearing the prejudice of the community.[95]

The 6th Regiment proceeded down Chestnut Street and turned south on 9th Street. They passed the Continental Hotel without incident.

The final destination of the march was the Union Volunteer Refreshment Saloon, located on Swanson Street below Washington Avenue. The citizens of Philadelphia had organized this extensive eating facility in order to feed the thousands of Northern volunteers as they passed through

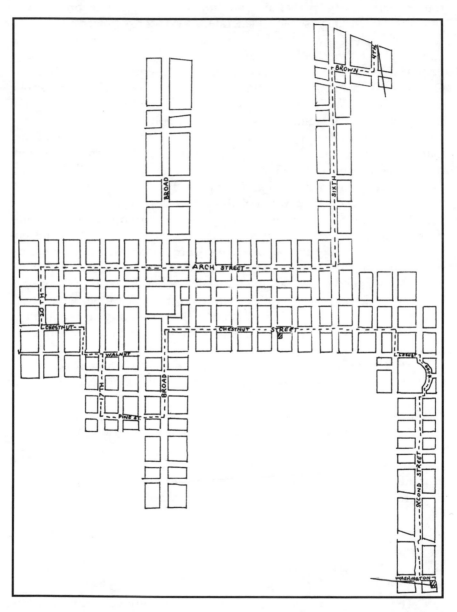

Map 1 — Philadelphia, October 6, 1863, Parade Route of 6th USCI

Philadelphia on their way south. Some of the saloon's volunteer workers, however, had "doubted the propriety of feeding colored troops."[96]

The 6th would again test public opinion by being the first Blacks to be served at this facility. The volunteers did serve the regiment. The men were "sumptuously fed."[97] This ground-breaking event caused no opposition, and donations to the saloon did not suffer. A Philadelphian observed that on that day "prejudices vanished and ever since that day, black men have been fed the same as white."[98]

After dining, the troops made their way back to Fourth and Master Streets for the return to camp. That night the 6th Regiment could reflect upon the events of the day with a feeling of accomplishment. It had not yet fired a shot at the enemy, but had already won a satisfying victory.

CHAPTER 4

THE MEN

The members of the 6th varied in age, place of birth, profession and manner of enlistment. All of the commissioned officers were white, while the noncommissioned officers, sergeants, corporals, and company musicians and rank and file were black.[1]

The regiment was fortunate to have a commander of intelligence and courage in Colonel John W. Ames. Born in 1833 in Lowell, Massachusetts, he graduated from Harvard College in 1854 and became a civil engineer. Enlisting at the war's outset in 1861 he was appointed captain, Company C, 11th Regiment of U.S. Infantry and was active in nearly every major battle in the East including Yorktown, Gaines Mills, Malvern Hill, Second Bull Run, Antietam, Shepherdstown Ford, Leetown, Snicker's Gap, Fredericksburg, Chancellorsville, and Gettysburg. Ames was wounded in the shoulder at Chancellorsville and brevetted for gallantry at both Gaines Mills and Gettysburg.[2]

Other officers in the regiment also possessed combat experience. Ames' second in command, Lieutenant Colonel Clark E. Royce, had previously served as captain with the 44th New York Regiment. First Lieutenant Maro J. Chamberlain and Second Lieutenant Edward Field came from New Hampshire units, the 14th and 4th respectively. Second Lieutenant Asa L. Jones had served in the 39th Massachusetts. First Lieutenant Charles V. York transferred from an artillery unit. Major Joseph B. Kiddoo had been with the 63rd and 137th Pennsylvania Infantry, and Captain Robert B. Beath of Company A had been a second lieutenant with the 88th Pennsylvania. Several others had also served with Pennsylvania regiments, including Captain John McMurray of the 135th; Second Lieutenant Frederick Meyer, the 112th; and First Lieutenant William A. Glass, who served with the 38th Pennsylvania Volunteers (9th Reserve Regiment). Captain Girard P. Riley came from the 15th Regiment of Ohio Volunteers. Second Lieutenant Frank A. Osborne was also a veteran, having lost an arm in the Peninsula Campaign the previous year.[3]

Colonel John W. Ames

Courtesy Donald McMurray

The white officers who served in colored regiments tended to be more antislavery in their political beliefs than most Northern Whites. It has even been suggested that "Of course, most of the whites who joined the USCT were ardent Republicans."[4] Captain McMurray supported this notion when he recalled: "Among all the officers who served in the regiment from first to last, I was the only Democrat, so far as my knowledge extended on that subject."[5] In spite of the preponderance of Republicans, there was still "a substantial cluster" of loyal Democrats among the officers. In the 6th Regiment, however, amicable coexistence was apparently not a problem, because "politics cut no figure. The subject was never mentioned, and no one in the regiment knew what my politics were, as far as I ever learned."[6]

Chaplains in the United States Army had always been white Christian ministers or priests. When the government began to form black regiments, government officials, including President Lincoln, considered assigning African American ministers to the post of chaplain in some of these regiments. The American Baptist Missionary Convention appointed a committee of black Baptist ministers to visit Lincoln and petition him for approval of such clergymen and afterward issued a letter addressed "To whom it may concern":

> To-day I am called upon by a committee of colored ministers of the Gospel, who express a wish to go within our military lines and minister to their brethren there. The object is a worthy one, and I shall be glad for all facilities to be afforded them which may not be inconsistent with or a hindrance to our military operations.[7]

Although well over one hundred regiments of African American troops were raised in the American Civil War, which were served by 133 chaplains, only fourteen black ministers were officially appointed. The 6th Regiment received one of these, the Reverend Jeremiah Asher.[8]

Asher was born October 13, 1812, in North Branford, Connecticut. He became pastor of the Shiloh Baptist Church, a black church in Philadelphia, and actively campaigned for racial justice. He also actively campaigned for the raising of colored troops. The pastor was urged early in his career to write his autobiography, and he did so. It was published in London in 1850.[9]

Army chaplains were not always accorded the respect that that position ordinarily elicits. This was especially true for "colored" chaplains. Asher along with the chaplains of three other Black regiments petitioned Secretary Stanton to provide them with insignia designating a chaplain to insure that they would be treated with some respect. Another black chaplain, Henry M. Turner of the 1st USCT, pointed out to Stanton that having no insignia

> ...subjects us to a thousand inconveniencies, [sic] especially at Hospitals where we are the most needed, unless the gaurds [sic] know us personally, we are often treated below a private, not allowed to enter where we have important business, and sometimes driven away unless we show our Chaplain's appointment.[10]

While the 6th Regiment had good fortune in securing a chaplain, obtaining a surgeon was not so easy. On December 3, 1863, an impatient Colonel Ames wrote to Major Charles W. Foster, Assistant Adjutant General: "I have the honor to request that Surgeon G. Stegman...be ordered to join this regiment at this point without delay—Surgeon Stegman has never reported to this Regt. either in person or by letter."[11] Foster replied to Ames on December 7:

> Surgeon Stegman was on duty in the South West at the date of his appointment, Sept. 11th, 1863. It is thought that he was captured at Chickamauga. If he is not heard from by the 1st of January, a new appointment will be made and you will please call attention to the matter at that time.[12]

About 43 percent of the 6th Regiment had volunteered for military service. Another 31 percent were drafted, and over one-quarter of the regiment were listed as "substitute." A conscriptee could avoid military service if he furnished an able-bodied substitute to take his place. Most substitutes in this regiment were young, usually in their early twenties. A youth might well agree to be a substitute; he might likely be drafted anyway; better to join and accept a substantial cash payment for taking someone's place.[13]

But there were also some older men who entered the service as substitutes. It may be that they had already raised their family, were no longer needed as urgently at home, and their families would benefit from the money earned as a substitute.[14] Muster rolls indicate that volunteers, substitutes, and draftees of the regiment were distributed unevenly among the different companies.[15]

The median age of a soldier in the 6th Regiment was almost twenty-three years. The most common ages were twenty and twenty-one years. The oldest member of the regiment was fifty-one years of age, while the youngest was only fourteen.[16]

Members of the regiment averaged about 5 feet, $6^1/2$ inches in height. They ranged in height from 4 feet, $10^1/2$ inches to 6 feet 11 inches. This tallest soldier (if his height was correctly recorded in the muster roll) constitutes quite a statistical aberration; the soldiers nearest his height are one man 6 feet, $3^1/2$ inches and two men 6 feet, $2^1/2$ inches. More than half of the regiment ranged from 5 feet, 5 inches to 5 feet, 8 inches in height inclusive. *Table 5* and *Graphs 9 and 10* reveal the variations in height and their frequencies of occurrence.[17]

The soldiers hailed from twenty-three different states, both North and South, as well as the District of Columbia. Muster rolls do not indicate place of residence at the time the soldier enlisted, but they do list the place of birth of each inductee. The most common state of birth was Pennsylvania. Of those whose birthplace is listed, over 36

Reverend Jeremiah Asher, Chaplain, 6th USCI

Courtesy William Gladstone and Thomas Publications

percent of the men of the 6th Regiment claimed Pennsylvania as their birth place. Delaware and Maryland claimed 16 and 15 percent respectively, and Virginia, another 12 percent. Canada, providing twenty-two soldiers, stood as the most frequently listed birthplace of any foreign nation. Six were born in the West Indies, and two in Jamaica. The other foreign birthplaces listed were Great Britain, and the Sandwich Islands. *Tables 6 and 7* and *Graphs 11–21* present a breakdown of places of birth by company.[18]

African Americans in the 1860s, even in Northern states, had only limited occupational opportunity. This restriction is reflected in the heavy preponderance of "laborer" as the most common prewar occupation listed on the 6th Regiment's muster roll. The only other occupation that even approaches laborer in frequency is "farmer." Curiously, Company D does not list a single farmer on its muster roll. Considering the high frequency of this occupation occurring in other companies, it is highly likely that the recorder of this company considered farmers to be "laborers" working on a farm.[19]

Laborers would certainly be put to work at their occupation. Like most black units, the 6th Regiment would be assigned to an unusually high amount of physical labor particularly at building fortifications. There is little indication that many other soldiers in the regiment had the opportunity to ply their trades, although some of the many barbers in the regiment may have been called upon for grooming assistance by their comrades. William J. Tyddings of Company I listed his occupation as blacksmith, and elsewhere in the Muster Roll it is noted that he was assigned to become brigade blacksmith.[20]

A significant number had worked in service occupations as barbers, waiters and servants. Several were miners; a number did brickwork and carpentry. A number had worked in the shipping trade as sailor, seaman, boatman, ship carpenter, or waterman. Others worked in land transportation as coachman, driver, drayman, hackman, teamster, or wagonier.[21]

Interesting characters filled the regiment. One such was twenty-six-year-old Private Isaac Smith. Smith, a barber from Adams County, Pennsylvania, was the son of Lydia Hamilton Smith, the black housekeeper of United States Congressman Thaddeus Stevens of Pennsylvania.[22] Smith's passion was playing the banjo; he was rarely seen without his beloved instrument. Many of his fellow soldiers enjoyed his music. One officer recalled:

> Many a time when we were lying in camp did I go down into the company street, near the "cook house", and listen for an hour to him "picking on the old banjo." The men from other companies would often gather in Company D's street, and many a lively "hoe-down" have I witnessed there, as their feet beat time to the pulsing music of Isaac's banjo.[23]

Private Smith's mother, a devout Catholic, worried about his free-spirited ways. She visited Camp William Penn and convinced his company and regimental commanders to give permission for Isaac to accompany her into the city where he might talk to a priest, and mend his ways before he faced the dangers of the battlefield. No sooner had they reached the city, however, than Isaac was able to lose his mother and head for a drinking establishment. She searched for him in vain, and at sundown she reluctantly returned to camp without him. Not until after midnight did Isaac himself return to camp, singing "We won't get home until morning." He spent the rest of the night in the guard house and the next day sweeping up the camp as punishment.

Lydia tried again to reform him with no more success than in her first attempt. Discouraged, she finally returned home, but did not give up hope. She later visited the 6th Regiment when it was stationed in Virginia, and she stayed there for several days. Again her attempt at spiritual reclamation of her son failed.[24]

Another colorful character in the regiment was Private Hubbard Ceaser. He was born in Morristown, New Jersey and was thirty-eight years old when he signed on as a substitute. Ordinarily, soldiers try to lighten their load as much as possible when they go on the march. But Hubbard Ceaser was a notorious collector. Not only did he throw away as few of his things as possible, but neither did he want to see anyone else's belongings go to waste. When others in the regiment discarded excess possessions to lighten their load for the march, Caeser would grab up whatever he could use. His studied accumulation reached the point where his tent began to resemble "a pawn shop, or a second hand clothing store."[25] Whenever the regiment would break camp and start out on a march he systematically secured all of his possessions:

> He would usually have two pairs of trousers; always two shirts and usually three; never less than two blouses; his knapsack full and bulging out and two woolen [sic] blankets strapped on top; and in addition to all this, a frying pan, coffee pot, tin cup and various other cooking utensils tied to his load here and there with strings. How he carried his burden was always a wonder to me and to others who saw him.[26]

He did at times discard some of his impediments. But his comrades expressed amazement at how much he could bear and how long he could bear it. His efforts were even more remarkable considering his diminutive size of 5 feet, 4 1/2 inches.[27]

Another memorable personality in the regiment was that of "Big Sam" Johnson. The reason he was called "Big Sam" remains a mystery. At 5 feet, 7 inches in height, he stood at only the average height for his regiment. His company commander surmised two possible explanations for his nickname. Although Johnson was of short stature, weighed only about 130 pounds, and should have needed only a size 7 shoe, his huge feet required a size 11 shoe.

Another possible explanation of his nickname arises from the big stories that he told. He spun tall tales that would captivate listeners. His reputation as a storyteller spread well beyond his own regiment, as soldiers from other regiments in the brigade sought him out. It became a common sight in camp in the evening to find Big Sam surrounded by a crowd of intent listeners as he regaled them with strange yarns, making even the weirdest and most far-fetched of tales sound believable.[28] Captain McMurray characterized his tales as

> ...pleasant fictions, creations of his fertile imagination, intended only to amuse his hearers, although he told them with an air of the most serious truthfulness. I have often thought a liberal education would have placed him as a liar far in advance of Eli Perkins and Mark Twain.[29]

Johnson often uplifted the morale of the regiment. On the march when weariness overtook others, he continued his bright and cheerful demeanor. On long, demanding marches his company commander would drop back toward the end of the line of march where Big Sam usually took his position. Listening to what he had to say, "seeing his cheerful spirit, and hearing his pleasant stories, I would go forward with renewed energy."[30]

The men of the 6th Regiment represented a wide spectrum of backgrounds and personalities. Brought together at Camp William Penn, they would move on to share an unforgettable common experience.

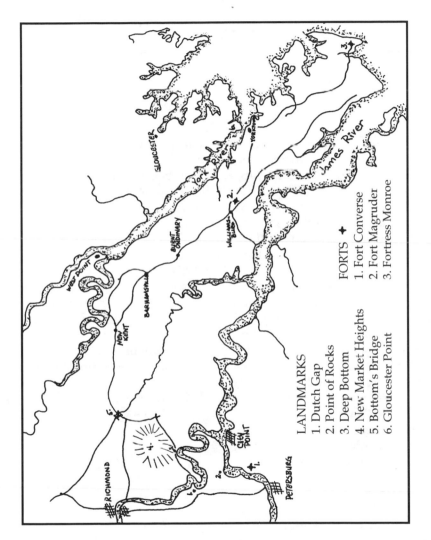

LANDMARKS
1. Dutch Gap
2. Point of Rocks
3. Deep Bottom
4. New Market Heights
5. Bottom's Bridge
6. Gloucester Point

FORTS ✝
1. Fort Converse
2. Fort Magruder
3. Fortress Monroe

Map 2 — Virginia, 1863–1865

CHAPTER 5

THEY ALSO SERVE

On October 14, 1863, the regiment left the Chelten Hills camp for the last time. A train carried them to the North Philadelphia railroad station. They then marched to the Delaware River and boarded a transport ship, the USS *Conqueror*,[1] awaiting them at the wharf at the foot of Washington Street.[2] Their destination was Fort Monroe on the Yorktown Peninsula in Virginia. The voyage, although a short one, was a memorable experience. Many of them encountered sea travel and sea sickness for the first time.[3]

The ship arrived at Fort Monroe on October 15, and was immediately sent to Yorktown, where the regiment disembarked. It marched up the Peninsula, and set up camp about a mile southeast of Fort Yorktown. Three of the companies of the regiment began submitting bi-monthly reports of their movements as early as October.[4] Captain McMurray recalled, "The weather was pleasant, and we at once set about making ourselves a comfortable home, expecting to remain there several months."[5]

Camp routine was soon formalized. Colonel Ames established the regiment's daily schedule as:

Reveille	Daybreak
Breakfast	7 1/2 AM
Surgeons Call	8 AM
Guardmounting and Policing	
Camp and Quarters	9 AM
Drill	10 AM
Dinner	12 M
Drill	3 PM
Parade and retreat	Sunset
Supper, immediately after parade	
Tattoo	8 1/2 PM
Taps	9 PM[6]

A few days after the 6th arrived on the Peninsula, the 4th and 5th Regiments of U S. Colored Infantry set up camp alongside them. In mid-February of 1864 the 22nd USCI, fresh from its training at Camp William Penn, joined them.[7] These four regiments were brigaded together under Colonel Samuel A. Duncan. Duncan's Brigade served under General Isaac J. Wistar, Commander of U.S. forces at Yorktown, which was part of Major General Benjamin F. Butler's Department of Virginia and North Carolina.[8]

The first two months in Virginia were spent in preparation. The regiment's stay at Camp William Penn had been hardly long enough for the men to acquire and practice battlefield skills. In addition to company and regimental drill they kept busy working on the fortifications of Yorktown and Gloucester Point.[9] They also took part in "raids, or tramps, up the Peninsula toward Richmond, or expeditions north of the York River in the direction of the Rappahannock." Those movements were largely conducted to provide practice in marching.[10]

Nearby Yorktown may have been rich in history, but it seemed dreary to an observer from the regiment who described it as

> a village of only a few houses, and all the residents were "poor whites" or colored people. Not a well-to-do person remained in the place. Outside of the fortifications, distant less than a mile, was a collection of nearly half a hundred cheap, frail houses, occupied by colored families.[11]

Local white women did their best to make the black troops feel unwelcome. The women would gather along the parade route when the men would march "to jeer and shake their fists."[12] According to the *New York Tribune*, the men responded with "good-natured laughter."[13]

The town of Williamsburg, through which the regiment would march several times, was not much more impressive than Yorktown. "The town was about a half mile long and seemed to have only one street," observed Captain McMurray.[14] But this town did supply inspiration to the soldiers every time they would march through it. On those occasions, "both sides of this Main street would be lined with colored people, old and young, male and female, to see the colored soldiers, of whom they were very proud." The sight of a unit of colored soldiers marching through their Virginia town gave a great thrill to the black townspeople. The troops saw one black woman dancing ecstatically as they reached the town. She continued to dance "in an ecstasy of excitement" until they had all marched by, and she collapsed from exhaustion.[15]

Such a reception must have been exhilarating. On at least one occasion they could not keep themselves from reciprocating the greeting they received. As they marched through Williamsburg a group of Blacks stood on the portico of a large house to view the parade. Among them was an attractive young woman, talking and laughing as she watched the soldiers pass by. A handsome young soldier in Company D, Nathaniel Danks, caught sight of her and ran out of ranks. He quickly ran onto the pavement and up the porch steps. He put his arm around her neck and "kissed her with a resounding smack that was heard half a square away, and was down on the pavement on the other side before the girl had time to realize what had happened." A "mighty cheer" went up from the regiment and Danks was the hero of the day.[16]

The day to day tedium of drill, fatigue duty, and seemingly pointless marching was wearing.

> Every soldier who has lain in camp any length of time knows how monotonous camp life becomes after a while. Almost any occurrence that would break in upon this monotony would be hailed as a welcome visitor. Day after day brings the same weary round of detailing so many men for "guard tomorrow"; guard mounting in the morning; the steady tramp, tramp of the sentinels on their beats; and "dress parade" in the evening.[17]

One day a local black resident called upon the officer in charge of the regimental camp. Captain McMurray happened to be the officer of the day. The resident complained that the previous night several chickens had been taken from his hen house. He also said that he had witnessed soldiers performing the deed and that he would be able to identify the perpetrators. McMurray had plenty of time on his hands and, "anticipating some fun," escorted the plaintiff through the camp. They had not gotten far before the accuser pointed out the culprits. The soldiers owned up to the deed, and McMurray let them off as easily as he could.[18]

On December 13 the regiment awoke early, and by 4 o'clock they were on the march. They advanced about twenty-five miles to a point twelve miles northwest of Williamsburg called "Burnt Ordinary" or "12 Mile Ordinary." The regiment arrived before dark, and Colonel Ames selected a good defensive position. Because the road forked at this point, Ames sent pickets ahead down both roads. The rest of the regiment bivouacked at Burnt Ordinary.[19]

The purpose of this march was to support Union cavalry and infantry units engaged in a surprise attack on a Confederate cavalry battalion camped at nearby Charles City Courthouse. The success of this operation depended on the swift movement of the raiders. No ambulance accompanied the attacking units, nor did they carry extra rations to slow their march. The 6th brought with them to Burnt Ordinary the needed ambulances and a wagon loaded with rations. The regiment remained bivouacked at Burnt Ordinary until the raiding party returned to camp about one o'clock on the morning of December 14.[20]

General Wistar saw the raid as a "complete success." His forces took the Confederates almost completely by surprise. They captured the entire enemy force, three companies including eight officers and eighty-two enlisted men. They also captured fifty-five horses and three mules as well as some 100 carbines, 100 sabers, 100 sets of horse equipment, ammunition, provisions, and new tents. They burned all that they could not carry.

The ambulances and rations brought by the 6th were much needed. Union troops had lost two men killed and four wounded including a captain. The exhausted troops turned over their prisoners to the also tired 6th.

The 6th had marched about twenty-five miles on the thirteenth, setting out by 4 A.M. Needing a good night's sleep, they were instead aroused at 1 A.M. by the return of the raiding party. Later the same morning they set out on the thirteen-mile march back to Union lines, bringing with them the prisoners and captured property. This march would have been demanding even under ideal conditions, but the expedition was plagued by a drenching rainstorm that continued throughout most of the operation. Reports described the downpour as "a severe storm of wind and rain" and "a pelting, pitiless storm."[21]

The weather turned roads that were normally muddy anyway into torturous quagmires. Some New York infantrymen involved in the raid reported walking right out of their shoes.[22] Wistar appreciated the hardship when he commended the troops in his official report. Of the 6th he reported:

> Colonel Ames' colored infantry did what was required of them, which would be considered very severe duty (weather and roads considered),...Their position at Twelve-Mile Ordinary, in readiness to receive and guard prisoners and horses, issue rations, attend to wounded, and do picket duty, on the return of the other exhausted troops, was found of extreme advantage.[23]

The regiment slogged on through the thirteen miles between Burnt Ordinary and Fort Magruder, where they turned over their prisoners. The men were glad to be back behind their own lines again. They had been campaigning miles in advance of Union lines and had lost one man of the regiment who was captured by the enemy.[24] They remained at Fort Magruder until Christmas Day, when they marched the final twelve miles back to their old camp near Yorktown.[25]

The next major action in which the 6th was involved was Major General Benjamin F. Butler's raid. Butler had been greatly concerned about the many captured Union soldiers being held in prisoner of war camps in and around Richmond. His spies in Richmond had reported that its garrison had been sent to operations in North Carolina. The Confederates felt safe in taking this measure because of the "almost impassable" condition of the roads. They had left only a small guard, less than a company of artillerymen, stationed at Bottom's Bridge over the Chickahominy River eleven miles from Richmond. No other Confederate troops stood between Bottom's Bridge and Capitol Square in Richmond.[26]

A rapid march might allow Butler to take the Confederates by surprise, and if the bridge could be seized, he could penetrate the city and free the many Union prisoners there. The Union command also planned a secondary objective of capturing members of the Confederate Cabinet and perhaps even Jefferson Davis himself. Davis's own gardener had crossed over to Union lines and would serve as guide on the expedition.[27]

After nightfall on February 5, 1864, the combined force of 4,000 infantry, 2,200 cavalry, and two batteries of light artillery concentrated behind Union lines at Williamsburg. The infantry force composed of three white and three colored regiments including the 6th moved out sometime between 9 A.M. and 11 A.M.[28] on the morning of the sixth. Colonel Samuel P. Spear's cavalry moved out two hours later.

Spear was to arrive at Bottom's Bridge by 3 A.M. on the seventh, take the troops there by surprise, and move quickly on to Richmond. The infantry would follow in support. Wistar understood clearly how essential secrecy was to the success of the mission. As he told Butler, "Of course the success of the enterprise was based upon the sudden and noiseless surprise of the strong picket at Bottom's Bridge." Otherwise the Union cavalry could not possibly get past the Confederate artillery.[29]

McMurray recalled that "Most of the officers in the expedition knew what its purpose was, and were prepared for any emergency."[30] If most of the officers knew the purpose and some did not, enlisted men were even more likely to be left uninformed. The men were issued six days' rations at the outset, however, a sure sign that they were in for more than a short trek.[31] An even more ominous sign of impending action came when each man of the regiment was issued seventy cartridges. They filled their cartridge boxes with forty rounds each and stashed the other thirty rounds in their knapsacks.[32]

Unknown to any of the raiders, however, the secrecy had already been shattered. A soldier from a New York regiment, awaiting execution for the willful murder of an officer, had escaped from Williamsburg the night before the expedition had begun. He fled to the enemy and warned them of the coming raid. And so the Confederates were well prepared for the raiding party.[33] McMurray strongly suspected that the operation was no longer secret. He recalled: "We felt sure before midnight of the first day's march that our coming was known, for two or three times we saw sky rockets go up some distance in advance of us, no doubt as signals of approaching danger."[34]

The 6th performed admirably throughout the entire episode. The day before the raid began, the regiment left its camp near Yorktown at 2 P.M. By the end of the day it had marched the entire twelve miles to Williamsburg, where they bivouacked near "Fort McGruder" [sic].[35] All through the day and the night of February 6 they marched. The cold February night chilled the men but they pressed steadily onward. This forced march tired out the troops even in the absence of opposition or obstructions of any kind. By early morning of the second day, they had come within two miles of Bottom's Bridge. At that point the cavalry passed them, taking the lead for the first time.[36]

As the horsemen now quickly approached the bridge, through the darkness they suddenly found themselves looking down the barrels of two artillery pieces set up waiting for them at the far end of the bridge.[37] The enemy stood in strong force with infantry and cavalry supporting the artillery. They had learned of the coming attack some sixteen hours previously and had made good use of the time making preparations. They had torn up the planks on the bridge and effectively obstructed the fords across the Chickahominy River both above and below the bridge with fallen timbers, "extensive earthworks and rifle pits."[38] Even more Confederate reinforcements were on their way by means of the York River Railroad.

The horsemen approached the bridge moving forward two abreast. The Confederate artillery blasted them with canister, and three or four of the lead horses fell. Realizing the hopelessness of trying to cross the bridge with the floor torn off, the cavalrymen abandoned altogether the idea of taking it. The cavalry lost nine men killed or wounded and ten horses killed. They reconnoitred the river both above and below the bridge for some miles, "but at every possible crossing the enemy was found in force with newly placed obstructions."[39] All hope of success extinguished, the dismayed cavalry turned about and headed back the way they had come.

The horse soldiers again passed the infantry at New Kent Courthouse. The men of the 6th could easily assess what had happened when they saw the "sad, disappointed, dejected" horsemen pass by them.[40] The frustrated infantry turned around and headed back toward their own lines. The 6th Regiment had marched twelve miles on February 5 and over thirty miles on the sixth, and it would march another twenty-seven miles before the next day ended. The march would be even harder going back.[41] Besides physical weariness the men had to deal with their own feelings of frustration as well as the harassment of the enemy:

> Without rest, and many of us wondering why we had been brought on this long, hard, fruitless march, we all started back. For several miles the rear of our retreating column was harrassed by pursuing cavalrymen, but before noon they ceased to annoy us, and the next day we reached Williamsburg, as tired and disgusted a lot of soldiers as ever marched up and down the Peninsula.[42]

The regiment was not yet finished marching. It would only return to its camp near Yorktown on the ninth, after a two-day march of another forty-three miles.[43] The official reports from the individual companies of the regiment indicate that the men had been both dependable and durable. Company B reported that on the demanding first day's march they "withstood a forced march of 32 miles exceedingly well, but for one man falling out." Company D indicated that officers and men "behaved admirably on the march. No stragling [sic] whatever." Reporting on the whole operation, Company F reported returning to camp "having marched in about 4 days about one hundred and twenty-five miles. During the whole march not a man fell behind his Co[mpany]. nor rode in any ambulance."[44]

The remainder of February would be uneventful. On the thirteenth the regiment was ordered again to Williamsburg. They arrived there about noon of that day and formed camp near Fort Magruder. They remained there doing picket duty on the right of Williamsburg until February 26. On that day the regiment was relieved by the 22nd USCI and returned to their camp near Yorktown.[45] The rest of the winter they would spend wondering about what might have been. "How often in the days that followed we wondered and speculated as to what would have happened had we been able to cross Bottom's Bridge."[46]

By the end of February, Union Brigadier General Hugh Judson Kilpatrick had developed a plan for another raid on Richmond with similar goals of freeing Union prisoners. Kilpatrick launched his cavalry raid on the evening of February 28 and reached Richmond's intermediate defense line the next day. At that point the operation fell apart. The lightly defended Confederate defensive line intimidated Kilpatrick, and he halted. A pursuing force of only 300 Confederate cavalry attacked the 3,000 invading troopers. Kilpatrick chose to abort the mission and head for the safety of the Union-occupied Yorktown Peninsula.[47]

Butler ordered some of his infantry, including the 6th U.S. Colored Infantry, to march to New Kent Court House to rendezvous with Kilpatrick. They were to both aid Kilpatrick and cover his march to Fort Monroe.[48]

On the afternoon of March 1, the 6th Regiment began their relief march. By 3 o'clock in the afternoon of the next day they had reached New Kent Court House after a march of forty-two miles. On the morning of the third, the regiment moved a few miles farther and met Kilpatrick's cavalry. They marched back through Barhamsville, a comparatively light march that day. Company K calculated a march of eighteen miles on the third and twenty-six on the fourth, continuing beyond Williamsburg to Fort Magruder. After ten more miles of marching, they reached the Yorktown camp, the lead company arriving at noon on the fifth, other companies as late as the morning of the sixth.[49] One unit calculated that the regiment had been absent from camp 102 hours during which they had marched ninety-two miles.[50] Company H reported the loss of Corporal John Smith and Private Richard P. Armistead, "probably taken prisoner between Williamsburg and Burnt Ordinary."[51]

The very day they arrived in camp they embarked on transports. At this point the reports of the various companies of the regiment differ. Activity and movement filled the month of March, which may explain the diversion of accounts. Companies wrote and submitted their official reports for two-month periods. Only at the end of April did they put together their reports for the period March–April. The passage of time and the abundance of movements to recall may have caused confusion. Different companies may also have been detached from the rest of the regiment or may have marched different routes, followed different schedules or taken different transport ships.[52]

According to the headquarters staff the regiment returned to camp on the fifth and on the evening of the same day left camp and went aboard transports, landing the next day at Portsmouth, Virginia and proceeding to Getty's Station. According to Companies A, B, and C they returned to Yorktown on the morning of the sixth and the same day embarked and landed at Portsmouth.[53] They mention no marching as part of this movement. Company D, on the other hand, reported taking transports to Getty's Station and marching from there to Portsmouth. Companies F and K in more detailed reports state that they arrived in camp at Yorktown at noon of the fifth and embarked that evening for Portsmouth. They arrived the next morning and immediately moved out to Getty's Station, arriving at 3:00 P.M. On the eighth they both marched back to Portsmouth.[54]

The next expedition in which the men of the regiment participated would take them north to another part of Virginia. Companies A, B, and C embarked March 10 on the steamer *Champion* and disembarked at Shepherd's Landing on the Mattaponi River. The remaining companies according to headquarters boarded transports and steamed up the York River to West Point. At West Point the river forks, and the ships proceeded up the right fork, the Mattaponi.. They landed at Shepherd's Landing in King and Queen County, arriving at 2 o'clock the next morning.[55]

Orders had been given to march inland quickly, "seize all suspicious characters, and take such private property as might be useful to contrabands, and to prevent any plundering by the men."[56] For the next three days they tramped through King and Queen County and Gloucester County, traveling ten miles on the tenth, twenty-four miles on the eleventh, and twenty miles on the twelfth. They arrived at Gloucester Point on the twelfth. The troops returned to camp near Yorktown between the thirteenth and the fifteenth.[57]

Another excursion began on the seventeenth and eighteenth, when the regiment boarded transports yet again. The transports, including one steamer named the *Thomas A. Morgan*, probed up the Piankatank River. At some point on this river they landed and marched through Matthews County and part of Middlesex County. The men returned to Yorktown on March 21 or 22 and remained there until April 20. On that day they marched to Camp Hamilton near Fort Monroe, covering twenty-eight miles in eighteen hours.[58] As April gave way to June of 1864, the 6th Regiment had still experienced only the fringes of war. That would soon change.

CHAPTER 6

THE ASSAULT ON PETERSBURG

By May of 1864 sweeping changes had taken place and momentum was building toward a major offensive operation. Major General Ulysses S. Grant, after a series of notable military successes in the west, had been brought to Washington, promoted to the newly recreated rank of lieutenant general and placed in command of the combined armies of the United States. Grant would exercise command from the east. His main objective in the east would be to engage and defeat Robert E. Lee's Confederate Army of Northern Virginia. To accomplish this goal he had at his command two armies, the Army of the Potomac under Major General George G. Meade and the Army of the James under Major General Benjamin F. Butler.[1]

If properly utilized, the 35,000-man Army of the James could be a decisive factor in the coming struggle. The 6th USCI along with the 4th and 5th USCI composed the brigade of Colonel Samuel E. Duncan. Duncan's and one other brigade of Colored Troops made up a division under the command of Brigadier General Edward W. Hinks. Hinks' Division, along with two divisions of white troops, served as part of the XVIII Corps under Major General William F. Smith. The XVIII and X Army Corps formed by Butler's Army of the James.[2]

Grant would use his two armies in a coordinated drive toward Richmond. On May 4 the Army of the Potomac began crossing the Rapidan River as the first step in its thrust toward the Confederate capital. Within two days that army would become locked in a deadly struggle with Lee's army in the dense woodlands known as the Wilderness.[3] On the very day that Grant began the crossing of the Rapidan, Butler also set his army in motion.

On May 4 the 6th left Fort Hamilton and boarded transports at Fort Monroe.[4] A huge fleet of transports of all types, "a motley array of vessels,"[5] began ferrying the 25,000 troops. In order to mislead the Confederates, the ships first steamed northward as if to ascend the York River. At midnight, however, the ships reversed course and steamed up the James River with ironclad ships leading the way.[6] They landed that evening near the mouth of the Appomattox River at City Point, a position from which a detachment of sharpshooters had earlier driven off the Confederates. These sharpshooters, selected from several "colored" regiments, were under the command of Captain Philip Weinmann of Company I, 6th USCI.[7]

The African American troops took control of City Point while the white troops secured control of Bermuda Hundred to the north. They encountered no opposition because the move had achieved complete surprise. On May 6 the men began to throw up entrenchments about a half mile from the landing.[8]

While Butler's ultimate goal was the capture of Richmond, his important intermediate objective was to cut off Richmond from the rest of the Confederacy by severing its railroad lifeline south of the capital. This aim could be effectively accomplished by capturing the city of Petersburg, the last key railroad link to Richmond, or by cutting the Richmond & Petersburg Railroad to the north or the Weldon Petersburg Railroad to the south of Petersburg.

On May 7 Butler sent a reconnaissance force toward the Richmond & Petersburg Railroad, and after a fight the troops were able to destroy a portion of the line.[9] Butler's efforts, however, were ineffective. He allowed his army to be "bottled up" at Bermuda Hundred, for the time being ruining Grant's plans for a two-pronged advance on Richmond. Grant could not hide his disappointment.[10]

McMurray also felt exasperation. His regiment did extensive entrenching, but was completely left out of combat actions such as that against the railroads. He complained: "Day after day we lay there, inactive, knowing of the fighting that was going on, but required to take no part in it."[11]

On May 9 the 6th Regiment moved out and made a reconnaissance toward Petersburg, but they returned the same night. On the twelfth they again moved out, this time marching six miles toward Petersburg and going into camp at Spring Hill. Their new camp stood in a large field perched on a high point near the Appomattox River. From camp they could see the spires of churches and public buildings in Petersburg. The city lay only four miles away in a straight line, but a good six miles by local wagon road.[12]

Here a picket line was set up and cavalry videttes were sent out towards Petersburg. The 6th went to work alongside the 4th USCI building fortifications. They built a strong earthwork, afterward known as Redoubt Converse, to protect the pontoon bridge that crossed the river at that point. The 4th was soon withdrawn. This left the 6th as the sole unit manning the nearest outpost to Petersburg.[13]

Here at Spring Hill the regiment would experience its first combat of any kind. It was no encounter of any consequence, only a "little skirmish or two," according to McMurray. Several times small forces of Petersburg defenders attacked the picket line. Each time the enemy drove back the outposts but inflicted no serious losses beyond the wounding of a few soldiers. But, insignificant as it may have been, it became their baptism of fire and the men remembered it well.[14]

At least two of these attacks were important enough to be recorded in company reports. On May 18 Confederates attacked the picket line. The blue-uniformed pickets fell back a short distance. The enemy then retired.

The Rebels returned on May 31. This time they came in force. They "vigorously" attacked and drove in the Union pickets, who fell back fighting about 200 yards. For a short time Confederate cannons poured shot and shell on the 6th Regiment's works. Union artillery then opened heavy fire upon the attackers, silencing the Confederate artillery in the process. That afternoon the 4th and 5th USCI arrived as reinforcements. The 4th pushed out to the former Union picket line, where the Confederates at this time waited in force. After some fighting the Petersburg defenders fell back and withdrew sometime during the night.[15]

Company reports indicate that the Federals had inflicted a number of casualties on the Southerners, but that they themselves had suffered only a few men wounded. Company I reported firing forty rounds per man in the fighting. Since the men were armed with single-shot muzzle-loading rifles, each soldier was likely to fire no more than two rounds per minute in the heat of battle. Fighting must have continued that day at some length.[16]

McMurray recalled an incident at Spring Hill that provided amusement for him and others in the regiment, but embarrassment for First Lieutenant George E. Heath of his Company D. While the rest of the regiment had been engaged in the grueling work of building fortifications, Heath had been enjoying himself in Philadelphia. He had stayed behind at Camp William Penn as part of the camp administration when the rest of the regiment marched off to war. He joined his company eight months later and stood out in his pristine uniform, "as if he had just stepped out of a band box," in sharp contrast to the men who had spent their last eight months roughing it in the field.[17]

Heath's dapper appearance, however, did not save him from a picket duty assignment his first morning in camp. With a gleaming sword and a portfolio of fancy stationery he went out to his station, fancifully intending to send home letters writen on the picket line. But Heath left his picket station on the road to Petersburg and walked up the road about an eighth of a mile to where he talked with a farmer while writing a letter to his wife. McMurray narrates:

> Suddenly he heard a noise up the road toward Petersburg, and looking that way saw half a dozen cavalrymen coming down the road

at a brisk trot. He took in the situation at a glance, and leaving his portfolio with all its fine stationary, and the half written letter to his wife on
the upper fence rail, ran for dear life toward the picket post he had left
only a little while before. Just then the approaching cavalrymen espied
him, and then it was a race for life. The men on the picket line saw him
coming, with the cavalrymen in hot pursuit, and to help him all they
could, began shooting at the approaching horsemen. The firing checked
their speed a little, and Lt. Heath got safely inside our lines, leaving
behind him his portfolio, his haversack, and some other nice articles
that tended to impede his progress on the retreat. If he had had thirty
rods further to go to reach our picket line, he doubtless would have
been captured.[18]

Those horsemen were the advance guard of a reconnoitering party of
fifty or more sent out to determine the strength and position of the Union
forces there. On that day, probably May 31, the Confederates preceded their
attack by firing their two artillery pieces at the Union reserve position. One
of the shells struck an old building that was serving as shelter for a score of
men at the time. The soldiers tumbled headlong out of the building, re-
minding McMurray of "bees swarming out of their hive when it was rudely
disturbed in summer."[19]

McMurray had his own close call. Just about the time of the attack
he was walking alone in a plowed field bordered by woodlands. Unknown
to him, riflemen were perched in these trees barely 100 yards away. They
opened fire on him point-blank. He ran as bullets struck the plowed ground
a few feet ahead of him. He was not hit.[20]

Two or three companies including a unit of about twenty-five colored cavalrymen, came to the aid of their embattled pickets. As he watched
the cavalry charge the two cannons that had been firing at them, McMurray
saw several black horsemen tumble from their saddles. But the counter-
charge was a success as the Rebels hitched their two cannons to limbers
and departed, never to return to this site.[21]

Early in the fighting as the picket line was falling back, McMurray
went to assess the situation. On the way he met young Private Alphonso
Cherry, a five-foot, two-inch, eighteen-year-old member of Company D
from Harrisburg. After firing one or two shots, Cherry began falling back
in seemingly good order for his camp, and McMurray asked him why he
was doing so. He explained that in the heat of fighting he had shot his
ramrod away, a fairly common error for raw troops in their first battle.
This meant that he could no longer load his rifle and was of no use on the
firing line. McMurray told him to go to camp, get another gun, and return. But instead, Alphonso continued to fall back and fall back, and did
not stop falling back until he reached Norfolk.

Strangely enough, some seven months later McMurray would spot a
familiar-looking sergeant in a regiment of colored cavalry. Cherry explained

that he decided that if he had to stay in this war he would rather do it riding than walking. At his old captain's insistence he returned to Company D and served until the end of the war, April of 1865. "By hard pleading with Colonel Ames" McMurray got him off with only a few days in the guard house.[22]

After Spring Hill came the major turning point for the 6th. Up to this point:

> We had considerable experience in marching, some in throwing up earth-works, and were fairly well trained in company, regimental, and brigade drill, but in fighting we were novices. But now we were at the turning point, and from this time forward we were destined to experience our full share of the vicissitudes of war.[23]

On the morning of June 9 Major General Quincy A. Gillmore of the X Corps led a reconnaissance toward Petersburg. The 6th saw action during this demonstration as their force encountered enemy pickets about noon that day. The blue-clad troops continued to advance to within a short distance of the works in front of Petersburg and withstood fire from them for about two hours before withdrawing. They returned to Spring Hill that same day. A number of companies in the regiment suffered casualties. Company A reported one killed and three wounded, one private of Company D was wounded, two wounded from Company F.[24]

Grant wrote to Butler on June 11 directing him to move against Petersburg, to seize and hold the city.[25] Early in the morning, June 15, Major General William F. Smith's XVIII Corps began crossing the Appomattox River at Point of Rocks, using the pontoon bridge that the 6th had been protecting. They watched Smith's troops pass by their camp. They then immediately followed them together with several other "colored" regiments who formed the all-black division of Brigadier General Edward W. Hinks.[26]

On June 15, General Grant ordered Major General William F. Smith's XVIII Corps and Major General Winfield S. Hancock's II Corps of the Army of the Potomac to attack the Confederate lines near Petersburg.[27] Later that morning, the XVIII Corps would face the earthworks in front of that city, and several sharp skirmishes would break out throughout the day.[28]

Duncan's Brigade, including the 6th, broke from line of march and formed a line of battle. They advanced through dense woods, and about a mile away from the main line of works they suddenly came upon a clearing. Directly in front of them stood a small redoubt holding two pieces of artillery and a company or two of supporting infantry. The brigade continued advancing and a sharp fight broke out. The entire regiment for the first time came under fire. Company D had the bad fortune to be located directly in front of the Rebel cannons. As soon as the blue line emerged from the woods the artillery opened fire and poured grape and canister into them.[29]

Even the bravest of men would be severely tested by charging straight toward cannons aimed directly at them. As a first time in combat, the experience must have stretched beyond the capacity of some men to handle. The color bearer holds the most conspicuous and perilous position of all. Carrying a bright banner in advance of all other troops transforms him into the most likely target of all. The regimental color bearer going into this fight was William Law of Company D.

Enlisting at age twenty-one, the six-foot, one-inch youth was immediately selected as color sergeant because of his stature and his strong and neat appearance. As the cannons ahead exploded in fire and sprayed deadly canister on the regiment, Law could stand no more. He turned around and attempted to run back into the woods, but was stopped by the officer directly behind him, who took his arm and pushed him back into his place in line telling him to go ahead. He went forward a few more steps but again turned around to run. This time even "a smart blow across the shoulders" with the officer's sword could not stop his retreat. He threw the flag to the ground and crawled on his hands and feet to the rear. Because of his conduct he was reduced to the ranks and was never again permitted to carry the flag.[30]

The actions of the color bearer stood out in contrast to the seemingly intrepid deportment of the rest of the regiment. Even seeing the uninspiring behavior of their flag bearer the men continued their advance, suffering several killed and wounded. Company D in this charge lost two mortally wounded and three less severely wounded. The attacking force quickly drove off the small force of defenders and captured both of the artillery pieces.[31]

The assault on the main Confederate works had not yet come. It seemed to many participants that the attack should have been made much earlier in the day, but in fact it would not be launched until sundown, giving the enemy an entire day to reinforce their lines. Many officers and enlisted men judged that the Confederate line earlier in the day was little more than a skirmish line. More than one officer believed:

> Had we moved forward promptly we would have been in possession of Petersburg before the middle of that afternoon. Petersburg could have been taken that day with a loss of just a handful of men, whereas its final capture cost possibly a hundred thousand Union soldiers' lives, and many millions in money.[32]

Finally that afternoon Hinks reordered his troops in preparation for the charge on the enemy's main works. While waiting for the order to advance, the Union troops were severely harassed by enemy artillery, which rained upon them "an unremitting and very accurate and severe fire."[33] Company B reported being under heavy artillery fire from 8 o'clock A.M. to 6 P.M.[34] McMurray remembered:

From about ten or half past ten in the morning until nearly sundown, we lay exposed to the enemy's fire, which was mostly of spherical case shot. While this fire was not very effective, it was quite annoying. The little shells sent every few minutes to greet us were not as large as hornets' nests, but their contents were more annoying. They were filled with little metal bullets nearly as big as hickory nuts, small pieces of broken metal, etc. We had no means of protecting ourselves from them, as when they would burst over our heads their contents would come down in all directions.[35]

A metal fragment struck Second Lieutenant Asa Jones of Company A behind his ankle, crushing his large tendon. A week later he would be discharged, a cripple for life.[36] Another officer, First Lieutenant Enoch Jackman, received a slight wound on the hand or wrist, barely a scratch, but enough to send him to the rear. The well-timed wound left him "seemingly as happy as though he had been promoted to Colonel." Two able-bodied men accompanied him to the rear.[37]

That afternoon, as McMurray and some other officers lay under a tree, a Confederate cannon fired a solid shot at the group. They could plainly see the shot bounding toward them, ricocheting over the open field. It came directly at the captain, who leaped out of the way just in time. But a soldier from another regiment who was in this group did not move and was struck in the side and killed instantly.[38]

Captain Harvey Covell of Company B described the action on the fifteenth in a letter written five days later to his wife. The Confederates had several pieces of artillery and "quite a force" ensconced in a rifle pit. The regiment was ordered to advance to get in position for an attack, but the men were so eager that at the command, "Forward," they charged with a yell. An unidentified colonel had to ride in front of them and tell them to halt and reverse, and most of the companies fell back into the woods in some disorder. Colonel Ames, however, stayed in the advanced position in front of the woods along with Companies A, B, and C until the rest of the regiment had disappeared into the woods. At that time the Confederates concentrated their fire, including ten artillery pieces, on those exposed troops. Their position became, in Covell's eyes, "about as hot a place as I ever saw." The enemy then moved in on their left and gave them a terrible raking fire killing or wounding several men. Ames then ordered them back into the woods where they awaited the order to advance.[39]

As artillery continued to pound them, the troops would move to avoid their shells. Ames had his men keep down, but they could only find small hollows in the ground and a few scattered small trees. They were forced into a deadly game of dodging cannon balls:

> I had one as narrow escape as I wish to have the shot and shell
> now all around us all the time but we could see when they were about
> to fire and if the shell was coming directly for us we could dodge it if

it struck the ground before it reached us as it usually would. I was behind a little tree a shell struck within a few feet and as it struck it exploded among us....[40]

Covell escaped injury from that explosion, but no sooner had he side-stepped that explosion than he looked up to see another cannon shell heading directly towards him. He had no time to act because it never struck the ground, and with it coming right at him he could not decide which way to dodge. He froze. It exploded a few feet in front of him, showering iron balls and fragments all around him but miraculously missing him.[41]

As the sun was about to set, General Smith finally started his assault. His artillery opened up an impressive barrage against the Confederate works in preparation for the attack. The distance from the woods to the Confederate line was about 360 paces by one account but as much as 800 yards according to other observers. The advancing skirmish line, which had already driven back the Confederate sharpshooters with repeated advances, again drove forward toward the earthworks. The two Union divisions advanced and emerged from the woods, Smith's white troops on the right, Hinks' Colored Division on the left. They were aiming for the earthworks extending from Confederate Battery 5 through Battery 10.[42]

The first line of colored troops included the 1st, 4th, and 22nd Regiments, followed by the 5th and 6th in support. The line advanced at the double-quick, bayonets glittering obliquely in the fading sunlight. Heavy musket and cannon fire erupted from in front of them. Crossing a burned over slash, the lead regiments met stiff resistance and suffered grim casualties. They were at first repulsed, but surged forward again overpowering the defenders. Led by Colonel Joseph B. Kiddoo, formerly a major with the 6th, the 22nd poured into Battery 7. The 1st Regiment pushed on to Battery 8 and captured it against heavy resistance.[43]

At this point the 6th was directed against Battery 9. The men continued to surge forward in the growing darkness through the mud and tangled underbrush, having already crossed the slashing. They then ran into breast high blackened logs. They had to climb over them in some places and go under them in others. The redoubt appeared increasingly formidable in the twilight as they came near it. Yet not one shot had been fired at them from the redoubt. They reasoned that the defenders were holding their fire until the attackers came close. Then they encountered their last two obstructions, a line of abatis and a ditch.[44]

As quickly as possible the troops made their way through the abatis, an arrangement of felled trees with branches facing toward them to slow their attack.[45] Soon they surged into the ditch, expecting a rain of musket fire at any moment. The ditch filled with men and they began to climb the face of the fortification. Soldiers stabbed their bayonets into the side of the parapet and climbed them as a ladder. The first men to reach the top lifted their heads over the wall expecting to be shot instantly. But they found the redoubt empty. The Rebels had fled, leaving nothing behind save the body of a teen-age defender. After they had climbed into the redoubt the soldiers buried the young soldier with care.[46]

The 6th Regiment's assault on Battery 9 proved to be mercifully anticlimactic. But although not a man was killed nor a shot fired by either side, "some were nearly scared to death."[47]

By 9:00 P.M., five redans and the connection rifle pits for a distance of over two and one-half miles were in Federal hands.[48] The assault also netted fifteen artillery pieces and 300 prisoners.[49]

At this point, instead of following up on his success, Smith halted the advance and sent out his pickets. All through the night they could hear Confederate reinforcements moving into position to defend Petersburg. The Union's best opportunity to capture the city slipped away that night. McMurray lamented: "Twelve hours earlier General Smith could have marched into Petersburg at will. Now, Grant's whole army was unable to force its way in."[50]

The next day Grant declared: "Smith has taken a line of works there, stronger than anything we have seen in this campaign! If it is a possible thing, I want an assault made at six o'clock this evening!"[51] He saw a great opportunity and thought that Smith should have pressed the attack. He judged:

> Between the lines thus captured and Petersburg there were no other works, and there was no evidence that the enemy had reinforced Petersburg with a single brigade from any source. The night was clear — the moon shining brightly — and favorable to further operations.[52]

In later years he would insist: "I believed then, and still believe, that Petersburg could have been easily captured at that time."[53] Even more bluntly it might be said: "Petersburg had scarcely more than 2,000 men in its earthworks. It was a sitting duck that could have been bagged easily."[54] Smith's Confederate counterpart, General Pierre G. T. Beauregard, thought it "strange" that Smith did not press his advantage.[55]

The impressive achievements of the attacking Union forces on June 15 have come to be eclipsed by the discouraging failure of their commanders to follow through. The significance of the initial deeds, however, was certainly appreciated at the time. On the morning of June 17, Grant himself paid tribute to Butler's men saying:

> Too much credit cannot be given to the troops and their commanders for the energy and fortitude displayed during the last five days. Day and night has been all the same, no delays being allowed on any account.[56]

An observer testified:

> The success has a peculiar value and significance from the thorough test it has given of the efficiency of Negro troops. Their losses

were heavy. In the thickest of the fight, and under the most trying circumstances, they never flinched. The old Army of the Potomac, so long prejudiced and so obstinately heretical on this subject, stand amazed as they look on the works captured by the Negroes, and are loud and unreserved in their praise.[57]

In a message to his corps, Smith lavishly praised his black soldiers:

To the Colored Troops comprising the division of General Hinks, the General commanding would call the attention of his command. With the veterans of the Eighteenth Corps they have stormed the works of the enemy and carried them, taking guns and prisoners, and in the whole affair they have displayed all the qualities of good soldiers.[58]

Smith also declared: "No nobler effort has been put forth today, and no greater success achieved than that of the Colored Troops." And he predicted that their work on June 15, "one of the greatest of the war," would "make the old Army of the Potomac open its eyes wide."[59] That is exactly what did happen when the II Corps of the Army of the Potomac arrived and relieved the "Colored Troops" from their advanced positions. Harvey Covell recalled:

It was rather exciting to see the old veterans of the A.[rmy of the] P.[otomac] stare when they saw the works we had captured. There were [13 ?] artilry [sic] captured our division captured 8 and Brook 5. The old soldiers would hardly believe that colored troops had done it but had to do so.[60]

The night of June 15 soldiers from the II Corps of Major General Winfield S. Hancock replaced the black troops on the picket line. An officer of the 3rd New Jersey Regiment accompanied the officer in charge of the 6th Regiment's pickets as they exchanged places. The men of the 6th settled down to sleep that night inside the Battery 9 redoubt.[61]

The next morning the black soldiers were sent a short distance to the rear where they set up camp. For these next three days they rested quietly in camp while white troops of the Army of the Potomac slugged away at the increasingly formidable Confederate works defending Petersburg. Throughout those anxious days they could hear the roar of artillery mixed with the occasional sound of muskets and yelling and cheering men. The wounded and stragglers passing to the rear could tell them little more than what they already suspected—the Rebels were holding. Reduced to the role of by-standers, the 6th would have no hand in concluding the work that they had so successfully begun. McMurray steamed: General Grant didn't seem to have any use for us. He hadn't learned yet that black men were just as good fighters as white men.[62]

Hancock's corps had made one of the costliest of the attacks on June 18. It had charged through a cornfield and been driven back, leaving a large number of dead and seriously wounded behind. The enemy refused permission for the Northerners to bury their dead or attend to their wounded, so they lay there in "no man's land" day after day. Ten days after this assault a detail from the 6th went out under cover of darkness to bury the dead.[63]

That new-moon night was a particularly dark one. As silently as possible they passed through the breastworks at about ten o'clock. They would attempt to bury as many as they could, as well as they could, as quietly as they could. Their grim work was indescribably distasteful. Groping through the darkness, the burial detail could not distinguish by sight the difference between a body and a flattened section of corn row. They had to feel their way with their hands. The task was made all the more horrible by the extensive deterioration of the bodies during those ten summer days.

As they would come upon a corpse they would dig a hole beside it as quietly as possible, roll the body into the shallow grave and cover it. The men had to do this work within 150 yards of the enemy's works. McMurray confessed: "This was possibly the saddest experience of my service in the army."[64]

In addition to this gruesome assignment the 6th was assigned to hold the front line opposite Petersburg from about June 20 through July 29. The troops occupied the rifle pits at the point where they cut the road between Petersburg and City Point. For the duration of this assignment they would alternate three days in the front works with three days back at camp.[65] Another source indicates that the men remained "in the trenches the entire month of July with the exception of five days, when we camped in the rear of them."[66] Manning those rifle pits proved to be perilous duty. Confederate riflemen stationed opposite them learned that they were black soldiers, and took special interest in shooting them. This continual rifle fire inflicted casualties each day they manned the line.[67] One account of Company A's stint in the trenches indicates that so many corporals of that company were killed or wounded by snipers that no enlisted man wanted to accept a promotion to that rank. Records indicate, however, that most of those wounded corporals, at least three, were actually wounded during the action of June 15.[68]

The men dared not lift their heads above the top of the breastwork for fear of drawing fire. The men tried to wait until nightfall to relieve themselves physically if they possibly could. A trip to the "sinks" in the daytime would be accompanied by a hail of Confederate bullets. The sinks for their section of the line lay in a small clump of woods consisting of saplings and small trees. A later examination of these trees would uncover scars made by the hundreds of bullets shot at men who could not wait until dark.[69]

When time came for the soldiers to be relieved of front-line duty at the end of its three days under fire, the men of the regiment all left together. They would leave about sundown from a point where the breastworks were high enough to shield them from the enemy. For example, one relief from this duty came on the afternoon of July 29. At that time the regiment pulled out of its position and moved to the left to a point where the enemy's works stood only 150 yards from the Union position.[70] Grant had approved a scheme to dig a mine from the Federal line across no-man's land and under the Confederate line. Thousands of pounds of gunpowder were to be placed there and the resulting explosion would create a huge gap in the Confederate line through which troops would charge.[71]

The 6th would take no active part in this assault, but would occupy a part of the line that had been held by Major General Ambrose E. Burnside's IX Corps. When the time came for the explosion one member of the regiment was looking directly at the Confederate line. Here was the earthwork:

> ...moving slowly, as if by tremendous effort. Then all at once it seemed to leap up quickly to a height of perhaps a hundred and fifty feet, breaking into fragments of timber, stone, broken gun carriages, muskets, tents, and black and mutilated human bodies, all falling back quickly with a dull, sullen sound.[72]

After a long delay white Union troops charged across to the gap in the line. Instead of charging through the gap and exploiting the break-through, the troops charged into the huge crater created by the explosion and remained there. This mistake gave the Confederates time to recover and counterattack forcefully. They poured heavy fire into the troops in the crater inflicting dreadful casualties. At this point, Burnside threw into the slaughter Brigadier General Edward Ferrero's 4th Division, IX Corps, black troops who were mowed down mercilessly. McMurray observed:

> Never in all my experience did I see artillery do such awful execution as was done that morning in the ranks of those black men by a Confederate battery that stood in an apple orchard. It looked as if one side of hell had opened, and fire and brimstone were belching forth.[73]

Those who tried to return to their lines were hit with murderous fire. Those who remained in the crater were doomed. Many black troops were killed as they attempted to surrender. The Battle of the Crater had been an unqualified disaster.[74]

That night the 6th drew the unhappy assignment of manning the picket line between the two lines. They remained there through the next day as well. For many this would be the worst day of picket duty that they ever experienced. Their picket line sat on a hillside in plain view and within easy rifle range of the enemy. Their only protection was a series of holes dug in the ground. They stretched their shelter tents over them-selves to shade them from the July sun. The Confederates, enraged by the events of the previous day, sought every possible opportunity to shoot at them. The day seemed interminable to the men on picket. As the day wore on, the men, for amusement, would intentionally draw enemy fire by placing a cap or a shoe on the butt of a musket and lifting it over the top of the rifle pit. When night finally fell, the men were relieved from picket duty and happily resumed their place behind the shelter of their own works.[75]

CHAPTER 7

DUTCH GAP

Confederate forces had long frustrated Union naval attempts to steam up the James River toward Richmond. At Trent's Reach, a bend in that river on the approach to Richmond, weighted hulks had been sunk as obstructions and well-placed Confederate artillery made that section virtually impassable. A scheme was proposed to dig a canal across a narrow neck of land near that loop. Doing so would enable Union ships to completely bypass that section of the river. The men of the 6th would be among those providing the muscle to excavate this canal at Dutch Gap.[1]

On August 4 the regiment marched away from the Petersburg front to Point of Rocks on the James River, where they remained encamped until August 17. On August 9 some of the men were detached to work on the Dutch Gap Canal. Company K reports seventeen of their members taking on this assignment. Each day about 100 men worked at this task. The men may have volunteered to take part in this project because it was designated as "extra duty," which entitled them to extra pay. The added demands included both "hard digging" and exposure to enemy fire. On the seventeenth the whole regiment moved to Dutch Gap to protect the working party. They set up camp on the river bank near what was to be the lower opening of the canal.[2]

Black troops often took on heavy fatigue duty. From the time Blacks had first been recruited it generally had been understood that they were to serve as laborers, and they were used disproportionately often in that role.[3] Their work at Dutch Gap would have been physically demanding under the best of circumstances, but this assignment included a complication that made it especially difficult and dangerous—they would have to do the work within range of Confederate artillery.

Under cover of night the first work detail crossed the river in boats. They carried with them picks, shovels, rifles, and provisions. As soon as the engineers set up two lines of stakes they broke ground. They easily

Dutch Gap – Beginning the Canal

shoveled through the light soil and quickly made significant progress. The men appeared "enthusiastic" and "light-hearted," punctuating their digging with laughter.[4]

As the night wore on weariness set in and the vigorous work pace began to trail off. The men anticipated the dawn with anxiety. Reveille woke the nearby Union troops, and distant bugles could be heard arousing Confederate troops as well. As the sun came up the workers could see a Confederate-held bluff and could eventually make out the artillery pieces. From that battery two silent puffs of white smoke appeared in quick succession, followed by distant booming. At the same time they began hearing "the scream of the shells far above our heads." The shells landed far enough away that they caused no harm, but the gunners were just getting their range.[5]

Again the guns fired. This time the shells landed nearer to the workers. With that, the Union batteries replied. An artillery duel continued for hours "with no perceptible result." The Southern artillerists, outgunned, were being hit with more shots than they were able to return. Their fire slackened, then stopped altogether. Those shots could do little harm to the canal workers anyway. Confederate fire came perpendicularly to the canal. Because of the relatively low trajectory of their cannons the shells, even with a perfectly aimed shot, could only slam into the walls of the deep ditch. They were unable to drop down into the ditch in the way only mortars could. Fortunately, no mortars were there.[6]

The diggers went back to work, apparently safe from enemy fire, and progressed rapidly at first. Their ditch became large enough for mule teams and carts to enter and haul away the earth. After cutting through the top layers of soil and loose clay, their digging became more difficult and progressed more slowly.[7]

Far worse for the workers, the Confederates had crossed to the north side of the river and set up batteries on the heights flanking the canal where they could fire down the length of the ditch. The guns began to lob shells so that they just cleared the bulkhead, dropped into the canal, and exploded. The workers had no shelter from this fire and had to make their own.[8]

They burrowed into the steep walls of the canal to make caves for shelter. The sides were of hard clay, but the protection afforded by the holes made it worth the effort to build them. To make matters even worse, the Confederates set up a mortar battery less than three quarters of a mile away in a bushy meadow beyond the river.[9] The mortar shells were deadly. They were fired high into the air "and then fell by their own weight, with no warning scream, and, dropping in the midst of busy groups, burst into ragged fragments of iron, which maimed and killed."[10]

Union artillery was brought in to silence those mortars, but its task was nearly impossible. Not only were the mortars well hidden among the thickets and brushes, but they often moved to avoid counterbattery fire. The cannoneers kept a sharp lookout for a puff of smoke whenever a mortar would fire. Then they would try to direct their fire at that spot. But Confederate sharpshooters stationed in hiding near the riverbank would open fire on the artillery crews and distract them from their task.[11]

The work crews eventually had to rely on their shelters, which they called "bombproofs" or "dugouts," along with a primitive early warning system. Lookouts were stationed at points from which projectiles could be watched through the entire course of their flight. After a little practice the spotters could predict with accuracy where each shot would land. Whenever work on the canal was in progress the observers would be on duty. Whenever an incoming shell was fired they would calculate whether it was likely to land in the ditch. If so, they would shout out, "Holes!" and the workers would scurry to their shelters. After the shell exploded they would come out and resume work.[12]

While the work at Dutch Gap was in progress Butler learned that captured black Union soldiers had been put to work building Confederate fortifications. That work enforced the often-stated policy of the Confederate government that captured black soldiers would either be executed or sent into slavery. The fortifications to which they were assigned included some that were under fire from Union guns. Butler, a staunch defender of black troops, retaliated. With permission from Grant, Butler sent Southern prisoners into the canal to work and notified the Confederates that they would remain there under fire from their own forces until captured black soldiers were treated properly as prisoners of war.[13]

The appearance of Rebel prisoners working alongside them provided an unexpected sight and a source of amusement for the Union soldiers. Southern commanders were well aware that some of their own men were in the canal, but the shelling continued. McMurray noted: "... several times I was looking on when shells exploded among the prisoners thus at work, and saw them scamper with our boys to places of partial safety as they could find."[14] After a few days Butler removed the prisoners from the canal on order of Grant. Grant had received assurances directly from Robert E. Lee that black prisoners of war had been released from the offending work assignments.[15]

General Butler later noted that the bombproofs built by the canal workers provided good protection that made Confederate fire ineffective. He stated after the war that the Rebels dropped shells into the canal "with considerable frequency, but did very little damage, and scarcely any harm to the workmen."[16] But Butler did not spend day after day in that ditch, and those who did told a different tale. According to McMurray the hiding places dug in the sides of the canal "afforded only partial safety." Moreover, he said, even when the men were promptly warned of incoming shells they often could not get out of the way in time. "There was

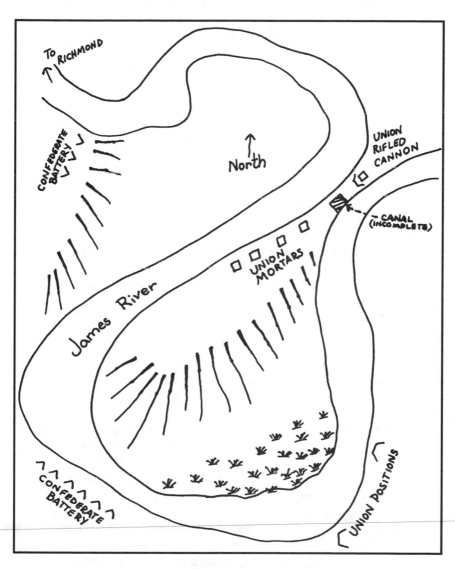

To Richmond

Confederate Battery

North

Union Rifled Cannon

Canal (Incomplete)

Union Mortars

James River

Confederate Battery

Union Positions

Map 3 — Dutch Gap

scarcely a day passed without us having one or more men killed or wounded in the ditch."[17] Another observer reported nightly boat loads of hospital transfers to the other side of the James River. He remembered: "...now no day passed without death and wounds in the deepening channel."[18] McMurray recalled the casualties at Dutch Gap:

> A small boat was always ready to convey the wounded across the river to the hospital, and it usually made two or three trips or more daily for that purpose. Occasionally a dead man had to be carried over. I went to the hospital one day and found there thirty or forty men being treated for wounds received in the canal. In the course of the hour I spent there I saw two or three legs or arms amputated. Going to the rear of the amputating tent I saw a pile of legs and arms lying on the ground there as large as a small "potato hole".[19]

At first this assignment looked like a welcome opportunity to get out of duty on the front-line rifle pits of Petersburg. It turned into a miserable experience. The sun beat down on the working party who had no shelter from the heat; on the contrary, the walls of the canal seemed to radiate the heat. The walls also "stifled the breezes, and exhaled miasma," according to one observer, and the digging "set free the malaria of newly turned earth and sedgy shores." Being forced to spend time in the "cellar-like holes" used for protection further worsened living conditions.[20]

Accordingly, the sick list swelled quickly. Before a month of labor had finished, half of the laborers were listed as "*hors de combat*," out of combat and unfit for duty.[21] Death from disease ran unusually high.[22] The army high command must have been aware of the nature of the work and the aggravating conditions. Some soldiers convicted by courts-martial were punished by being sentenced to "two years hard labor at Dutch Gap Canal."[23]

The men had to fight psychological affliction as well. A feeling of helplessness hung over those at the bottom of a pit, defenseless against the silent and deadly shells. Daily the same unnerving routine continued. The mortar shells would fall "as silently as snowflakes," until:

> ...the quiet and stealthy fall ended in a sudden roar of explosion, which reverberated with horrid exageration from the upright walls. Then crouching figures rose slowly from the sulphurous cloud of the gunpowder smoke; or there were some who did not rise, and a blanket was made to do duty as a stretcher, and something limp and bloody was carried down to the outer bank, by the mouth of the canal.[24]

The effect on morale was devastating. The men no longer sang songs at night around the campfire.[25] One participant observed:

> The effect upon *morale* can not, of course, be estimated but to live in putrid holes; to be exposed daily to hostile fire, with no chance to retaliate; to suffer a soldier's dangers, while deprived of his spirit as a

combatant; to wield a spade only under fire—all this is depressing and demoralizing, and...was doing much to deprive him of his soldierly ardor.[26]

Thomas Morris Chester, a black newspaper correspondent, visited Dutch Gap and sent out a dispatch on September 9 praising the men laboring there but perhaps exaggerating their cheerfulness:

> To the labors of the colored troops, who, amid the showers of shot and shell, are industriously prosecuting this great enterprise, will be ascribed the glory of its accomplishment. Though batteries, forts, and a ram continually hurling their messengers of death to interrupt the work and drive them off, our black troops, who have become seasoned to this kind of exercise, which they regard as sport, continue on in their operations as cheerfully as if nothing was happening.[27]

Chester particularly commented on the 6th's imperturbability:

> Yesterday I saw a shell explode in the camp of the 6th (Penna.) U.S.C.T., and expected to see some uneasiness manifested by the close proximity of these ugly customers, but was surprised to observe no more commotion than if the occurrence had been on of the most ordinary circumstances. It will be gratifying to the people of Pennsylvania to learn that this gallant regiment, raised near Philadelphia, is doing a service, under trying circumstances, in connection with others equally as brave, that commends it to the consideration of the country. That colored troops should be selected to perform such an arduous duty, exposed as they are to the raking fire of the enemy from several batteries, is an evidence of their high standard in the estimation of their military chieftain.[28]

Commotion arose among the Dutch Gap troops at midnight of September 27 as their officers spread the word that the regiment was moving out. The men were to prepare at once to march. They welcomed the news that they would be relieved of the drudgery of canal digging, and quickly prepared to depart:

> Down with the shovel and the hoe, and up once more with the rifle and the knapsack. In an hour or two we had turned our backs on the now enormous gash of the canal and the putrid holes where we had camped, had crossed the river to the Federal lines once more, and were in joyful, light-hearted march for a new crossing of the river two miles below.
>
> With every step away from the grim horror of the canal our spirits rose till at length the night-march at route-step fell into cadence with the first song for week.[29]

They would not have been singing if they had known what awaited them. The regiment was marching toward New Market Heights where the 6th Regiment would experience their bloodiest day of the war.

Dutch Gap Canal – Fall 1864

CHAPTER 8

NEW MARKET HEIGHTS

The 6th USCI was among the units designated to take part in a major offensive. The regiment reunited with the 4th and 22nd. Their XVIII Corps had nearly lost its identity since July when its various regiments were separated and sent out to garrison scattered posts in the area.[1]

Grant's central idea for his fall 1864 campaign was to put pressure all along the stretched-out Confederate line defending Richmond and Petersburg, forcing it to break at some point. Brigadier General Charles J. Paine's Third Division, XVIII Corps which included the 6th Regiment, would attack the enemy lines at New Market Heights in order to keep forces there from reinforcing nearby Fort Harrison, which would also be attacked at the same time.[2]

Speed of movement was crucial to the success of the operation. The men were instructed to leave everything behind except a single blanket rolled up and slung over their shoulders, a haversack with three days' cooked rations, and sixty rounds of cartridges, forty filling their cartridge boxes and twenty in their pockets. They left behind all tents, cooking utensils, and other camp equipment. Wagons would not accompany them, but would follow them with six additional days' rations and forty more rounds of ammunition for each man.[3] Anyone not fit for a heavy march was also left behind.[4]

Approval of requests to be excused because of illness did not come automatically. While the regiment was preparing to leave Dutch Gap, Private Emanuel Patterson of Company D told McMurray that he was ill, and the captain sent him to the surgeon to be excused. The surgeon said that he was all right and had to go along.[5]

Before dark on September 28, the men climbed aboard a transport. They steamed downriver to Deep Bottom, where they disembarked about midnight. Before the sun came up they were on the march heading two miles up the road to New Market Heights.[6]

John McMurray

Courtesy Donald McMurray

On the morning of September 29, before beginning the march to New Market Heights, Patterson again reported to his captain that he was sick. To make sure that he was excused this time, McMurray accompanied Patterson to the doctor. But even with his captain's intercession the doctor refused to excuse Patterson, sending him back to his company.[7]

Before sunrise the 6th finished their march and formed a line of battle. It held the left of the line, the 4th Regiment forming up just to their right.[8] A heavy fog surrounded them, limiting their ability to see far ahead. They moved forward emerging from the woods into an open field at the top of a hill. The first signs of sunrise began to appear. The men could make out the enemy picket line falling back toward their entrenchments as they advanced. About twenty Confederates could be seen hurrying across the field, turning to shoot back at the advancing Federals.[9]

As the whole brigade moved forward into the open field they could see for the first time the ground over which they would have to charge. The field initially sloped downward toward the enemy, but the Confederates were well-positioned in the heights beyond. Entrenchments stretched along the foot of these heights from which riflemen could pour devastating fire on any attack.

The attacking troops would first have to cross a small, shallow creek, about twelve feet wide and only a few inches deep. Once across it, they would have to cross marshy terrain, deep and muddy, all of the while in range of Confederate rifles. They would next encounter the first of two lines of abatis running parallel to the entrenchments, which were well-designed to snare them and slow down the attack. The first line was fashioned from felled trees. The pointed branches facing the attackers would entangle them snaring their clothes. This would hold them up long enough to make them perfect targets directly in front of the Confederate rifle pits. If they were able to force their way through this line of obstructions they would shortly run up against a second such line. This line was made up largely of *chevaux-de-frise*, an intimidating obstruction of large sharpened wooden stakes facing the attacking force. This device was similarly designed to bring the attacking men to a halt just as they came into point-blank range.[10]

They gazed across the field, and as McMurray remembered years later:

I know there was a big lot of thinking done by us while we stood there. We knew there was a strong line of Confederates behind the rifle pits, across the slashing from us. We knew that as soon as we would move forward they would open fire on us. We knew the order to move forward would soon be given. But beyond that what? Would it be death, or wounds, or capture? Would it be victory or defeat? How the scenes and deeds of the past came rushing in on the mind like a might flood! That was perhaps the most trying five minutes or ten minutes we endured in all our army life. It would require the pen of the mightiest angel that ever stood before the throne of God to write down the thoughts of the men who stood in that line that bright September morning. My heart almost stands still now, as I write these lines, and try to recall some of the thoughts that came to me then.[11]

Companies A and K of the 6th were detached and sent out as skirmishers. They would not take part in the main assault. The remainder of the regiment lined up with its brigade, dressing its lines "with as much care and accuracy as though we had been on parade." The companies lined up in two ranks, the captain or company commander in the front rank, the first sergeant standing directly behind him in the rear rank. A step or two behind the rear rank stood the lieutenants and the other sergeants, serving as "file closers," to "encourage" the others to continue to advance. Behind the file closers stood the regimental field officers, who were followed in turn by their brigade commander, Colonel Samuel A. Duncan, and his staff.[12]

They stood in plain view of the Confederates as they prepared for the attack. But all the while that they stood there not one shot was fired at them. McMurray reflected, "I have no doubt but they [the enemy] looked on with great interest, thinking no doubt, what a lot of fools we were."[13]

Butler personally addressed his black troops before the attack. Pointing toward the enemy he exhorted: "Those works must be taken by the weight of your column; not a shot must be fired." They were not to stop to fire which would only break the attack's momentum and cause confusion. To prevent it from happening they were ordered before the charge to remove the percussion caps from the locks of their rifles.[14] Colonel Duncan could finally be heard calling out the order, "Forward," and the men immediately surged forward at "right shoulder shift" as if on parade.[15]

As they started down the sloping field First Lieutenant John Johnson began excitedly to swing his sword in circles over his head. He had completed only three or four of these circles when a Rebel bullet tore through the wrist of his sword arm. The sword flew off at a tangent, landing on the ground some twenty feet away. The lieutenant was taken to the rear. The rest of the regiment pressed on as the Texas Brigade poured murderous fire on them.[16]

As they splashed across the stream and ran into briars and swampy ground their once neat battle lines broke into some disorder. The men struggling through the marshy morass held their guns over their heads to keep them dry.[17] Their guns were of no use to them at this point; in some ways they were a hindrance to them. McMurray remembers the helpless feeling of being "unable to protect ourselves in any way." As he looked about him he saw the ranks becoming thinner and thinner and saw fewer and fewer of his own men. He looked about anxiously and carefully for men from his company. He soon found a horrifying sight. Patterson, who had asked to be excused earlier that day because of illness, appeared before him with a ghastly wound, "He was shot in the abdomen, so that his bowels all gushed out, forming a mass...which he was holding up with his clasped hands, to keep them from falling at his feet." McMurray never forgot that terrible sight and confessed years later, "Then, and a hundred times since, I wished I had taken the responsibility of saying to him that he could remain in the rear."[18]

But it was not possible to dwell for long on any individual, no matter how tragic his fate, while under enemy fire and with death on all sides. The 6th continued to advance. McMurray next found his first sergeant, Miles Parker, sitting down, shot through the leg. Sergeant Parker gave the captain a cheerful greeting and said, "Never mind 'em, Captain; I'll get along all right."[19]

As he pushed forward he found more of his men killed or wounded. Rebel fire was also bringing down many officers. Duncan was wounded four times. Command of the brigade then devolved to Colonel John Ames, who was the senior regimental commander. Fire also struck down Captain Robert Beath of Company A with a wound that cost him his leg.[20]

Halfway across the field a large oak tree partially blocked the Union advance. It had been chopped down and lay where it had fallen next to its stump. Captain McMurray was about to pass through the narrow gap between the stump and the trunk when three or four members of the color guard arrived there at the same time. Almost reflexively he gave way to the color bearer and followed right behind. Just as the flag bearer passed through the gap he was shot through the chest and fell back onto McMurray with a force that almost knocked him over. He clearly realized that the color bearer had saved his life by his death.[21]

Rebel sharpshooters as usual chose flag bearers as prime targets. Many paid with their lives for the honor of bearing the Stars and Stripes or the regimental flag. The color-guard of the national flag was decimated in the attack at New Market Heights. The color-sergeant was shot down early in the attack. An officer picked up the fallen Stars and Stripes and was shot down, himself, within seconds. Second Lieutenant Frederick Meyer of Company B picked up the flag to carry it forward.[22]

Ames by this time had reached one of the lines of abatis, where McMurray encountered him for the first time in this fight. Ames appeared to be incredibly cool under fire, "as though there wasn't an enemy within miles of us." As the two officers stood together, McMurray happened to be looking over at Meyer and saw him struck through the heart by a Rebel bullet. The instant he was shot he spun about and leaped toward the rear over a pile of brush, falling dead on the other side.[23]

At that point First Lieutenant Nathan H. Edgerton, the regimental adjutant, came upon the scene and spotted Meyer lying on top of the flag, still grasping it with his dead hands. Edgerton pulled the flag away and carried it toward the front. He was soon knocked to the ground by a force that he could not

Nathan Edgerton
Courtesy Donald McMurray

identify. He immediately leaped up and tried to raise the flag, but it would not move. Looking down to see why he could not lift the flag he saw his hand covered with blood and the flag staff lying there, split into two pieces. The same bullet had shattered both his wrist and the flag staff. He sheathed his sword with his remaining hand, then picked up the flag and broken staff and continued forward.[24]

Just at the time Meyer was killed Ames asked McMurray: "Captain, don't you think we had better fall back? We haven't force enough to take this line, and if we remain here we will probably all be killed." The captain agreed that would be the best course of action.[25] Edgerton then joined Ames and the mere handful of men still advancing. The smoke had grown so thick that no one could see more than a few feet ahead. Ames said: "We must have more help, boys, before we try that. Fall back."[26]

Ames realized that calling off the attack would create a new danger. Falling back under enemy fire, retreating soldiers may panic if their morale broke or if they were not kept under control. Lack of control can turn an orderly withdrawal into a panicky rout. He directed McMurray to "take the men back as quickly as you can, but keep them well in hand, and don't let them get demoralized."[27]

Edgerton had become too weak to continue carrying the Stars and Stripes. Sergeant Alexander Kelly of Company F took the flag, raised it up and rallied the men in the midst of the confusion and gunfire.[28] The other flag, the regimental colors, was safe in the hands of Sergeant Major Thomas Hawkins of Company C. Hawkins had been wounded at Petersburg on June 15, a bullet passing through his arm near the elbow. But when he saw the color bearer killed he seized the fallen flag and carried it through

Alexander Kelly   **Thomas Hawkins**

Library of Congress   Library of Congress

the remainder of the fight. In spite of receiving three more wounds, he bore the flag safely from the field.[29] So many bullets had ripped through these flags that they had both been turned into mere strips of cloth.[30]

The men started back, flags still flying to rally them. But going back may have been worse than the advance. As vulnerable as they felt during the attack, they felt "utterly helpless" with their backs toward the gunfire.[31] Companies C and F lost all their officers by the end of the assault, leaving the black noncommissioned officers or the men themselves to direct their safe return to friendly ground.[32] Some companies began to withdraw in good order; others began rushing back in a complete rout. Some sought safety by dropping to the ground, sheltering themselves in the contours of the earth. But this apparent safety proved an illusion as they became merely challenging targets to Confederate riflemen.[33]

Brigadier General John Gregg's Texas Brigade (now under Lieutenant Colonel Frederick S. Bass of the 1st Texas) counterattacked, swarming out of their rifle pits onto both flanks of the troops closest to the Confederate line. Many of the black troops were killed, while others threw down their weapons and surrendered. Some of the surrendering soldiers were seized as prisoners, while others were simply murdered.[34]

The Texas defenders gave a somewhat different account of the battle. Throughout the early morning they were unable to see much through the "dense, obscuring fog" that was "so thick as to render large objects, a hundred feet distant, indistinguishable."[35] Not until their attackers had closed to within one hundred feet could they see anything at all. Even then they could make out nothing more than "a wavering dark line." In spite of the unclear target and without orders to do so, the Confederates rose up to the top of the breastworks and opened fire, "shooting at shadows."[36]

An uncomplimentary Texan described the black troops as being "hurled upon us, driven on by white leaders at the point of the sword." He continues to describe the heavy fire that the Texans poured into the advancing infantry until, as he says, "They reel and fall by the scores; now they waver and now they run, and they go to the rear as fast their — — — legs can carry them & the artillery opened with terrible slaughter."[37] A Union officer then shouted the order to charge, but only those Union troops directly in front of the 1st Texas Regiment obeyed. They rushed the breastworks and in some places crossed them and plunged into the Texas troops. But after less than three minutes of struggle all of these attackers were casualties, half shot or bayoneted and half taken prisoner. Those troops who had not rushed the breastworks and who had not yet been cut down by the withering Confederate musket fire threw down their guns and ran for the rear or fell to the ground where they lay until taken prisoner.[38]

The survivors retraced their steps back toward the safety of their lines. As they crossed the field they passed many dead and wounded comrades. McMurray passed Captain Charles V. York of Company B, who lay on the ground unable to walk, suffering from a painful wound. McMurray could not stop to help him, but took note of the wounded man's location so that he could return to him as soon as his men had fallen back in good order. Sergeants Kelly and Hawkins bore the two flags safely back from the field of battle in spite of wounds. For the heroism that they displayed in this battle, these two along with Edgerton would earn the Congressional Medal of Honor.

As Duncan's Brigade came reeling back, Brigadier General Alonzo G. Draper's Brigade of Colored Troops moved forward and covered the retreat. Duncan's Brigade fell back past them and Draper's Brigade renewed the assault. They also met the deadly Confederate gunfire. Finally they drove the defenders from their entrenchments.[39] When the 6th Regiment was safely clear of the field of fire, the officers tried to re-form their units as best they could. They also collected what information they could on who had been killed or wounded. As they counted their survivors the grim truth became clear.[40]

Because of the many sick and unfit for duty, only about thirty men per company went into battle that day. Companies A and K, skirmishers who had not been part of the main assault, had suffered the least. Company A's commander, Captain Robert B. Beath, had been shot in the leg and would lose it later. Three of his enlisted men had also been wounded. Company C suffered four men killed, sixteen wounded; Company E, three killed, five wounded, one missing; Company F, five killed, thirteen wounded; Company G, four killed, fourteen wounded. Company H lost its commander, Captain George W. Sheldon, killed, five enlisted men killed, and one officer and sixteen others wounded. Company I suffered four killed and twenty wounded.[41]

The most staggering loss of all was suffered by Captain McMurray's Company D. The captain had gone into battle leading thirty-two men. Forty minutes later twelve of them were killed or mortally wounded, while sixteen others including one officer were sent to the hospital with wounds. McMurray gathered together all of his company's survivors — there were only three. The company had lost over eighty-seven percent of its men, the heaviest loss ever reported by any company of Union troops in a single charge. The regiment had lost three officers and thirty-nine men killed, eleven officers and 150 men wounded, and seven men missing. Of the 367 men who made the charge, 210 were casualties.[42]

When Draper's Brigade finally drove the Texans from their works, the men of the 6th Regiment could return to attend to the wounded and identify the dead. McMurray found the body of Captain York, who had been stripped of everything but his undergarments. They also found the body of Captain George W. Sheldon lying face-down in the little stream. They spent a sad hour searching the battlefield for the dead. Here they found the body of Nathaniel Danks, the handsome young man who had bolted from the line of march a year before to kiss a pretty young girl to the cheers of his comrades. But the loss that most affected Captain McMurray was that of "Big Sam" Johnson:

> Going over the battle field after the fight was ended, I found "Big Sam" shot dead, lying as comfortably apparently as though he had lain down to sleep. I couldn't help shedding a few tears when I realized that he was indeed dead. And even now when I think of him I feel a pang of sorrow that his cheerful light of life was extinguished so early. He was probably about twenty-five years old. I looked at him a few moments, said "goodbye, Sam," and was compelled to go on without seeing that he was decently buried.[43]

There was no time for burials. The 6th received orders to march immediately to Fort Harrison. The attack made that morning at New Market Heights, as costly as it was, had accomplished its purpose. It tied up the Confederates who were defending New Market Road and prevented them from reinforcing Fort Harrison. This action helped enable the XVIII Corps to capture the fort on the same day.[44] The regiment began its march to the fort by crossing over the undefended Confederate entrenchments for which they had sacrificed so much earlier in the day.[45] That afternoon, while en route to Fort Harrison, they witnessed a failed attack on Confederate Fort Gilmer by a combined force of black and white Union troops.[46]

The regiment arrived at Fort Harrison and soon saw indications that the Confederates were planning a counterattack. The Union force, now the defenders, observed the enemy shifting regiments and building up an assault column toward a grove of oak trees only a few hundred yards away. That concentration revealed the point of the Union line that the attack would strike. Armed with this knowledge, the troops began elaborate preparations to repel the attack.[47]

The 6th occupied the formerly Confederate works just outside of Fort Harrison. Ames at this time commanded not only the 6th but all of Duncan's Third Brigade as well. The black troops manned the reverse side of the earthworks. The Confederates had constructed the works by throwing the earth up against the outside of their line, creating a ditch in the process. Ames' troops now occupied this ditch and enjoyed breastworks three and one-half or four feet high in front of them. Brigadier General George J. Stannard's First Division, XVIII Corps occupied the fort itself, where the attack was anticipated. Some of those men were armed with Spencer repeating rifles, which increased their firepower tremendously.[48]

The Confederates opened fire with a deafening barrage from some forty cannon. The Union defenders recognized the cannonade as a prelude to an infantry assault. Through the bombardment, as shells burst around them, more regiments rushed into position to repel the impending attack. An unidentified Union staff officer from another regiment crept along the breastworks, keeping as low as he could, showing a great deal of fear of the rebel fire. His behavior was apparently demoralizing the men. Colonel Ames saw him and angrily swore at the officer. He ordered him "to walk upright like a man." Then, to reassure the men, Colonel Ames jumped up to the top of the breastworks and walked back and forth two or three times the length of the regiment. His intrepid performance must have inspired the men he led; one of them swore: "After that we would have followed him into the very jaws of the inferno if he had asked it of us."[49]

The Confederate artillery fire tapered off and stopped. Shortly afterward the attack began out of the oak grove and across a ravine. The advancing Southerners were described as a "mighty, resistless, human machine," and as a "solid mass of men, with the steadiness of a great machine, and the determination of death."[50] Union troops held their fire until the Confederates came close. The attackers drew to within 200 yards, and still the defenders had not fired a shot nor had the Confederates made a sound. Then, as they closed to within 100 yards, the Southerners let out the dreaded "Rebel Yell" and charged almost at a run. With that the Union defenders unleashed a devastating volley, the Vermonters firing at the attackers head-on while Ames's regiments tore up the Rebels' flank. After the Union front rank had fired their single-shot muskets the rear rank

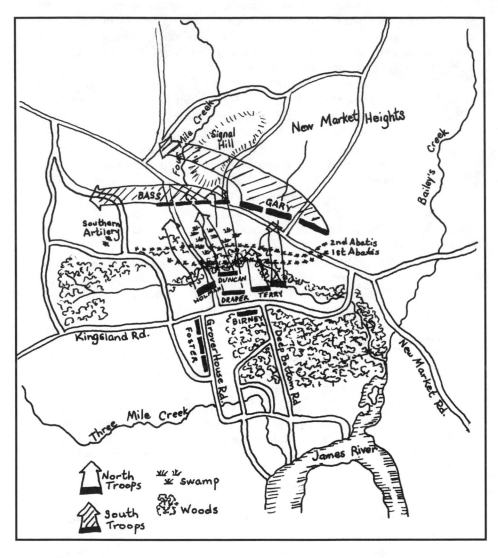

Map 4 — Battle of New Market Heights

passed them loaded guns. The troops armed with Spencer repeating rifles simply kept up their deadly fire.

The Confederates advanced until they were within forty feet of the Union muskets. When they could no longer stand the heavy fire poured on them from three directions, they broke in complete disorder and began running back to the Confederate lines as quickly as they could. The Union soldiers shouted in triumph, some even leaping over the breastworks and chasing after the retreating enemy. Ames's men did not know the identity of the men who had attacked them. They would have to confess, though, that they "would have felt a savage satisfaction had we been assured that they were the same men who handled us so roughly in the morning."[51]

With the attackers driven off, the 6th was pulled out of the line of earthworks and sent back to set up camp for the night. The enlisted men pitched their shelter tents at a spot used as a Confederate campsite the night before. Most of the officers found shelter in some wooden huts recently abandoned by Confederate officers.[52]

So ended the bloodiest day in the regiment's history. General Butler lavished praise upon his soldiers in a general order issued October 11, which read:

> Of the colored soldiers the general commanding desires to make special mention. In the charge on the enemy's works by the colored division or the Eighteenth Corps, at Spring Hill and at New Market, better men were never better led; better officers never led better men. .... A few more such charges, and to command colored troops will be the post of honor in the American armies. The colored soldiers, by coolness, steadiness, and determined courage and dash, have silenced every cavil of doubters of their soldierly capacity, and have drawn tokens of admiration from their enemies.[53]

Butler also felt personally moved by the deeds of his troops. As he looked out on the bloody field of New Market Heights after the battle, Butler later said that he swore an oath "to defend the rights of those men who have given their blood for me and my country that day and for their race forever.... " The general directed that the words "Petersburg" and "New Market Heights" be inscribed on the flags of the regiments that had fought in those battles.[54]

The 6th would carry along with it for the rest of the war a battleflag inscribed with "New Market Heights." But each man in the regiment who lived through that battle would carry the recollection of a nightmare inscribed forever in his memory.[55]

CHAPTER 9

THE LAST CAMPAIGNS

The men remained in camp near Fort Harrison through all of October and November. They needed that time to recover from the wounds of New Market Heights and from the illnesses contracted while at Dutch Gap. The regiment also received reinforcements at this time. The arrival of new recruits brought the number present for duty up to about 400 men.[1]

November brought with it the crucial presidential election of 1864. By that time the Confederates had lost hope of winning independence by victory on the battlefield. Their only serious chance of achieving independence was the defeat of the Lincoln Administration and the election of a peace-seeking Democratic president.

Union soldiers voted in that election heavily favoring Lincoln's return to office. African American soldiers especially felt support for the Lincoln Administration because of its policy of pursuing the war to a military victory. If successful, that policy would strike a death blow against slavery.[2] The election results boosted morale in the regiment according to Chaplain Jeremiah Asher:

> The general health of the reg.[iment] is very good. There is a few cases of chills and fever but most of them are light. I have never known the men in better health and in higher spirits never more helpful of success than today. The election has had a very happy effect upon the soldiers.[3]

The autumn passed without much activity. But Company K, which had only been deployed as skirmishers at New Market Heights, lost three killed and 19 wounded between September 29 and October 31. They had spent this time "behind the breastworks in front of Richmond, Virginia on the South side of James River."[4]

Religious pursuits often occupied the men during this time of reduced activity. The Christian Commission had erected a large tent for conducting religious services near the camp. They were well attended. On one occasion when the large tent was filled with enthusiastic soldiers a witness observed:

> At the far end of the tent from where I was standing was a platform two or three feet high, reaching across the end of the tent. A nice looking young man had charge of the meeting. He seemed to be greatly interested for the colored men. After singing and praying he told them the meeting was for them, specially, and he wanted them to feel at home in it. He asked some of them to come onto the platform, and hoped they would be prompt to do so. Well, they were not at all backward about going forward, and in a few minutes the platform was filled with stalwart negro soldiers, who seemed to be entirely at home in a meeting of that sort. They took entire charge of the meeting, and did it so promptly and so readily that the young man who gave them the invitation wondered how it was accomplished. The young man was completely crowded out, and the last I saw of him he was jammed away back in the farthest corner of the tent, and the colored brethren were running the meeting, under a full head of steam.[5]

A pleased regimental chaplain, Jeremiah Asher, made the observation that the religiosity of the men extended beyond religious services. As he noted:

> With regard to the moral condition of the regiment there is much which is encouraging. 1st I am happy to mention the fact since the last pay our Reg.[iment] have sent home to their families and friends more than eight thousand dollars. Exclusive of the officers.

> 2nd for the last three months I have taken considerable pains to ascertain moral condition of a number of the regiments both white and colored and it is my honest conviction that there is less profanity in the 6th USCT than in any one I have seen[;] this I have no doubt is owing in a great [effect?] to the force of example. I am happy to state that some of our officers are religious men and those who are not professed Christian seldom indulge in the foolish Crime of Profanity. The same may be said of intemperance. I have never seen any of the officers intoxicated and very few of the soldiers.[6]

In December, Union forces prepared for a major expedition to North Carolina to capture the powerful Fort Fisher, which guarded the approach to Wilmington, North Carolina, the last open and active Confederate seaport. Grant directed Major General Godfrey Weitzel to lead the joint army-navy assault. About 7,000 troops of Butler's Army of the James would take part in this expedition. Paine's Division, including the brigade of which the 6th was a part, would participate. Colonel Samuel A. Duncan, the brigade's former commander, was recuperating from wounds suffered at New Market Heights. Colonel John W. Ames of the 6th took his place while Major Augustus S. Boernstein took over as new commander of the regiment.[7] Paine's division joined organizationally with two other divisions to form the all-black XXV Corps.[8]

A detachment of soldiers from the 6th became part of the sharpshooters of the 3rd Division, XXV Corps. They left their camp on December 7 for Bermuda Hundred, where they embarked on the *Admiral Dupont* and the steamer *Empire City* on the twenty-second and sailed to New Inlet, North Carolina. Most of Butler's other troops had already left Virginia by transports on the fourteenth and reached the North Carolina coast by the fifteenth.

At this point the plans fell apart. Butler, never known as a competent commander, took it upon himself to take charge of the operation. Due to poor coordination, the transports waited so long for the navy to rendezvous with them that they had used up their coal and drinking water. The transports were forced to take an unplanned side trip to resupply at Beaufort, where poor weather conditions held them up for another six days. Meanwhile, many of the soldiers had become severely seasick and were in no condition for a fight. To make matters worse, the Confederates had taken advantage of the delays to reinforce their positions around Fort Fisher. Only a relatively small force of Union troops landed near Fort Fisher, enough to capture some weakly held Confederate outer works. None of the black troops landed; they could only watch the action from their vessels.[10] After a 12-hour naval bombardment on December 25, Butler determined that the fort could not be taken and returned with his transports to Fort Monroe.[11] The 6th arrived back in Virginia on December 28 or 29. The detached sharpshooters rejoined the regiment and they all returned to their old camp near Fort Harrison on December 20.[12]

Grant was furious that Butler had so badly botched the operation. He relieved Butler of command and began preparations for another, more determined, strike at Fort Fisher.[13] During the expedition some 200 men from Ames' Brigade had become unfit for duty due to seasickness. These men were sent with McMurray to Fort Harrison to recover while the rest of the regiment prepared for a second attempt to capture the fort.

Grant quickly organized the second expedition against Fort Fisher, to be led by Brigadier General Alfred H. Terry. On January 3, 1864, the 6th received order to march. They reached Bermuda Hundred that evening and bivouacked for the night. The next day they boarded the transport *Herman Livingston*, which moved to Fort Monroe and put to sea on the morning of January 6. On January 11 it entered Beaufort Harbor, North Carolina.[15]

The operation involved 59 warships and 21 transports carrying almost 9,000 troops including Paine's black Division. The expedition could not leave Beaufort until the morning of the twelfth. Progress was halted by "a punishing gale that tossed sailors from their bunks, washed at least one sentry overboard and infected thousands of soldiers with rail-hugging seasickness." They proceeded south and anchored off Fort Fisher.[16]

Fort Fisher stood at the southern end of a narrow peninsula. On the morning of the thirteenth, with fixed bayonets and forty rounds of ammunition each, the 6th landed on the beach a few miles north of the fort and marched across the peninsula. They struggled in a line of battle through swampy terrain covered with thickets. As they neared the river they found higher ground but thicker undergrowth. As night fell, the men had to push their way through the underbrush single-file. The tangle of natural obstructions became so disorienting that the lead officer was forced to stop frequently to consult his compass by match light. Finally, after nearly four hours of fighting their way through "jungle-like thickets," they reached the banks of the Cape Fear River.[17]

There they built defensive works across the peninsula to help prevent Confederate reinforcements from coming down the peninsula to aid the garrison. Confederate Major General Robert F. Hoke commanded rebel forces at Sugar Loaf, a fortified position just to the north of the position Paine's Division had reached. Farther north at Wilmington, General Braxton Bragg commanded still more troops. Paine's Division and a brigade of white troops under the command of Colonel Henry L. Abbott took on the responsibility of holding these enemy forces at bay while the rest of the Union expedition attacked Fort Fisher.[18]

At 2 A.M. they reached the site chosen to build the defensive line. Eight hundred spades were issued to the men. They took turns all night long shoveling the earth in the darkness. They also hauled logs to the trench and used them to strengthen the earthworks. They even set up some abatis. When the sun rose, it shone on a line of defensive works that extended all the way across the peninsula from the Cape Fear River to the ocean, a defensive line strong enough to easily repel an attack by a force twice their size.[19]

On January 15, about the same time that Union forces began their assault on Fort Fisher, the Confederates unleashed an attack on Paine's and Abbott's troops in their new entrenchments. The enemy advanced in a "strong skirmish line at the double-quick" along the entire Union front. They quickly drove back the pickets of Abbott's Brigade on the right flank. After driving the brigade out of their earthworks, the Rebels moved into the trenches that had been held by Abbott's men.[20]

Meanwhile, on the Union left, Paine's Division held firm. A hot exchange of gunfire had erupted on that front until the heavy guns of the Union navy joined in the fighting hurling huge shells into the Confederate positions. Bragg eventually recalled the Southerners back to their original positions.[21] Fort Fisher surrendered that evening. The black troops had done their job, keeping possible reinforcements from reaching Fort Fisher and from attacking the Union rear.

Confederate Major General William H. C. Whiting identified General Bragg's intimidation at Sugar Loaf as the chief reason for the Southern defeat. Whiting had emphatically urged Bragg to attack, but to little avail.[22] Before he died in a Northern hospital of wounds received defending Fort Fisher, Whiting complained to a friend:

> That I am here and that Wilmington and Fisher are gone is due wholly and solely to the incompetency, the imbecility and the pusillanimity of Braxton Bragg,...Bragg was within two and a half miles [of the fort], with 6,000 of Lee's best troops, three batteries of artillery and 1,500 reserves. The enemy had no artillery at all. Bragg was held in check by two negro brigades while the rest of the enemy assaulted and, he didn't even fire a musket.[23]

On January 15, Company C, 6th USCT was ordered detached from the regiment for provost duty at Third Division Headquarters. On the sixteenth Captain John F. Devereux and his Company I were detached from the 6th Regiment. They were to join the division sharpshooters, Third Division, XXV Army Corps under Major Philip Weinmann, formerly Captain of Company I, USCI, who had been promoted on January 1, 1865, to major in the 37th USCT. Those two companies would be absent from their regiment until mid-March.[24]

On January 18 Ames led the 4th, 6th, and 13th Regiments of his brigade along with the division sharpshooters on a reconnaissance. His troops drove in the rebel pickets and caught a view of the Confederate main line on the left. They returned with the needed information losing one killed and one wounded. The 6th probed the enemy again the next day. In a sharp encounter with Hoke's force at Sugar Loaf Hill the regiment lost Captain Newton J. Hotchkiss of Company F, mortally wounded. Four of five other men were killed in the fight and about fifteen wounded.[25]

February 9 or 10 McMurray returned from Fort Harrison with about 200 recovered "invalids." The regiment since January 15 had been living in a swamp, where they had built a corduroy road, the only means by which troops could move from one part of the line to another. On February 10 the regiment conducted another reconnaissance toward Sugar Loaf. The next day the division broke camp and advanced in force with Ames's Brigade taking the lead. In a "brisk skirmish" the division lost two officers and fourteen men killed and seven officers and sixty-nine men wounded. First Lieutenant Daniel K. Healy of Company F was severely wounded and Second Lieutenant Edward Field, commanding Company A, was killed. When Field, the company's last commissioned officer, fell, First Sergeant Richard Carter, a black man, took charge of the company and "commanded with great skill and courage until the company was relieved." The Union troops drove off the skirmishers and took possession of their rifle pits. They entrenched and held that position. Men who were killed in the fight, such as Corporal Edward Cummings of Company F, were buried on the field.[26]

On the nineteenth, the Southerners withdrew from in front of Paine's Division and Northern forces again moved forward, pressing the Rebels.

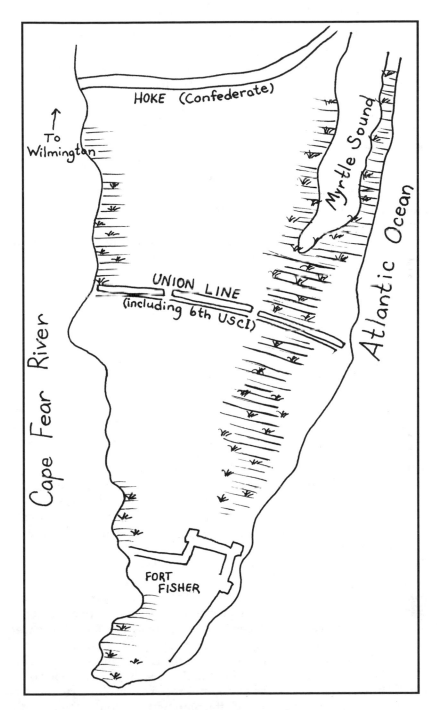

Map 5 — Fort Fisher Campaign

Skirmishing broke out again on the twentieth and the Union pursuit continued until they came upon the entrenched enemy, this time only six miles from Wilmington, North Carolina. The Confederate works were well-manned and included six or seven artillery pieces. February 21 was spent preparing to advance against that line. The rising sun on the morning of the twenty-second revealed that the Confederates had evacuated their works the previous night. The men in blue crossed the abandoned works and headed toward Wilmington. The thick black smoke that they could see coming from the direction of Wilmington clearly indicated that the Rebels were burning anything that might be useful to their conquerors.[27]

Union troops who reached the deserted city at 2 P.M. found only smoking ruins where the wharves and storage buildings had once stood along the riverfront. The soldiers were able to save some tobacco from the flames and to pick up more tobacco that they found in the streets of the town. They maintained good discipline and touched no property besides the abandoned tobacco. The men passed through the town with mixed feelings:

> We cheered a little when we entered the first street, but the awful quiet of the place seemed to be infectious, and in a few minutes our march was as noiseless and as solemn as if we had been on our way to a funeral.[28]

They marched through the city without stopping and came to a halt beyond the town in an open field near the tracks of the Wilmington and Weldon Railroad. They rested here for about an hour, making coffee and dividing the newly found tobacco. At three o'clock that afternoon they continued to march along the course of the railroad toward Goldsboro. After marching nine more miles they reached the point where the railroad crossed the North East River, a branch of the Cape Fear. In addition to a railroad bridge, a pontoon bridge crossed the river at this point. Hoke's troops had just crossed this river and opened fire on the approaching Federals. For an hour or more the Northerners kept up only "a desultory fire." But at least one member of the regiment was wounded in this exchange as reported by Company G.[29]

The men were exhausted by their 25 miles of marching that day. Sending out pickets, they strongly secured the railroad bridge. Even the proximity of the enemy could not keep them from their much needed slumber. McMurray recalls, "...we prepared and ate our suppers, and then lay down and enjoyed a good sleep, although we knew the Johnies were just across the stream from us."[30]

The opposing forces remained across the river from each other from January 22 to March 16. "They did not molest us, and we did not trouble them." This camp location was sometimes referred to as "North East Station." One afternoon early in March the regiment was told to prepare dinner for several hundred Union prisoners of war who had just been released from Rebel prisons. The men immediately set to work clearing a camp-ground and cooking a meal for them. A locomotive whistle on the Rebel side of the river signaled the arrival of the former prisoners. Across the pontoon bridge came men who were "a sorry looking set—ragged and dirty," but exceedingly happy to be safe behind their own lines again.[31] Some of the officers found old comrades among the men released:

> If we had had a fatted calf we would have killed it. In the absence of such we gave them the best our camp afforded—good bread and butter and beef steak and coffee, and plenty of each. We stuffed them till they couldn't eat another bite, and then insisted on them eating more.[32]

The ex-prisoners stayed for at least two hours before they moved on to Wilmington where they boarded a ship the next day for Annapolis.[33]

March 16 the regiment broke camp and with its division crossed the North East River on the pontoon bridge. The long trek toward Goldsboro followed the general course of the Wilmington and Weldon Railroad. They went north to Burgaw Creek.[34] Private Hubbard Ceaser, as was his custom, carried an excessive burden. The unusually hot weather and the "sultry" air made the march especially demanding. The men sweated profusely and discarded unessential items to lighten their loads. Captain McMurray caught sight of one soldier who staggered from the ranks and collapsed. It was Ceaser. McMurray and others tried to revive him, thinking that he had fainted. When he did not respond they did everything they could to resuscitate him, but to no avail. He had died, but they could not take time then to bury him. They placed his body in an ambulance and when they stopped a few hours later, buried him in an unmarked grave. McMurray reflected on Ceaser's life and death and how callous he and his men had become:

> How war hardens the hearts of its votaries, crushing out, utterly obliterating all tender feelings. We dug a hole in the ground there in North Carolina, and put Hubbard Ceaser into it, and covered him over and then turned away as we would from the grave of a faithful horse or a treasured dog. I wonder now that we could have had such feelings then. But it had to be. If it had been otherwise we would have been worthless as soldiers. He was a good soldier, but had to meet a soldier's fate. He gave his life there that day for his country just as much as if he had fallen in battle.[35]

The march continued. On the seventeenth they reached South Washington, on the eighteenth Island Creek. The nineteenth found them at a point eight miles northwest of Kenansville. They marched twenty miles on the twentieth and reached Cox's Bridge, about eight miles from Goldsboro on the Neuse River, on the night of March 21. The next morning they crossed the river by pontoon bridge and threw up breastworks on the other side. On the twenty-fourth the enemy made "a reconnaissance in considerable force." The Confederates opened up on their pickets with artillery and made a "vigorous attack" with their troops. The attacking force included cavalry under the command of Major General Joseph Wheeler. The black soldiers easily repulsed the assault and suffered very few casualties.[36]

That night the Union troops recrossed the river and the next morning marched to Faison's Station (or Faison's Depot) on the Wilmington and Weldon Railroad. While they encamped at Faison's Station General Terry arrived and held a four-hour elaborate review of his corps. They remained in camp there until April 10, when they left for Raleigh.[37]

One of the regiment's most memorable days of the war came during this five-day march. The division had just about passed a clearing and the head of the marching column was beginning to ascend a hill thickly covered with pine trees. There the 6th heard a faraway sound coming from the division that preceded theirs in line of march. It was "a faint sound like distant cheering":

> Gradually the sound came nearer and nearer, and grew louder and louder. Now I could hear the sound of shouting and cheering distinctly....As the cheering came nearer, and the noise increased to a great volume of sound, resembling the roar of the ocean when you stand near the shore, an officer came riding down the hill from the head of our column, carrying the news as he rode that Lee had surrendered, and the war was over. That was what had caused the cheering. And then my voice mingled with the rest, to swell the grand triumphant sound that rang through that old pine forest. It was the gladdest sound that ever rang through the old North State, and came from the gladdest men that ever trod its soil.[38]

Although Lee had surrendered his Army of Northern Virginia, General Joseph E. Johnston still commanded an active army in North Carolina. This army was opposed by Major General William T. Sherman's army. Sherman, after capturing Atlanta and marching through Georgia to Savannah, had then moved up through the Carolinas where Johnston confronted him with what was left of the once-powerful Confederate Army of Tennessee. While the 6th had been on the march to Cox's Bridge, less than fifty miles away Johnston's army had been struggling with Sherman's in a three-day battle at Bentonville, North Carolina, March 19–21.[39]

On April 11 the 6th with the rest of Paine's Division marched through Bentonville where they reviewed the scars made on the landscape during the recent battle. They pushed on for three more days of relatively easy marching and reached Raleigh on the afternoon of the fourteenth. The regiment made camp about a mile south of the city.[40]

At Raleigh they finally joined Sherman's troops. Sherman and Johnston at that time were arranging suspension of hostilities, anticipating the surrender of Johnston's army. On April 20 the 6th broke camp and marched through Raleigh where they were reviewed by Sherman himself.[41]

After the review they set up a new camp about two miles outside the city near the main road to Smithfield. They remained at that camp until after Johnston surrendered. While in the process of arranging surrender was in progress, many of the officers and men of the regiment paid visits to Johnston's army. Curiosity drew them to see the Rebels in their camp. After the surrender Sherman wasted no time reviewing his soldiers and setting off with them to Washington for the Grand Review of the armies on Pennsylvania Avenue. For Sherman's troops the war was over, but few in the 6th imagined that they would serve another five months before they could go home.[42]

The regiment set off for Smithfield on April 29 arriving there on the thirtieth. The next day they marched to Goldsboro and encamped just outside the town. They would remain here for over a month. With the fighting over, picket duty and drills were discontinued. Practically the only duty required was taking a turn at guarding the camp. Near the center of the town, a short distance back from the main street, stood a stark image—a slave pen. About sixty feet square and surrounded by a high board fence, the enclosure had been used on several occasions to confine Union prisoners for a short period. This human cage eloquently symbolized for the men the meaning of the war that had just ended.[43]

On June 3 the regiment was ordered into Goldsboro to relieve the 4th USCT as provost guards. They remained inside the town until June 5, when they were relieved in turn by the 3rd New Hampshire Volunteers and were transferred to Wilmington. They traveled by railroad the 152 miles from Goldsboro to Wilmington. They would be stationed in Wilmington doing garrison duty for over three months.[44]

There would be no more deaths from battle, but being stationed in one place for a long period of time increased the likelihood of contracting disease. The American Civil War saw twice as many soldiers die from disease as from battlefield wounds. Officers were by no means exempt from danger. While stationed at Goldsboro Captain Henry Herbert of Company G died of illness. His body was sent home. At Wilmington the list of sick men grew. At the hospital Chaplain Asher faithfully ministered to his soldiers who were suffering from "malignant fever." Finally Asher himself succumbed to severe illness and died in the line of duty July 27, 1865.[45]

CHAPTER 10

CLOSING THE BOOKS

The soldiers of the 6th Regiment of U.S. Colored Infantry would not be mustered out of the service until September of 1865. Their last months of service were not easy for the men to endure. Their enemy had surrendered and their fighting was over, and more than ever they longed to go home. But they remained in the South doing occupation duty as they watched other Northern units go home.

Nearly one thousand men were in the regiment when it left Camp William Penn in the fall of 1863. Its size varied continually from that point in time. Over the course of the war men separated from the regiment through discharge, death, and desertion. New men joined the regiment as well in distinct waves.[1] Draftees and substitutes were assigned to the regiment in a time pattern that reflected periods of conscription activity. The last draftee joined the regiment in December of 1864; no substitutes joined after January of 1864. A significant number of volunteers came into the regiment, however, between February and April of 1865. In fact, fifty-three volunteers were mustered into the regiment on a single day—March 13, 1865. The cumulative number of men in each of these categories over time can be compared in *Graph 33*.[2]

Even while the war was still being fought, the men of the regiment continually thought of home and family and how much they wanted to return to them. They went for months without pay and many of them felt a great need to return home to provide for their families. A member of the 6th who signed his letter "Bought and Sold," wrote an anguished plea to the *Christian Recorder* in February of 1864:

> I am a soldier, or at least that is what I was drafted for in the 6th USCT; have been in the service since Aug., last. I could not afford to get a substitute or I would not be here now and my poor wife at home almost starving. When I was home I could make a living for her and my two little ones; but now that I am a soldier they must do the best

they can or starve. It almost tempts me to desert and run a chance of getting shot, when I read her letters, hoping that I would come to her relief. But what am I to do?...When I was at Chelton Hill I felt very patriotic; but my wife's letters have brought my patriotism down to the freezing point, and I don't think it will ever rise again; and it is the case all through the regiment.[3]

It is no surprise to discover that some members of the regiment thought about desertion. Letters such as those received by "Bought and Sold" could only aggravate such inclinations. Wives had little choice but to protest to someone about the intolerable conditions that they were forced to endure. The New Jersey wife of a soldier in the same brigade as the 6th Regiment sent her plea directly to President Lincoln:

> Sir, my husband, who is on Co. K. 22nd Reg't U.S. Col[ore]d Troops. (and now in the Macon Hospital in Portsmouth with a wound in his arm) has not received any pay since last May and then only thirteen dollars. I write to you because I have been told you would see to it. I have four children to support and I find this a great strugle [sic]. A hard life this!
>
> I being a col[ore]d women do not get any State pay. Yet my husband is fighting for the country.[4]

When the fighting ended, the men saw all the more reason why they should be allowed to go home. An anonymous black soldier wrote to Secretary of War Edwin M. Stanton in July of 1865. He emphasized to Secretary Stanton the loyalty displayed by "colored troops":

> Sir   I adress you with a few lines in reference to colored troops doing duty in North Carolina who, are, troops organized in Northern State. for instance their is the 6th U.S.C.T. from Camp William Penn at Pennsylvania 4th U.S.C.T. from Baltimore, Md., 5th U.S.C.T. from Ohio 1st U.S.C.T. from Washington, D.C., who, Have Served the government faithfully two years, & the most of them free men, amongst them are a large number of farmers, & Mechanic who, could get employment if they were Mustered out of the Service they Have been Loyal, in all respects as, soon as the call for colored. Troops was made they rallied around the countries Standard & gave themselves to their country & now Since their is No More fighting to be done are desirous of turning Home to their families after two years Hard Service in the field. while their was fighting the colored troops in Division was Satisfied. if war was to break out again they would Serve 3 years longe without finding fault.[5]

He continued his letter with a list of the major battles and campaigns in which these troops had taken part. He ended the message with the plea: "...Now M' Secty dont you think we, Have done our duty as, men &

soldiers, & if you can Shorten our time as, their is an order to muster out more troops."[6]

Graph 34 depicts the pattern of desertion among volunteers, draftees, and substitutes. An examination of this pattern might lead one to conclude that as soon as hostilities ended, veteran volunteers staged a mass exodus. But this graph can be misleading. The statistics for the regiment are skewed by late-arriving volunteers.

Between March 2 and March 14, 1865, sixty-three new volunteers mustered into the regiment. On those dates the regiment had penetrated into the interior of North Carolina, and the new volunteers were probably swept up from among the local inhabitants as it advanced. In this group, forty-one of the forty-four men whose birthplace is listed give North Carolina as their birthplace. The other three, born in Virginia and Maryland, may well have moved to North Carolina. Of these sixty-five new recruits, forty deserted. All of those deserters whose birthplace is listed give North Carolina as their birthplace. Of the fifty-three who mustered in on May 13, 1865, thirty-three deserted; twenty-two of them departed within a month and a half of them joining the regiment.[7]

A very different pattern of desertion is shown for the veteran troops who enlisted between July and September of 1863. The troops who reported to Camp William Penn at the time of the regiment's formation would need to serve about 800 days before being mustered out and were not likely to desert at the end of hostilities. In fact, all but two of the deserters in their group left the regiment before Lee's surrender. Men in this group were most likely to desert either in their first one hundred days of service while stationed at Camp William Penn or sometime shortly after the Battle of New Market Heights. This original group was most likely to desert while stationed in Pennsylvania, and least likely to desert while in North Carolina. As the large number of deserters from North Carolina indicates, a soldier was most likely to walk away from the service if he was near a familiar, friendly refuge.[8]

Desertion statistics for the regiment as a whole are misleading. The desertion rate appears much higher when including the men who deserted from training camp, who never left Pennsylvania, and also including the eleventh-hour additions to the regiment. The men who marched out of Camp William Penn with the regiment were the heart of the unit. It was they who struggled through Petersburg, Dutch Gap, and New Market Heights, showing great unit cohesion and a very much lower rate of unauthorized leave.

Graphs 38 through 47 depict the losses suffered by each company of the great regiment. They illustrate over time the frequency of men killed, died of wounds, died of other causes, discharged, deserted, or missing.[9]

When the order came for the 6th to be mustered out of service, the men began their journey home. They boarded a train at Wilmington; most of the men had to ride on platform cars due to segregation or a shortage of transport. They traveled along the Wilmington and Weldon Railroad to Goldsboro, to Weldon, and finally to Petersburg. They stopped for an hour and had dinner in that town that they had wanted so badly to capture the previous year. They transferred to the railroad between Petersburg and City Point and were assigned to box cars furnished with benches for seats. The train carried them across former Confederate lines and across the positions held by Union forces from June 15, 1864, onward. They traveled from there to City Point over the same rail line, the United States Military Railroads, that had been used during the war to transport supplies from the supply base at City Point to the front. From City Point they traveled by steamer down the James River, past Fort Monroe, and on to Baltimore. From there they traveled "speedily and comfortably" to Philadelphia, where they went into camp at or near Camp William Penn. The enlisted men "were provided with good quarters in camp," while most of the officers stayed in hotels in the city.[10]

It took five days to muster out the men.[11] As the books were closed on their service in the war the men had time to reflect on the last two years of their lives. In the course of the war they had lost eight officers and seventy-nine men killed. Five officers and 132 men died of disease, and 169 officers and men were wounded or missing.[12] Officers were more likely to be killed or wounded in battle than enlisted men, but less likely to die of other causes. *Graph 37* compares the fates of officers and enlisted men.[13]

The flags of the regiment had been badly damaged in the course of their service. Colonel Ames as early as November 1864 realized that the national colors were in such a sorry condition that the regiment could no longer use them. He asked the chairman of the Supervisory Committee on Enlistment of Colored Troops if the committee members would be willing to accept "some very ragged pieces of silk" to decorate the committee headquarters or to store in their closets.[14] While he described the pitiful condition of the flag, he also reflected upon its deeper worth:

> I am quite anxious to consign the tattered fragments of our "stars and stripes" to some safe place, tho' I confess it is not a very valuable or desireable piece of property even to the ragman. It has been exposed to all weathers and som [sic] very rude winds—the red has stained the white to a dirty mixture and the blue has wept over both—the staff was shot in halves at Newmarket Heights, and in fact almost impossible to be carried in the ranks. It's a problem to unroll it and is [study?] to roll it up again. In fact—I am quite anxious to set it aside, as are all my officers, its period of usefulness is certainly over. But we all feel some respect and appreciation for it,—we think it has looked upon some very creditable performances,—it has been "in at the death" of some seventy of our men, and witnessed the blood and mutilation of more than two hundred others of us. I do not know that you would

consider it much of a boon, but I should feel very much pleased to have it in your committee rooms or even stored in your closets.[15]

The regiment presented the other standard, the Regimental Color, to Sergeant Major Thomas Hawkins, who had rescued that standard at New Market Heights. Years later Hawkins, along with Alexander Kelley and Nathan Edgerton, would be awarded the Congressional Medal of Honor.[16]

The men finally went home. The officers of the regiment held a farewell gathering at the Continental Hotel, at Ninth and Chestnut Streets. The regiment had triumphantly marched past this building two years earlier. The fact that the white officers stayed at hotels while the black enlisted men stayed in camp might serve as a sign that now that the war was over the two races would go their own ways and the Whites, who no longer needed black manpower would redesignate Blacks as second-class citizens. But the officers' experiences had forced them to reevaluate their thinking. The officers adopted a resolution to express their appreciation of the black troops who had served with them.[17] The resolution went beyond evaluating their performance as soldiers:

1. Resolved, that, in our intercourse with them during the past two years, they have shown themselves to be brave, reliable, and efficient as soldiers; patient to endure, and prompt to execute.

2. That, being satisfied with their conduct in the high position of soldiers of the United States, we see no reason why they should not be fully recognized as equals, honorable and responsible citizens of the same.[18]

Black soldiers were also changed by their experiences as soldiers. They returned to their homes knowing that they had taken an active and important part in their own liberation. When men were needed to strike a blow for freedom, they had answered the call and did themselves strike the blow.

APPENDIX A

PSYCHOLOGICAL WOUNDS

When the fighting of September 29, 1864, ended, the officers added up the fearful cost of the day's battle. The men had paid a heavy price that was clearly reflected in the number killed, wounded, and missing. But some wounds went uncounted — the invisible psychological wounds.

Private Thomas Anderson of Company E was one of many wounded in action on September 29, 1864. Anderson had enlisted in August of the previous year, a twenty-year-old farmer from Bucks County, Pennsylvania. After being wounded he was taken to the hospital at Point of Rocks, Virginia. Medical personnel must have determined his wounds to be serious enough to require more treatment than they were able to provide. He was taken on board a hospital steamer, the *Thomas Powell*, to be transported to the U.S. General Hospital at Hampton, Virginia.[1]

For Anderson the wound itself did not cause his death, but while the ship was en route to Hampton, according to one report, "His wound produced insanity." Another account reports that "...while insane from the Effects [sic] of his wounds, he leaped from the steamer into the James River, where he drowned."[2] One can only speculate why he would be so emotionally distraught that he would choose to end his own life. Perhaps the pain was simply beyond his endurance. Perhaps the wound had taken away a part of him or disabled him so much that he could not accept life as he would have to live it from that point onward. This tragic story indicates that the price paid by the fighting men of the regiment extended beyond the observable wounds.

The American Civil War predated the development of psychology as a formal academic discipline. The term "post-traumatic stress disorder" was, of course, unknown, and for the most part the concept behind the term was not accepted nor understood by the general population. But medical personnel became increasingly aware of what we would consider psychological disorders. In fact, of every thousand medical discharges from the Union army during the war, some fifty-eight were dismissed for reasons that would later be regarded as psychological. Army surgeons treating combat veterans in the field contributed a great number of articles on this subject to the *American Journal of the Medical Sciences*.[3]

One veteran of the 6th provided a frank and detailed description of his own bout with psychological trauma. McMurray's *Recollections* give insight into what went on inside the men of the regiment. As McMurray began to settle down for the night at the end of the regiment's most bloody day, September 29, powerful feelings overwhelmed him:

> What my feelings were after that day's work, I will not attempt to state. They were somewhat sad and gloomy, I admit. Less than a year before I left Camp William Penn, near Philadelphia, with over ninety men in my company, and two officers besides myself. Now I had just three enlisted men present for duty. Both officers of my company were in hospital, one sick and the other wounded. At that rate, where would Company D be in one year more? I was among strangers, with not an old-time friend to go to. My heart sank áway down toward my shoe soles, and sometimes it was hard enough to keep the tears back. I did think of home and the dear ones there, and wished the war would soon end.
>
> After eating some supper I began to have a strange, unusual feeling, a feeling of great oppression. I experienced a tingling, prickly sensation, as though a thousand little needles were jagging my flesh. The air seemed oppressive, and I breathed with difficulty. I couldn't remain in the hut, and felt I must be out in the open air. So I went out to get relief, and spent a good portion of the night walking round and round the little building. After a while I became wild, almost crazy, and had to be looked after by those near me. Dr. Barnes, the regimental surgeon was sent for. He gave me a potion that quieted me, and I rested till morning, when I was sent to the corps hospital, where I remained just ten days, and then returned to my company. And those ten days comprised all the time I was off duty during the two years of my service in the Sixth U.S. Colored Troops.
>
> What ailed me that night of September 29, 1864, I did not know at the time. But I found it out afterward, and have realized it many times since. The strain on me was so great through the day, that when the excitement passed over and quiet came, my nervous organization broke down temporarily. That was all. I was young, and strong, and had never suffered from any sort of dissipation, which was all in my favor. But I have suffered more or less every year of my life since from that day's experience. Over work, physical or mental, would bring me back to the place where I was that September night. On three different occasions, if not four, I have been brought to where I was that September night in Old Virginia, and have borne it all with a mighty

small amount of sympathy from those about me. Soldiers have lost a leg or an arm and never suffered as much as I have done from the breaking down of my nervous system there at Fort Harrison. My readers will pardon this short reference to my physical troubles resulting from the war. I will not offend in the same way again.[4]

McMurray left enough of a record of his experience for a psychologist to interpret it and determine the nature and severity of his reaction. Dr. Joseph A. DiIenno, a psychiatrist who has studied post-traumatic stress disorder, read the foregoing account and gave an explanation of McMurray's reaction. Some of this interpretation is, by necessity, conjectural, but much can be concluded with clinical certitude. Although some conclusions apply to only Captain McMurray, some universal principles apply to anyone in the regiment who took part in the attack.

McMurray's behavior indicates that he had a strong personality, a strong ego as the term "ego" is used in psychology to mean "self."[5] He had been thrust into a helpless position and, in his own words: "...we were utterly unable to protect ourselves in any way."[6] Dr. DiIenno explains:

A person who is in a defenseless position is in a situation where a whole man who makes choices about himself and decides what to do is now in a position where his body is being flung in a way that he no longer can decide what to do. He is experiencing "overwhelmingness."[7]

Besides being defenseless, McMurray saw people he knew getting killed. He did not know what would happen next, either to himself or to the people whom he could only helplessly watch being killed. He recalls: "I saw that my company was suffering heavy loss, but thought of little else than pressing forward."[8] That he could continue to function in his role while defenseless and in this situation indicates that this particular man "is not like ordinary men." The reaction of most people to such a situation is to just fall down in fear, and "You can just shoot them right on the ground, they just stay on the ground petrified."[9]

By reading from McMurray's *Recollections*, Dr. DiIenno concludes:

I don't see anything that would say that a post-traumatic stress disorder is necessarily the diagnosis here. Anybody would have some problem if out of thirty men, three returned. That is going to make you feel something; that is going to be devastating within. It's a devastating experience. What it does indicate to me, though, is a panic attack. In other words, he became acutely anxious when he was having this meal after the battle.[10]

The disorder that some may call a "panic attack" has until recently been called an "acute confusional state." That is the diagnosis offered. McMurray was in "a state of confusion that was time-limited. He was oriented to person, but not to time or place." In other words he knew who he was, but not the time or place where he was.[11]

One reason for making the distinction between the post-traumatic stress disorder (PTSD) and the reaction described here is the difference in the "flashbacks." With PTSD the flashback to the initial trauma happens at odd times. A person could be engaged in a simple conversation when he begins having some sort of disturbing reaction. Perhaps something reminds him of the battle. His reaction could continue for days. PTSD is ruled out here because the anxiety in this case recurs only when it is brought on by a stressor such as "overwork."[12]

Another major difference between PTSD and McMurray's reaction is the nature of the flashback itself. He stated that "Overwork, physical or mental, would bring me back *to the place where I was that September night.*"[13] He did *not* return to *the battle itself*. Rather, what repeated itself to him in his feelings was the original anxiety reaction, a confusional state that he had never before experienced. He did not say that the battle came back to him; he remembered instead the anxiety that followed the battle. This is typical of anxiety attacks:[14]

> It is not odd that he would go back to the anxiety and not to the battle itself. It is not odd because of the way the ego works. The ego tries to remove itself from the pain as far as possible at all times. The stronger the ego, the farther away from the pain it gets so that if it becomes just a memory you are as far away from it as you are ever going to get.[15]

Remembering the actual death of a loved one is much more painful than remembering the bad feelings that came at that time. In other words: "You would rather remember the anxiety than remember the actual thing, because if you remember the actual thing, instead of thinking of symptoms, which is what he thinks about, you would be thinking of persons — much worse, more painful."[16]

To explain why he felt an unconscious need later in life to return to that terrible night DiIenno speculates:

> The anxiety state that he experienced apparently is more overwhelming to him than the battle itself, which is a sign of ego strength. He is afraid, of course, of losing his boundaries, or losing his limits, or losing his identity as a reaction to the battle, that it might happen again, or something along those lines....Most likely he wants to go back into battle and either kill the enemy, (which he hates, although it is never indicated in here [McMurray's *Recollections*]) or help his friends which he missed.[17]

Some observations can be generalized and extended to all in the regiment, but the reaction of any individual could be completely different from that of other soldiers in the regiment. Many factors affected the way a soldier reacted, most importantly the individual's "ego strength," or strength of self. But regardless of ego strength, "everybody is maimed." "It is not possible to experience this and not be affected permanently in some way."[18] The nature of the stressor, itself, was shared by all in common:

> One of the key characteristics of a stress disorder is that the nature of the stress is such that it would stress anyone. No matter who is under the circumstances, everyone is altered by the experience.[19]

And war is unlike any other stressor:

> Every foot soldier and everyone who has ever studied wars knows that the situation of battle is an absolute horror. It is not reproducable by any games, you get into something that there is absolutely no way of getting used to and there is no way of preparing for it. Soldiers who have been in more battles are usually better soldiers than soldiers who have been in less battles, but that doesn't mean that they are all not petrified. Though more or less, there is still a lot of fear.[20]

The men of the 6th Regiment had to deal with this emotional trauma. Those who survived also had to carry with them the burden of dealing with this trauma for the rest of their lives. Undoubtedly many of the men experienced, as did John McMurray, "a mighty small amount of sympathy," for those suffering from the wounds that no one else could see.[21]

APPENDIX B

STATISTICAL TABLES AND GRAPHS

Table 1.   Numbers of Volunteers, Draftees, and Substitutes in 6th USCT by Company

Company	Vol	Draft	Sub	Totals
A	81	19	24	124
B	103	19	16	138
C	92	28	14	134
D	39	44	52	135
E	75	26	31	132
F	30	35	53	118
G	26	53	41	120
H	52	38	33	123
I	35	65	22	122
K	16	64	46	126
Totals	549	391	332	1,272
Percentages	43.2	30.7	26.1	100.0

Table 2.   Percentages of Volunteers, Draftees, and Substitutes in 6th USCT
             by Company

Company	Vol	Draft	Sub	Totals
A	65.3	15.3	19.4	100
B	74.6	13.8	11.6	100
C	68.7	20.9	10.4	100
D	28.9	32.6	38.5	100
E	56.8	19.7	23.5	100
F	25.4	29.7	44.9	100
G	21.7	44.2	34.2	100
H	42.3	30.9	26.8	100
I	28.7	53.3	18.0	100
K	12.7	50.8	36.5	100

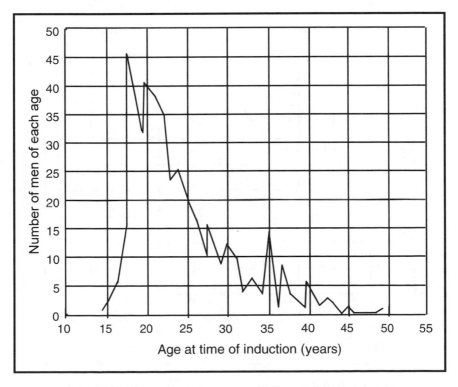

Graph 1. Distribution of Ages of Volunteers in 6th USCI.

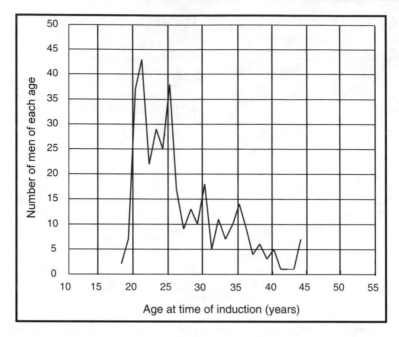

Graph 2. Distribution of Ages of Draftees in 6th USCI.

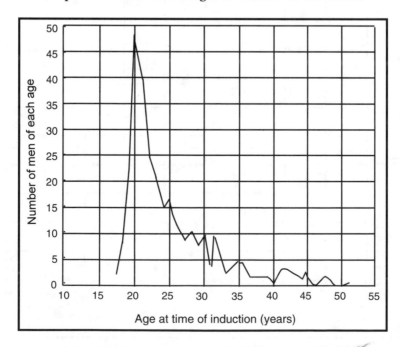

Graph 3. Distribution of Ages of Substitutes in 6th USCI.

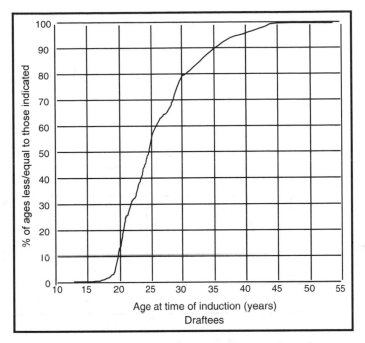

Graph 4. Cumulative Distribution of Ages of Draftees.

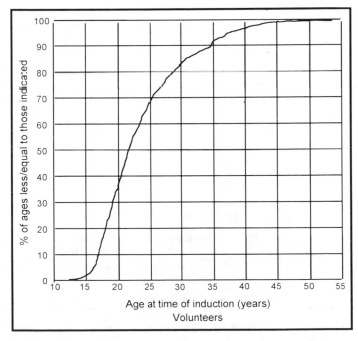

Graph 4a. Cumulative Distribution of Ages of Volunteers.

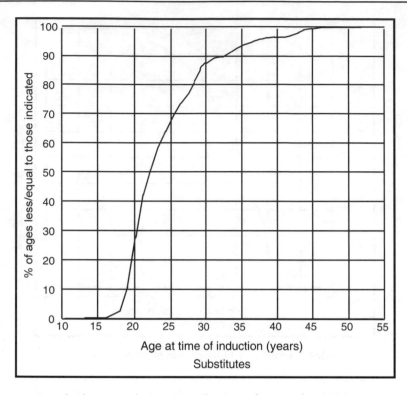

Graph 4b. Cumulative Distribution of Ages of Substitutes.

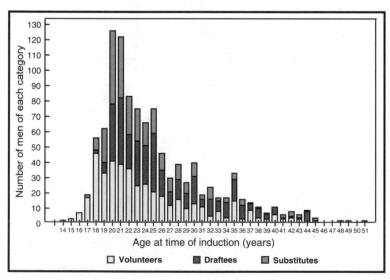

Graph 5. Distribution of Ages of Volunteers, Draftees, and Substitutes.

Table 3.   Distribution of Ages Report for All Companies of 6th USCT
            (Number of Men of Each Age)

Age	Vol	Draft	Sub	Totals
13	-	-	-	0
14	1	-	-	1
15	2	-	-	2
16	6	-	-	6
17	16	-	2	18
18	45	2	8	55
19	32	7	22	61
20	40	37	48	125
21	38	43	40	121
22	35	22	25	82
23	24	29	21	74
24	25	25	15	65
25	20	38	16	74
26	17	17	11	45
27	11	9	9	29
28	15	13	10	38
29	9	10	7	26
30	12	18	9	39
31	10	5	3	18
32	4	11	8	23
33	7	7	2	16
34	3	10	3	16
35	14	14	4	32
36	2	9	4	15
37	8	4	1	13
38	3	6	1	10
39	2	3	1	6
40	5	5	-	10
41	2	1	2	5
42	3	1	3	7
43	2	1	2	5
44	-	7	1	8
45	1	-	2	3
46	-	-	-	-

Table 3. Distribution of Ages Report for All Companies of 6th USCT (Number of Men of Each Age) (*continued*)

Age	Vol	Draft	Sub	Totals
47	-	-	-	-
48	-	-	1	1
49	1	-	-	1
50	-	-	-	-
51	-	-	1	1
52	-	-	-	-
Totals	415	354	282	1,051
Percentages	39.5	33.7	26.8	100.0

Table 4. Distribution of Ages Reported for All Companies of 6th USCT (Percentage of men of each age)

Age	Vol	Draft	Sub
13	0.00	0.00	0.00
14	0.24	0.00	0.00
15	0.48	0.00	0.00
16	1.45	0.00	0.00
17	3.86	0.00	0.71
18	10.84	0.56	2.84
19	7.71	1.98	7.80
20	9.64	10.45	17.02
21	9.16	12.15	14.18
22	8.43	6.21	8.87
23	5.78	8.19	7.45
24	6.02	7.06	5.32
25	4.82	10.73	5.67
26	4.10	4.80	3.90
27	2.65	2.54	3.19
28	3.61	3.67	3.55
29	2.17	2.82	2.48

Table 4.   Distribution of Ages Reported for All Companies of 6th USCT
             (Percentage of men of each age) (*continued*)

Age	Vol	Draft	Sub
30	2.89	5.08	3.19
31	2.41	1.41	1.06
32	0.96	3.11	2.84
33	1.69	1.98	0.71
34	0.72	2.82	1.06
35	3.37	3.95	1.42
36	0.48	2.54	1.42
37	1.93	1.13	0.35
38	0.72	1.69	0.35
39	0.48	0.85	0.35
40	1.20	1.41	0.00
41	0.48	0.28	0.71
42	0.72	0.28	1.06
43	0.48	0.28	0.71
44	0.00	1.98	0.35
45	0.24	0.00	0.71
46	0.00	0.00	0.00
47	0.00	0.00	0.00
48	0.00	0.00	0.35
49	0.24	0.00	0.00
50	0.00	0.00	0.00
51	0.00	0.00	0.35
52	0.00	0.00	0.00
Totals	100	100	100

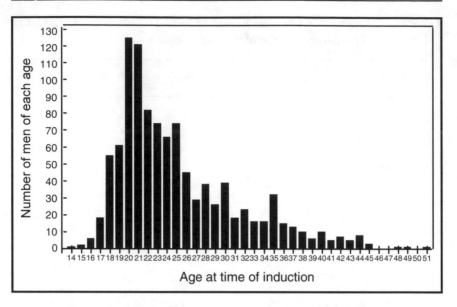

Graph 6. Distribution of Ages of Men in Regiment.

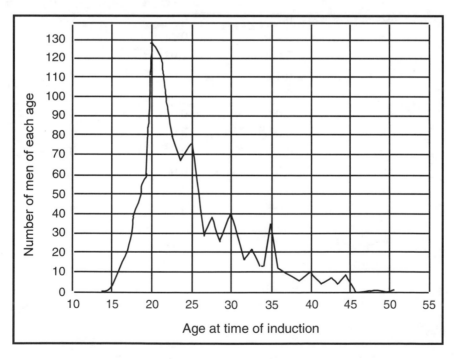

Graph 7. Distribution of Ages of Men in Regiment.

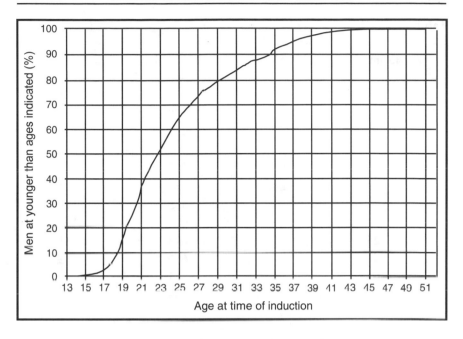

Graph 8. Cumulative Distribution of Ages.

Table 5.   Distribution of Heights of the Men of 6th USCT

Height	No. of Men	Cum No. of Men	Cum % of Men
58.5	1	1	0.10
59.5	1	2	0.20
60	13	15	1.46
61	11	26	2.54
61.5	7	33	3.22
61.75	2	35	3.42
62	21	56	5.46
62.5	12	68	6.64
62.75	1	· 69	6.74
63	59	128	12.50
63.25	2	130	12.70
63.5	22	152	14.84
64	59	211	20.61
64.5	35	246	24.02
64.75	1	247	24.12
65	100	347	33.89

Table 5. Distribution of Heights of the Men of 6th USCT (*continued*)

Height	No. of Men	Cum No. of Men	Cum % of Men
65.25	1	348	33.98
65.5	30	378	36.91
65.75	3	381	37.21
66	122	503	49.12
66.25	2	505	49.32
66.5	28	533	52.05
66.75	2	535	52.25
67	109	644	62.89
67.25	1	645	62.99
67.5	41	686	66.99
67.625	1	687	67.09
67.75	2	689	67.29
68	93	782	76.37
68.25	1	783	76.46
68.375	1	784	76.56
68.5	22	806	78.71
68.75	2	808	78.91
69	65	873	85.25
69.25	1	874	85.35
69.5	12	886	86.52
69.75	2	888	86.72
70	55	943	92.09
70.5	8	951	92.87
71	23	974	95.12
71.25	1	975	95.21
71.5	4	979	95.61
71.75	3	982	95.90
72	21	1003	97.95
72.25	1	1004	98.05
72.5	1	1005	98.14
73	12	1017	99.32
74	3	1020	99.61
74.5	2	1022	99.80
75.5	1	1023	99.90
83	1	1024	100.00

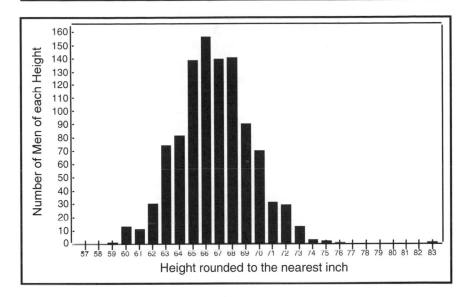

Graph 9. Distribution of Heights.

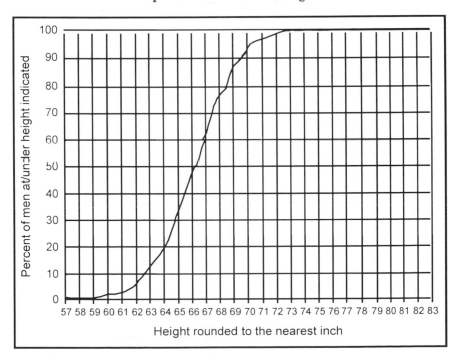

Graph 10. Cumulative Distribution of Heights.

Table 6. **Birthplaces of the 6th USCT**

BIRTHPLACE	NO. OF MEN
Pennsylvania	365
Delaware	161
Maryland	150
Virginia	122
North Carolina	54
New Jersey	52
New York	24
Canada	22
Georgia	6
West Indies	6
Kentucky	4
District of Columbia	3
Missouri	3
Ohio	3
South Carolina	3
Tennessee	3
Jamaica	2
Alabama	1
Connecticut	1
England	1
Florida	1
Great Britain	1
Illinois	1
Indiana	1
Louisiana	1
Maine	1
Massachusetts	1
Michigan	1
Sandwich Islands	1
Vermont	1
Total Reported	996

Table 7. Birthplaces and Numbers of Men from Each, Reported by Company

BIRTHPLACE	A	B	C	D	E	F	G	H	I	K	Totals
Alabama	0	1	0	0	0	0	0	0	0	0	1
Canada	1	7	7	1	2	0	0	0	2	2	22
Connecticut	0	0	0	0	1	0	0	0	0	0	1
Delaware	10	9	6	1	2	15	18	2	45	53	161
Dist of Columbia	0	1	0	1	1	0	0	0	0	0	3
England	0	0	0	0	0	0	0	0	0	1	1
Florida	1	0	0	0	0	0	0	0	0	0	1
Georgia	0	2	1	1	0	1	1	0	0	0	6
Great Britain	0	0	0	0	0	0	0	0	1	0	1
Illinois	0	0	0	0	1	0	0	0	0	0	1
Indiana	0	0	0	0	1	0	0	0	0	0	1
Jamaica	0	0	1	1	0	0	0	0	0	0	2
Kentucky	0	2	0	0	0	1	0	1	0	0	4
Louisiana	0	0	0	0	1	0	0	0	0	0	1
Maine	0	1	0	0	0	0	0	0	0	0	1
Maryland	13	16	9	26	10	9	29	8	18	12	150
Massachusetts	0	0	0	0	0	0	0	1	0	0	1
Michigan	0	0	1	0	0	0	0	0	0	0	1
Missouri	0	2	0	0	0	0	0	0	0	1	3
N. Carolina	3	10	7	8	13	0	0	1	7	5	54
New Jersey	9	5	5	3	10	5	1	8	6	0	52
New York	1	3	6	2	7	1	0	0	4	0	24
Ohio	0	0	2	0	0	0	1	0	0	0	3
Pennsylvania	36	46	48	48	33	33	32	49	22	18	365
Sandwich Islands	0	0	0	0	0	0	0	0	0	1	1
S. Carolina	0	1	1	0	0	0	0	0	1	0	3
Tennessee	0	0	0	1	1	0	0	0	1	0	3
Vermont	0	0	1	0	0	0	0	0	0	0	1
Virginia	11	12	7	22	14	5	19	9	7	16	122
West Indies	0	1	0	2	2	0	1	0	0	0	6
Totals	85	119	102	117	99	70	102	79	114	109	996

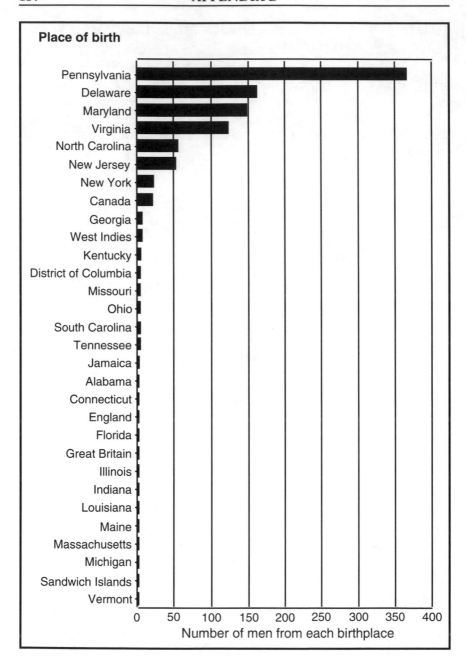

Place of birth

Number of men from each birthplace

Graph 11. Birthplaces, 6th USCI.

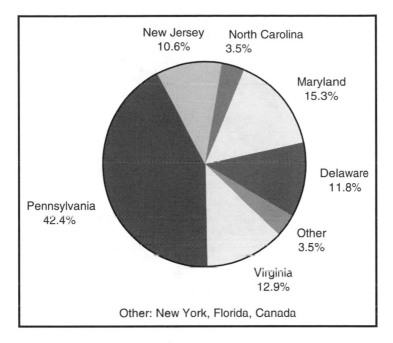

Graph 12. Birthplaces, Company A.

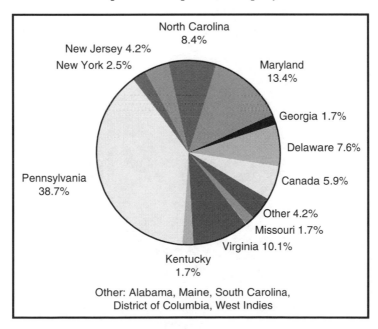

Graph 13. Birthplaces, Company B.

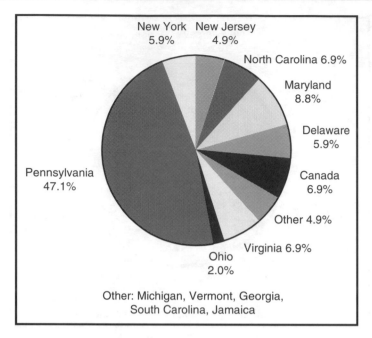

New York   New Jersey
5.9%   4.9%

North Carolina 6.9%

Maryland
8.8%

Delaware
5.9%

Canada
6.9%

Other 4.9%

Virginia 6.9%

Ohio
2.0%

Pennsylvania
47.1%

Other: Michigan, Vermont, Georgia,
South Carolina, Jamaica

Graph 14. Birthplaces, Company C.

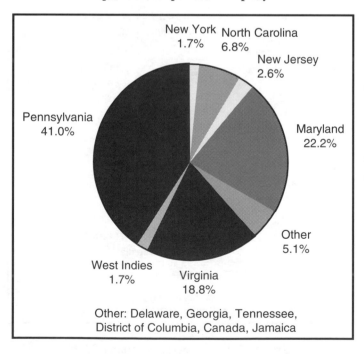

New York   North Carolina
1.7%   6.8%

New Jersey
2.6%

Maryland
22.2%

Pennsylvania
41.0%

Other
5.1%

West Indies
1.7%

Virginia
18.8%

Other: Delaware, Georgia, Tennessee,
District of Columbia, Canada, Jamaica

Graph 15. Birthplaces, Company D.

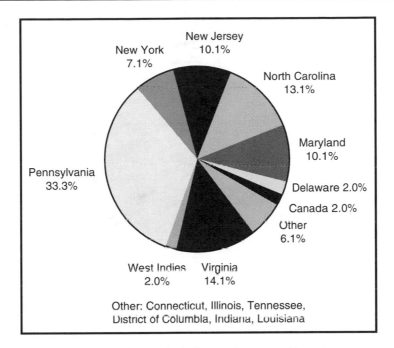

Graph 16. Birthplaces, Company E.

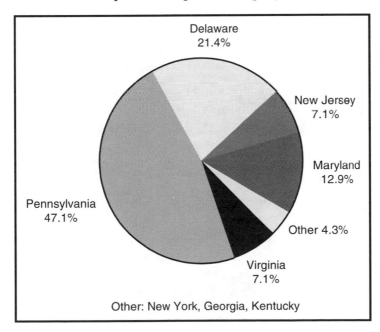

Graph 17. Birthplaces, Company F.

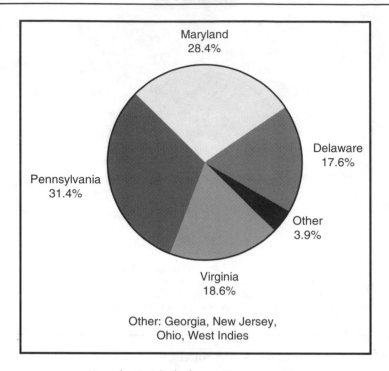

Graph 18. Birthplaces, Company G.

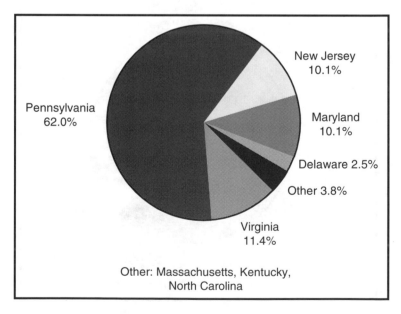

Graph 19. Birthplaces, Company H.

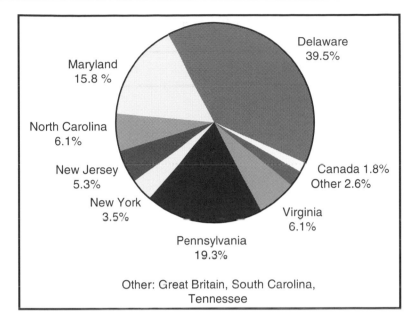

Delaware
39.5%

Maryland
15.8 %

North Carolina
6.1%

New Jersey
5.3%

New York
3.5%

Pennsylvania
19.3%

Virginia
6.1%

Canada 1.8%
Other 2.6%

Other: Great Britain, South Carolina,
Tennessee

Graph 20. Birthplaces, Company I.

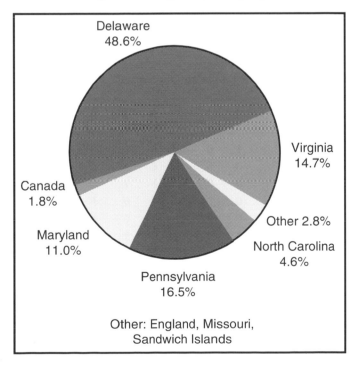

Delaware
48.6%

Virginia
14.7%

Canada
1.8%

Maryland
11.0%

Pennsylvania
16.5%

Other 2.8%

North Carolina
4.6%

Other: England, Missouri,
Sandwich Islands

Graph 21. Birthplaces, Company K.

Table 9. **Number of Men per Occupation for 6TH USCT by Company** (*continued*)

OCCUPATION	A	B	C	D	E	F	G	H	I	K	Totals
Cooper	0	0	1	0	0	0	0	0	0	0	1
Drayman	0	0	0	0	0	0	0	0	1	0	1
Driver	0	0	1	0	0	1	1	0	1	0	4
Engineer	1	0	0	0	3	0	0	0	0	0	4
Farmer	31	48	29	0	41	17	25	12	9	14	226
Fireman	0	0	0	0	0	0	0	1	0	0	1
Gardener	0	0	1	0	0	0	0	0	0	0	1
Hackman	0	1	0	0	0	0	0	0	0	1	2
Huckster	2	2	0	0	0	0	0	0	0	0	4
Laborer	39	41	46	107	31	47	63	37	85	86	582
Machinist	0	0	0	1	0	0	0	0	0	0	1
Makeman	1	0	0	0	0	0	0	0	0	0	1
Mechanic	0	0	0	0	0	0	0	0	0	1	1
Miner	1	2	4	0	2	1	1	4	0	0	15
Musician	0	1	0	0	0	0	0	0	0	0	1
Painter	0	1	0	0	0	0	0	0	0	0	1
Plasterer	0	0	1	0	0	0	0	0	0	0	1
Porter	0	2	2	0	1	0	0	0	0	0	5
Sailor	0	3	2	2	2	0	1	1	1	3	15
Sawyer	0	1	0	0	0	0	0	0	0	0	1
Seaman	0	0	0	0	0	0	2	0	0	0	2
Servant	0	0	0	3	0	0	0	1	0	0	4
Ship Carpenter	0	0	0	0	0	0	0	0	0	1	1
Shoemaker	0	0	1	0	0	0	1	1	1	0	4
Steward	0	0	1	0	0	0	0	0	0	0	1
Tailor	0	0	0	0	0	0	0	0	1	0	1
Tanner	0	0	1	0	0	0	0	0	0	0	1
Teamster	1	0	2	0	0	0	1	1	0	0	5
Tobacconist	0	0	0	0	1	0	0	0	1	0	2
Tradesman	0	0	0	1	0	0	0	0	0	0	1
Typeman	0	0	0	0	0	0	0	1	0	0	1
Wagonier	0	1	0	0	0	0	0	1	0	0	2
Waiter	2	4	2	1	6	1	2	3	3	0	24
Watchman	0	0	1	0	0	0	0	0	0	0	1
Waterman	0	0	0	0	0	0	0	0	1	0	1
Totals	83	118	100	119	97	70	102	76	111	109	985

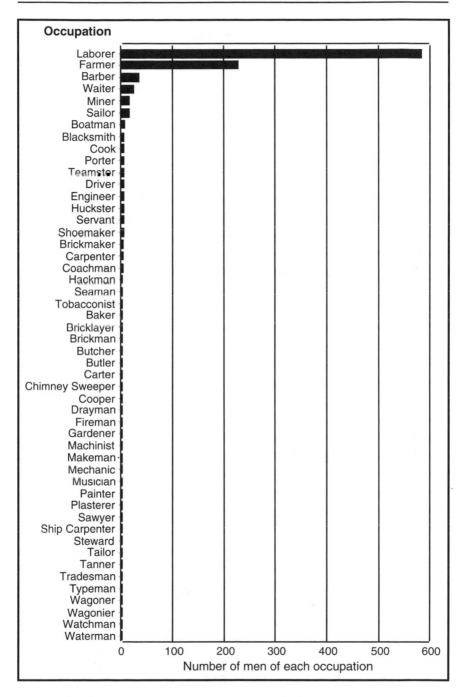

Graph 22. Occupations, 6th USCI.

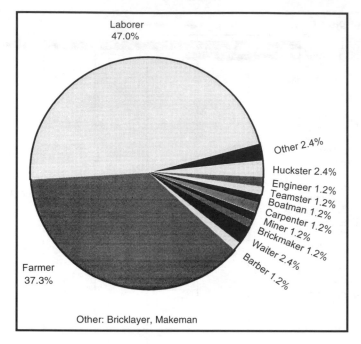

Graph 23. Occupations, Company A.

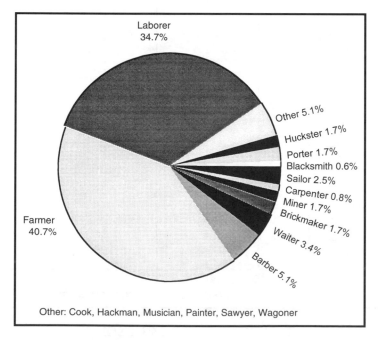

Graph 24. Occupations, Company B.

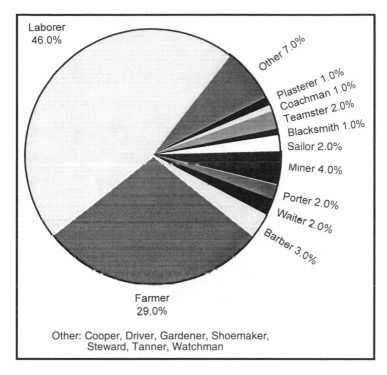

Other: Cooper, Driver, Gardener, Shoemaker,
Steward, Tanner, Watchman

Graph 25. Occupations, Company C.

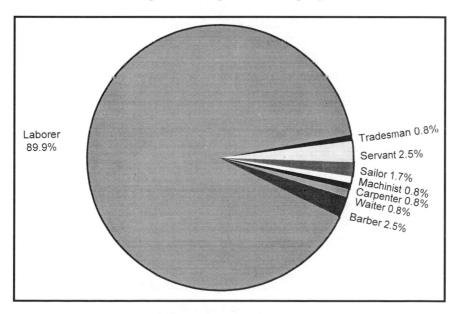

Graph 26. Occupations, Company D.

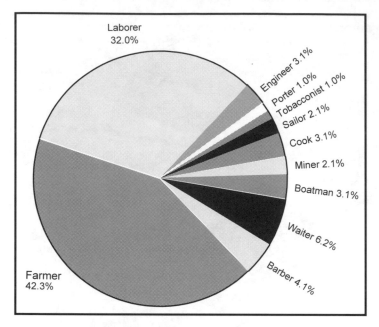

Graph 27. Occupations, Company E.

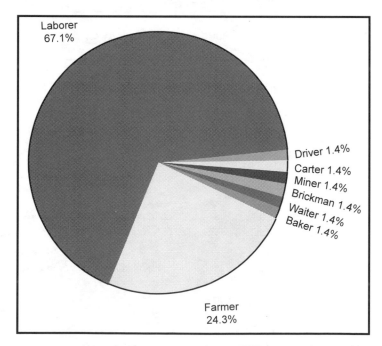

Graph 28. Occupations, Company F.

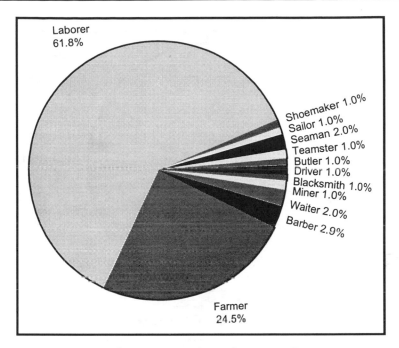

Laborer
61.8%

Shoemaker 1.0%
Sailor 1.0%
Seaman 2.0%
Teamster 1.0%
Butler 1.0%
Driver 1.0%
Blacksmith 1.0%
Miner 1.0%
Waiter 2.0%
Barber 2.9%

Farmer
24.5%

Graph 29. Occupations, Company G.

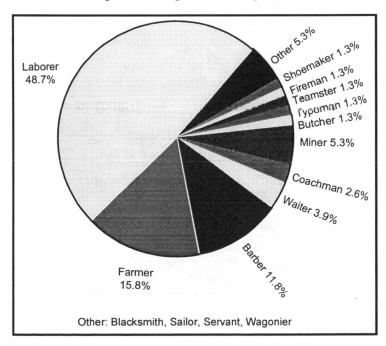

Laborer
48.7%

Other 5.3%
Shoemaker 1.3%
Fireman 1.3%
Teamster 1.3%
Typoman 1.3%
Butcher 1.3%

Miner 5.3%

Coachman 2.6%

Waiter 3.9%

Barber 11.8%

Farmer
15.8%

Other: Blacksmith, Sailor, Servant, Wagonier

Graph 30. Occupations, Company H.

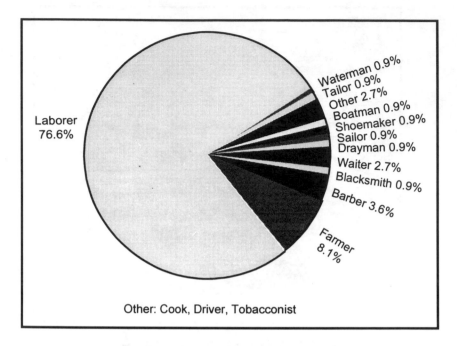

Graph 31. Occupations, Company I.

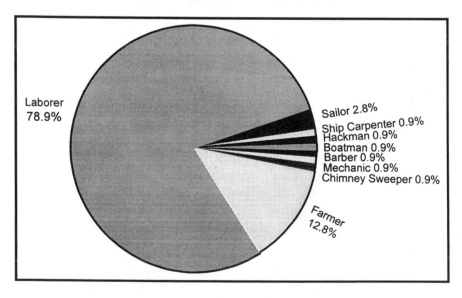

Graph 32. Occupations, Company K.

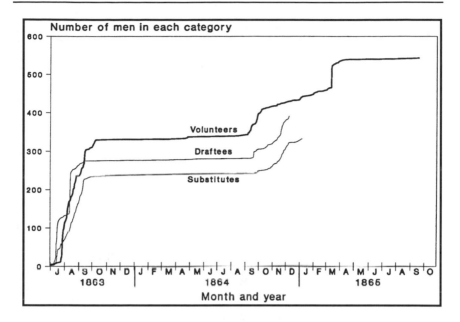

Graph 33. Cumulative Numbers Mustering In.

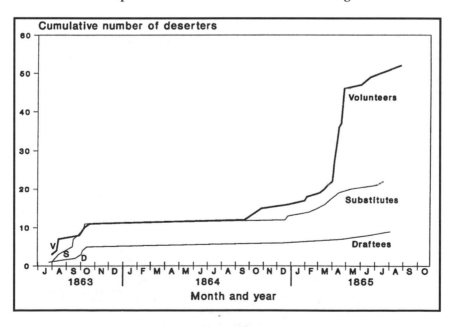

Graph 34. Cumulative Numbers of Deserters.

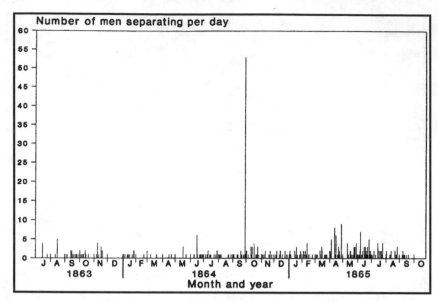

Graph 35. Number of Men Separating from Regiment prior to Muster
Out Date.

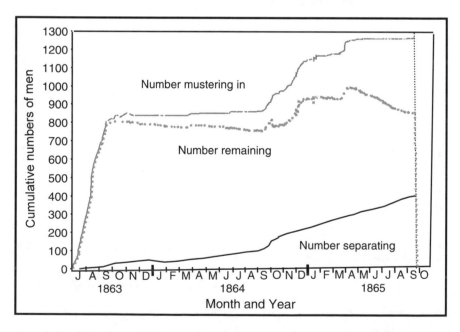

Graph 36. Number of Men Joining, Separating from, and Remaining with
Regiment.

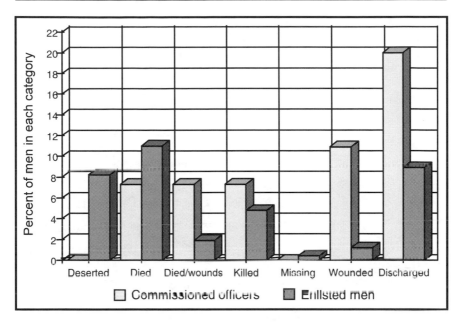

Graph 37. Fates of Commissioned Officers and Enlisted Men.

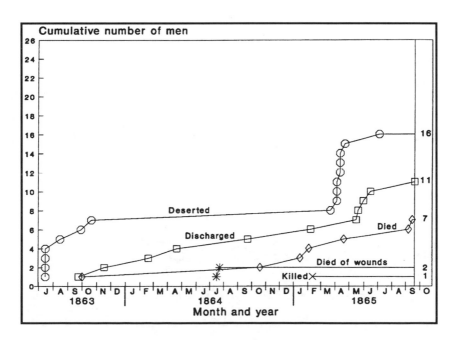

Graph 38. Cumulative Losses, Company A.

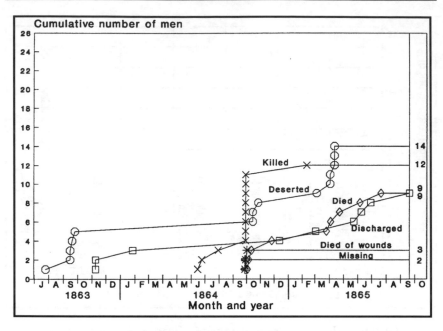

Graph 39. Cumulative Losses, Company B.

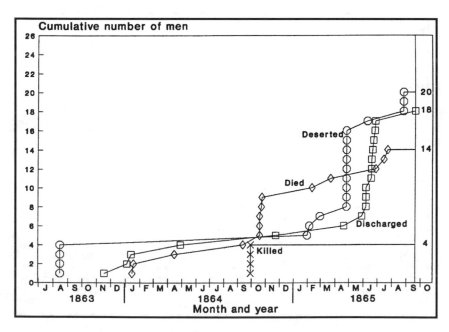

Graph 40. Cumulative Losses, Company C.

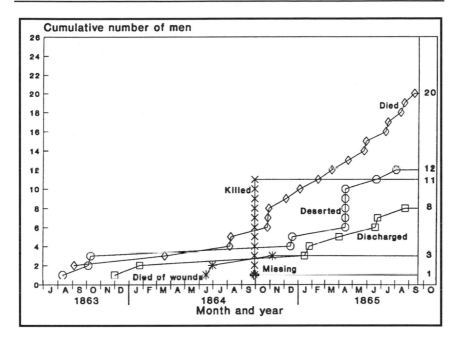

Graph 41. Cumulative Losses, Company D.

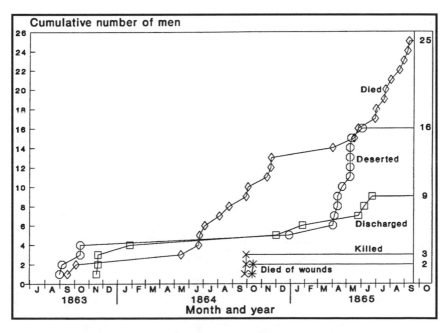

Graph 42. Cumulative Losses, Company E.

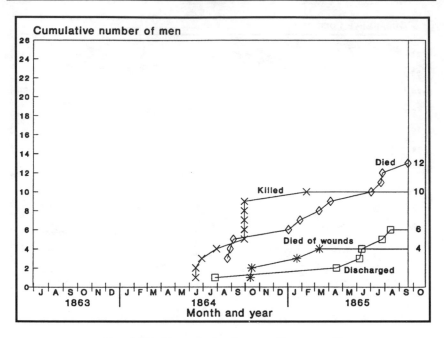

Graph 43. Cumulative Losses, Company F.

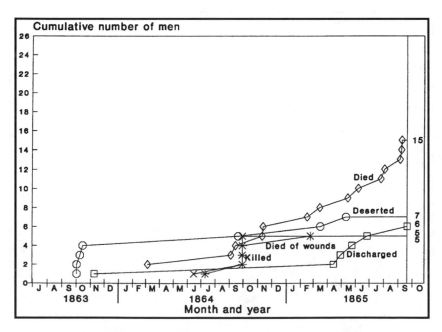

Graph 44. Cumulative Losses, Company G.

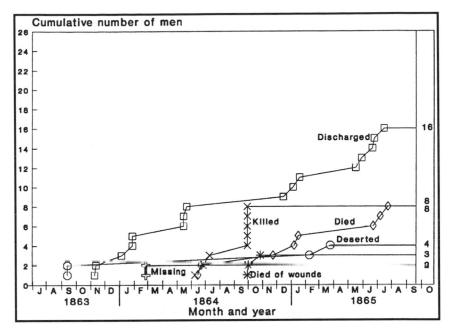

Graph 45. Cumulative Losses, Company H.

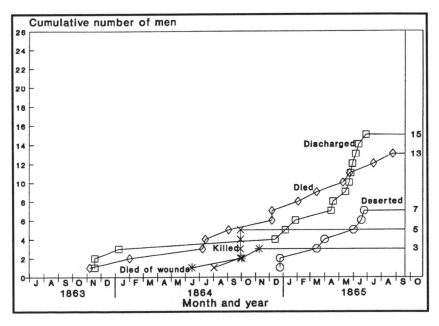

Graph 46. Cumulative Losses, Company I.

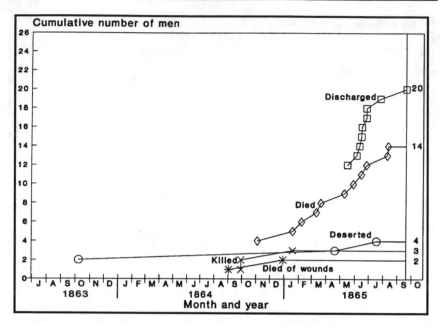

Graph 47. Cumulative Losses, Company K.

APPENDIX C

FIELD AND STAFF OFFICERS: 6TH REGIMENT OF UNITED STATES COLORED INFANTRY

Name	Rank	Date of Muster Into Service
James W. Ames	Colonel	May 14, 1861
Clark E. Royce	Lt. Colonel	October 5, 1863
Joseph B. Kiddoo	Major	October 5, 1863
Harvey J. Covell	Major	October 5, 1863
W. R. Hammond	Adjutant	August 22, 1863
Charles V. York	Adjutant	August 15, 1863
Nathan Edgerton	Adjutant	September 16, 1863
Lewis M. Hosfield	Quartermaster	August 22, 1863
Leeman Barnes	Surgeon	September 8, 1863
Columbus J. White	Asst. Surgeon	June 21, 1865
Edward H. Ware	Asst. Surgeon	August 24, 1865
George V. R. Merrill	Asst. Surgeon	October 5, 1863
Jeremiah Asher	Chaplain	December 4, 1863
John W. Jackson	Sgt. Major	July 30, 1863
Thomas R. Hawkins	Sgt. Major	August 4, 1863
William Watson	Qtrmaster Sgt.	September 10, 1863
Charles W. Jones	Qtrmaster Sgt.	July 29, 1863
T. O. W. Hamilton	Commissary Sgt.	July 28, 1863
Isaiah L. Lyons	Hospital Steward	September 4, 1863

MUSTER ROLL: 6TH REGIMENT OF UNITED STATES COLORED INFANTRY

Abs – absent at muster out	drp/rls – dropped from roll
arr – under arrest	fur – on furlough
cap – captured	GO – by general order
CM/GCM – general court martial	hab crp – habeas corpus
des – deserted	lv – on leave
det srv – detached service	M – mustered out
Dis – discharged	SO – by special order
dis/surg – discharged by surgeon	W – wounded

SIXTH REGIMENT OF THE UNITED STATES COLORED INFANTRY, COMPANY A

Last Name	First Name	Mid Init	Rank	Age	Hgt (in)	Birth-place	Occupation	Status	Muster-in Date	Separation Date	Separation Manner	Status	Casualty Date	Place
Beath	Robert	B	Capt					Vol	9/5/61	9/20/65	M	W	9/29/64	
York	Charles	V	Lt1					Vol	8/15/63					
Chamberlain	M		Lt1					Vol	8/22/63					
Phillips	Lionel	D	Lt1					Vol	1/7/65	9/20/65	Dis			
Jones	Asa	L	Lt2					Vol	9/23/63	9/22/64	Dis/W	W	6/15/64	
Field	Edward		Lt2					Vol	11/19/64	2/11/65	K	K	2/11/65	
Kaiser	Carl		Lt2					Vol	9/19/65	9/20/65	M			
Carter	Richard		Sgt1	26	66	PA	Teamster	Vol	7/27/63	9/20/65	M			
Milburn	John		Sgt	21	67	PA	Farmer	Vol	7/27/63	9/20/65	M			
Henry	Israel		Sgt					Vol	7/27/63	9/20/65	M			
Glasco	Benjamin	J	Sgt	20	67	PA	Farmer	Vol	7/27/63	9/20/65	M			
Scott	John		Sgt					Sub	7/13/63	9/20/65	M			
Jones	Theodore		Corp	24	71	PA	Farmer	Sub	7/14/63	9/20/65	M			
Johnson	Henry		Corp	20	64	NJ	Farmer	Vol	7/27/63		Abs/fur	W	6/15/64	Petersburg
West	Mordecai		Corp	22	64.5	PA	Farmer	Vol	7/28/63		Abs/sick	W	6/15/64	Petersburg

Last Name	First Name	Mid Init	Rank	Age	Hgt (in)	Birth-place	Occupation	Status	Muster-in Date	Separation Date	Manner	Status	Casualty Date	Place
Logan	Nathaniel		Corp	29	67	PA	Carpenter	Vol	7/27/63	9/20/65	M	W	6/15/64	Petersburg
Ross	John	W	Corp	23	70	PA	Waiter	Vol	7/27/63	9/20/65	M	W	6/15/64	Petersburg
Thomas	James		Corp	41	68	NJ	Laborer	Vol	7/28/63	9/20/65	M			
Davis	Francis		Corp	23	66	NJ	Farmer	Vol	7/27/63	9/20/65	M			
Dennis	Charles		Corp	21	66	PA	Farmer	Vol	7/28/63	9/20/65	M			
Alberts	Solomon		Corp	26	68	PA	Farmer	Sub	7/23/63	11/17/63	Dis/Surg			
Loper	Nehemiah		Corp					Vol	7/26/63	6/15/65	Dis			
Brown	William		Musn					Vol	7/27/63	9/20/65	M			
Anderson	Michael		Priv	42	69	MD	Laborer	Sub	9/20/64	9/20/65	M			
Adams	William		Priv	41	72	VA	Farmer	Sub	7/23/63	5/20/65	Dis/SO			
Belfield	Henry		Priv	18	64	VA	Farmer	Sub	7/16/63	9/20/65	M			
Blain	David	S	Priv	36	68	PA	Laborer	Sub	7/16/63	9/20/65	M	W	6/15/64	Petersburg
Bostick	Henry		Priv	23	68			Vol	7/25/63	9/20/65	M			
Brown	John	W	Priv	25	65	PA	Brickmaker	Vol	7/27/63	9/20/65	M			
Blackwood	Robert		Priv	19	65	MD	Laborer	Sub	11/22/64	9/20/65	M			
Brown	Perry		Priv	23	66	PA	Engineer	Dra	9/20/64	9/20/65	M			
Ball	Cyrus	A	Priv	20	68.5	VA	Farmer	Sub	7/23/63	9/23/63	Dis/Hab crp			
Brown	Landon		Priv					Vol	3/13/65	3/22/65	Des			
Cooper	Landon		Priv	22	70	VA	Farmer	Sub	7/17/63	9/20/65	M	W	6/15/64	Petersburg
Cooper	James	H	Priv	35	63.5	VA	Farmer	Vol	7/28/63	9/20/65	M			
Carroll	William		Priv	25	65	MD	Laborer	Dra	11/19/64	9/20/65	M			
Cajor	Richard		Priv	26	69	MD	Laborer	Dra	11/25/64	9/20/65	M			
Chaney	Alexander		Priv	25	61.5	MD	Laborer	Dra	11/20/64	9/20/65	M			
Chatman	Robert		Priv	25	67	FL	Laborer	Dra	11/23/64	9/20/65	M			
Chitman	Benj		Priv	22	73	DE	Laborer	Dra	11/25/64	9/20/65	M			
Cotton	Samuel		Priv	35	68	MD	Laborer	Dra	9/20/64	9/20/65	M			
Comminger	Benj		Priv	44	68	MD	Laborer	Dra	9/20/64					
Curry	Isaac		Priv	30	65	MD	Laborer	Dra	9/26/64					
Carr	William		Priv	40	69	DE	Farmer	Vol	7/27/63	4/20/65	Died	Died	4/20/65	Fort Monroe
Comminger	Aaron		Priv	28	66			Vol	7/28/63	7/31/63	Des			
Cromwell	William		Priv	20	66		Laborer	Dra	11/20/64	4/22/65	Des			
Davis	Emanuel	H	Priv	34	69.5	PA	Bricklayer	Dra	7/27/63	9/25/65	M			

COMPANY A (continued)

Last Name	First Name	Mid Init	Rank	Age	Hgt (in)	Birth-place	Occupation	Status	Muster-in Date	Separation Date	Manner	Status	Casualty Date	Place
Derham	George	W	Priv	27	70	PA	Miner	Sub	7/16/63	9/20/65	M			
Davis	William		Priv	19	63	VA	Laborer	Sub	11/19/64	9/20/65	M			
Davis	Elijah		Priv	21	68	DE	Laborer	Dra	11/23/64	9/20/65	M			
Dickinson	Daniel		Priv	35	69	MD	Laborer	Dra	11/20/64	9/20/65	M			
Driou	William		Priv	28	68.5	DE	Laborer	Dra	11/22/64	9/20/65	M			
Downs	John		Priv	21	71	DE	Laborer	Dra	11/22/64	9/20/65	M			
Dutton	Robert	H	Priv	23	61.5	MD	Laborer	Sub	11/25/64	9/20/65	M			
Dent	John	S	Priv	26	71.5	MD	Laborer	Dra	11/20/64	9/20/65	M			
Douty	John		Priv	35	73	NJ	Laborer	Vol	7/27/63	2/7/65	Dis			
Dorsey	Henry		Priv	18	68	PA	Waiter	Sub	7/24/63	2/3/65	Died	Died	2/3/65	Wshngtn DC
Ellenis	Stephen		Priv	24	66	DE	Laborer	Vol	7/28/63	9/20/65	Des			
Evans	James		Priv	31	69	PA	Laborer	Vol	7/25/63	10/20/63	Des			
Flemmer	Solomon		Priv	37	67	PA	Laborer	Vol	7/28/63	9/20/65	M			
French	Anthony		Priv	24	67	NY	Boatman	Vol	7/27/63	9/20/65	M			
Fiderman	Wm	C	Priv					Vol	7/27/63	10/1/63	Died	Died	10/1/63	Smyrna, DE
Fay	Tony		Priv					Vol		4/5/65	Des			
Gilliam	Harvey		Priv	22	69.5	PA	Farmer	Vol	7/27/63	9/20/65	M			
Ghant	Thomas		Priv	35	69	VA	Farmer	Vol	7/28/63		Abs/sick			
Green	Benjamin	C	Priv	21	69	NJ	Farmer	Vol	7/25/63	9/20/65	M			
Graves	Henry		Priv	39	69	MD	Farmer	Dra	9/20/64	9/20/65	M			
Grey	Andrew		Priv	36	61	DE	Laborer	Dra	11/22/64	9/20/65	M			
Green	Charles		Priv	23	63	VA	Laborer	Sub	11/22/64	9/20/65	M			
Gradus	James		Priv	19	67.5	DE	Laborer	Sub	11/25/64	9/20/65	M			
Greenwood	Jacob		Priv	21	70.5	DE	Laborer	Dra	11/22/64	9/7/65	Died	Died	9/7/65	Wlmngtn NC
Harris	Joseph		Priv	18	66	PA	Huckster	Vol	7/28/63	9/20/65	M			
Henry	Alphonso		Priv	21	67	NJ	Farmer	Vol	7/25/63	9/20/65	M			
Henson	Lewis	J	Priv	23	61	PA	Farmer	Vol	7/27/63	9/20/65	M			
Hopkins	Daniel		Priv	37	64	PA	Farmer	Vol	7/27/63	9/20/65	M			
Henry	Alexander		Priv	23	64	DE	Laborer	Dra	11/19/64	9/20/65	M			
Hearse	Emanuel		Priv					Vol		9/20/65	M			
Howard	Samuel		Priv	22	69	NJ	Farmer	Vol	7/27/63	4/20/64	Dis/SO			

Last Name	First Name	Mid Init	Rank	Age	Hgt (in)	Birth-place	Occupation	Status	Muster-in Date	Separation Date	Manner	Status	Casualty Date	Place
Hamilton	T	O W	Pr/Sgt	25	67.5			Vol	7/28/63	8/15/63	Des			
Hollinger	Charles		Priv	20	65.5			Sub	7/14/65	4/12/65	Des			
Hays	Jacob		Priv	18	70	NC	Laborer	Vol	3/13/65	4/12/65	Des			
Hays	Alfred		Priv					Vol	3/13/65	9/20/65	M			
Irons	Joseph	F	Priv					Vol	7/28/63	5/5/65	Dis/W	W		
Irons	David	H	Priv					Vol	7/24/63		M			
Jackson	James		Priv	19	68	VA	Laborer	Vol	7/25/63		Abs/furl			
Jones	Joseph	S	Priv	22	64	PA	Farmer	Vol	7/27/63		Abs/sick			
Jones	George	H	Priv	23	71	PA	Farmer	Vol	7/27/63		Abs/Fur			
Jones	Nathan	C	Priv	28	62	PA	Farmer	Vol	7/27/63		M			
Jones	Isaac	W	Priv	33	71			Vol	7/27/63		Abs/sick			
Johnson	John	W	Priv	25	74	PA	Barber	Sub	7/13/63		M			
Josh	Andrew		Priv					Vol	3/13/65	4/12/65	Des			
Josh	Ephraim		Priv					Vol	3/13/65		M			
Lee	Dandrich		Priv	36	66		Makeman	Sub	7/13/63	1/15/65	Died	Died	1/15/65	Fort Monroe
Lewis	Charles		Priv	21	65	PA	Laborer	Sub	7/24/63	2/5/64	Drp/rls			
Lyons	William		Priv	19	67	PA	Laborer	Vol	7/28/63	7/31/63	Des			
Lemon	George		Priv	24	68			Vol	7/28/63		M			
Martin	Jacob		Priv	25	65	NJ	Farmer	Vol	7/28/63		M			
Meads	David		Priv	27	64	PA	Laborer	Vol	7/25/63		Died	Died		
Miller	Cosson	L	Priv	28	66	PA	Farmer	Vol	7/27/63		M			
Miller	John		Priv	20	71	PA	Farmer	Vol	7/27/63		M			
Murray	Eli		Priv	20	63.5	PA	Farmer	Vol	7/27/63	9/15/65	Died	Died	9/15/65	
Moore	Thomas		Priv	20	68	PA	Huckster	Vol	7/28/63	10/19/64	Died	Died	10/19/64	Prtsmth Gr RI
Miller	Israel	W	Priv	24	72	PA	Farmer	Vol	7/27/63	7/16/64	Died/W	Died/W	7/16/64	Petersburg
Murray	Frederick		Priv	24	65			Sub	7/23/63	7/3/63	Des			
M'Pherson	Chas		Priv	24	66			Vol	7/23/63	9/28/63	Des			
M'Coy	Frederick		Priv					Vol	3/13/65	4/5/65	M			
NewKirk	Michael		Priv					Vol	3/13/65		M			
Nadine	Samuel		Priv	25	68.5	PA	Laborer	Vol	7/25/63		Abs/sick			
Penny	Joseph		Priv					Sub	7/17/63					
Prier	George		Priv	39	61	MD	Laborer	Vol	3/30/65		M			

COMPANY A (*continued*)

Last Name	First Name	Mid Init	Rank	Age	Hgt (in)	Birth-place	Occupation	Status	Muster-in Date	Separation Date	Manner	Status	Casualty Date	Place
Ralston	Andrew		Priv					Vol	7/27/63		M			
Robinson	William		Priv					Vol	7/25/63		M			
Rider	John		Priv					Vol	7/25/63	7/31/63	Des			
Somers	Frederick		Priv					Sub	7/13/63		M			
Thomas	Robert		Priv	22	66	PA		Sub	7/23/63	7/4/65	Des			
Viney	David		Priv	42	65	DE	Laborer	Vol	7/27/63		M			
Wilson	Willis		Priv	23	66	NJ		Vol	7/27/63		M			
Wright	Thomas	H	Priv	18	64	PA		Vol	7/25/63		M	W	6/15/64	Petersburg
Washington	Alfred		Priv	24	66	VA	Laborer	Vol	7/14/63		Abs/arrest			
Warren	Francis		Priv	40	65	Can	Laborer	Vol	3/28/65	5/31/65	Dis			
Wright	John		Priv	30	67	PA	Farmer	Vol	7/27/63		M			
Williams	David		Priv	26	72	NC	Farmer	Vol	7/28/63	7/23/64	Died/W	Died/W	7/23/64	Petersburg
Wright	Joseph		Priv					Vol	3/13/65	4/5/65	Des			
Young	Alexander		Priv	22	66	NC	Laborer	Vol	7/27/63		M			

SIXTH REGIMENT OF THE UNITED STATES COLORED INFANTRY, COMPANY B

Last Name	First Name	Mid Init	Rank	Age	Hgt (in)	Birth-place	Occupation	Status	Muster-in Date	Separation Date	Manner	Status	Casualty Date	Place
Covell	Harvey	J	Maj					Vol	10/5/63					
York	Charles	V	Capt					Vol	8/15/63	9/29/64	K	K	9/29/64	New Market
Buckman	Aaron	N	Capt					Vol	9/15/63					
Heath	George	E	Capt					Dra	8/24/63	9/29/64	K			
Hubbard	Nath'l	N	Lt1					Vol	10/8/63	9/20/65	M			
Sellew	George	E	Lt1					Vol		3/3/65	Dis/Surg	W	9/29/64	New Market
Meyer	Frederick		Lt2					Vol	8/22/63	9/29/64	K	K	9/29/64	New Market
Wallinus	Francis		Lt2					Vol	8/15/65	9/20/65	Dis			
Robinson	James		Sgt1	24	67	PA	Farmer	Dra	7/14/63	9/20/65	M			
Jackson	John	W	Sgt1	31	66	PA	Brickmaker	Vol	7/30/63					
Williams	James	B	Sgt	22	67	PA	Painter	Dra	7/13/63	9/20/65	M			
Stringfellow	Wm		Sgt	20	69	PA	Brickmaker	Sub	7/16/63	9/20/65	M			
Taylor	William	H	Sgt	21	67	PA	Huckster	Vol	7/31/63	9/20/65	M			
Vance	Joseph		Sgt	33	67.5	DE	Farmer	Vol	7/29/63	9/20/65	M			
Butler	Clinton		Sgt	21	68.5	PA	Barber	Vol	7/29/63	12/13/64	Dis/Surg			

Last Name	First Name	Mid Init	Rank	Age	Hgt (in)	Birth-place	Occupation	Status	Muster-in Date	Separation Date	Separation Manner	Status	Casualty Date	Place
Singer	Andrew	C	Sgt	36	75.5	PA	Barber	Dra	7/11/63	6/9/65	Dis/W	W		
Purnell	Larman	A	Corp	24	64.5	DE	Farmer	Vol	8/1/63		Abs/sick			
Hazzard	Wm	R J	Corp	22	68	PA	Laborer	Sub	7/16/63	9/20/65	M			
Ridgley	John		Corp	22	67	PA	Laborer	Dra	7/18/63	9/20/65	M			
Peterson	William		Corp	29	63	NY	Laborer	Vol	1/31/65	9/20/65	M			
Brown	Joseph		Corp	38	67	NC		Vol	3/29/65	9/20/65	M			
Jackson	Henry	A	Corp	31	72	VA	Farmer	Vol	10/4/64	9/20/65	M			
McCanty	Henry		Corp	21	67.5	Can	Farmer	Vol	9/29/64	9/20/65	M			
Freeman	James		Corp	22	71.5	VA	Laborer	Vol	9/29/64	9/20/65	M			
Greene	John		Corp	35	68	NJ	Farmer	Vol	7/29/63	9/29/64	K	K	9/29/64	New Market
Ridley	Anthony		Corp	22	66	PA	Barber	Vol	7/28/63	9/29/64	K	K	9/29/64	New Market
Anderson	Charles		Corp	24	63	Can	Laborer	Vol	10/4/64	9/20/65	M			
Adams	George	W	Priv	20	62	PA	Laborer	Vol	7/24/63	7/30/64	K	K	7/30/64	Petersburg
Bush	Thomas		Priv	23	67.5	DC	Carpenter	Vol	7/3/63		Abs/arst			
Balier	Abram		Priv	20	69.5	PA	Farmer	Vol	7/29/63	9/20/65	M			
Borton	Cyrus		Priv	21	64	PA	Laborer	Dra	7/13/63	9/20/65	M			
Burton	Major		Priv	27	66.5	DE	Laborer	Vol	7/29/63	9/20/65	M			
Buben	Asbury		Priv	20	63.5	MD	Laborer	Sub	7/28/63	9/20/65	M			
Brown	William		Priv	45	64.5	MD	Laborer	Sub	7/24/63	9/20/65	M			
Brown	Philip		Priv	20	65	VA	Laborer	Vol	9/28/64	9/20/65	M			
Brown	Moses		Priv					Vol	11/11/64	9/20/65	M			
Brewster	Edward	F	Priv	20	65	NY	Farmer	Vol	1/24/65	9/20/65	M			
Boyer	Enoch		Priv	27	66	DE	Farmer	Vol	7/29/63	10/2/64	Died/W	Died/W	10/2/64	
Beckley	Mortimer		Priv	20	66.5	MD	Laborer	Vol	2/4/65	3/25/65	Des	Died	3/26/65	Wlmngtn NC
Badson	Citizen		Priv	19	70	PA	Farmer	Sub	7/31/63	9/25/63	Des			
Beacham	John		Priv	21	65	DE	Huckster	Sub	7/29/63	10/15/64	Des			
Bird	Malachi		Priv	26	65	PA	Barber	Vol	2/7/65	3/5/65	Des			
Carter	John		Priv	22	65	PA	Farmer	Sub	7/13/65	9/20/65	M			
Crawford	John		Priv					Vol	7/31/63	9/20/65	M			
Cromwell	Obadiah		Priv					Vol	11/18/64		Abs/sick			
Coffee	Samuel		Priv	30	68	PA	Farmer	Dra	7/13/63	10/5/64	Died	Died	10/6/64	Fort Monroe
Clark	James		Priv	23	70	PA	Farmer	Sub	7/13/63	11/26/64	Died	Died	11/26/64	Prtsmth VA

COMPANY B (*continued*)

Last Name	First Name	Mid Init	Rank	Age	Hgt (in)	Birth-place	Occupation	Status	Muster-in Date	Separation Date	Manner	Status	Casualty Date	Place
Cummings	John	S	Priv	29	66.5	MD	Farmer	Vol	7/28/63	10/12/64	Died	Died	10/12/64	Pnt of Rcks
Clark	Robert		Priv	27	67.5	PA	Farmer	Dra	7/13/63	7/25/63	Des			
Davis	Abraham		Priv	24	64.5	MD	Farmer	Vol	7/29/63	9/20/65	M			
Dickinson	Abram		Priv	21	66	NC	Farmer	Vol	3/13/65	4/3/65	Des			
Evans	Thomas		Priv	25	74.5	PA	Miner	Dra	7/17/63	9/20/65	M			
Farris	William		Priv	21	68.5	NJ	Miner	Vol	8/1/65	9/20/65	M			
Francis	Robert		Priv	20	67	WIn	Porter	Vol	2/1/65	9/20/65	M			
Graver	Sidney		Priv					Vol	11/11/64	9/20/65	M			
Gibson	Joseph		Priv	17	62.5	NJ	Farmer	Vol	8/1/63	9/20/65	M			
Gost	Augustus		Priv	26	68.5	MD	Farmer	Vol	3/13/65	9/20/65	M			
Grigg	Jeremiah		Priv	25	64	PA	Farmer	Vol	8/1/63	6/15/64	K	K	6/15/64	Petersburg
Green	Charles		Priv	22	66	PA	Farmer	Vol	7/29/63	6/24/64	K	K	6/24/64	Petersburg
Glasgo	George		Priv	27	67	PA	Laborer	Dra	7/13/63	7/21/65	Died	Died	7/21/65	Wlmngtn NC
Halleger	William		Priv	27	69	PA	Farmer	Vol	7/28/63		Abs/sick			
Hilton	John		Priv	21	64	PA	Waiter	Dra	7/31/63	9/20/65	M			
Hill	Andrew		Priv	22	69	MD	Laborer	Sub	7/28/63		Abs/sick			
Hoffman	Peter		Priv	30	69	MO	Laborer	Vol	10/1/64	9/20/65	M			
Harvey	John		Priv	26	67	PA	Laborer	Sub	7/13/63	9/20/65	M			
Hunkson	Abraham		Priv	30	67	PA	Laborer	Dra	7/17/63	9/20/65	M			
Hurd	William		Priv	22	66.5	VA	Laborer	Dra	7/15/63	9/20/65	M			
Hull	Thomas	J	Priv	30	69.5	PA	Laborer	Vol	7/28/63	11/9/63	Dis/Surg			
Howard	John		Priv	45	63	GA	Cook	Vol	7/31/63	5/24/65	Dis/Surg			
Hazzard	Wilson		Priv	29	72	PA	Laborer	Sub	7/24/63	4/23/65	Died	Died	4/23/65	Wlmngtn NC
Huff	John		Priv	21	63.5	NY	Laborer	Vol	9/28/64	6/6/65	Died	Died	6/6/65	Gldsbro NC
Hill	John	W	Priv	21	64	DE	Laborer	Sub	7/15/63	9/15/63	Des			
Johnson	John		Priv	26	65	DE	Farmer	Vol	7/28/63		Abs/sick			
Johnson	Simon	M	Priv	16	62	PA	Farmer	Vol	7/28/63	9/20/65	M			
Johnson	Thos	W	Priv	24	67	PA	Barber	Vol	7/31/63	9/20/65	M			
Johns	Emanuel	H	Priv	33	64.5	NJ	Laborer	Sub	8/3/63	9/20/65	M			
Johnson	William		Priv	37	66	MD	Laborer	Vol	1/31/65	9/20/65	M			
Johnson	Thomas		Priv	31	66	PA	Farmer	Vol	7/31/63	11/9/63	Dis/Surg			

Last Name	First Name	Mid Init	Rank	Age	Hgt (in)	Birth-place	Occupation	Status	Muster-in Date	Separation Date	Separation Manner	Status	Casualty Date	Place
Johnson	Peter		Priv	26	66	VA	Farmer	Vol	7/31/63	9/29/54	K	K	9/29/64	New Market
Jones	William		Priv	27	67.5	VA	Sawyer	Vol	8/1/63	10/15/64	Des			
Kell	Moses		Priv	19	72	MD	Farmer	Vol	7/29/63	9/20/65	M			
Kinslow	Aaron	W	Priv	22	64.5	MD	Hackman	Vol	8/1/63	9/20/65	M			
Kaupt	Neil		Priv	25	66	VA	Farmer	Vol	9/26/64	9/25/64	K	K	9/29/64	New Market
Lewis	Gilbert	W	Priv	22	70	VA	Laborer	Vol	9/25/64		Abs/sick			
Lightfoot	Felix		Priv	20	68	GA		Vol	9/26/64	9/20/65	M			
Lynch	Spencer		Priv	26	63	VA	Laborer	Vol	9/26/64	9/20/65	M			
Lordon	Sandy		Priv	36	68.5	MD	Wagoner	Vol	3/13/65		AWOL			
Lewis	William		Priv					Sub	8/3/63	10/5/64	Died	Died	10/3/64	Prtsmth VA
Lamar	Boyd		Priv	20	66.5	PA	Laborer	Dra	7/13/53	9/19/63	Des			
Lewis	William		Priv	22	68	DE	Laborer	Sub	8/3/63	9/15/63	Des			
Magill	Briston		Priv	17	68	PA	Farmer	Vol	7/28/53	9/20/65	M			
Manning	Isaac		Priv	18	63.5	SC	Porter	Vol	7/30/53		Abs/sick			
Marshall	John		Priv	24	63.5	PA	Farmer	Vol	7/31/63	9/20/65	M			
Moore	Joseph	H	Priv	16	63	PA	Farmer	Vol	8/1/63	9/20/65	M			
Martin	Richard		Priv	20	68.5	KY	Laborer	Vol	9/22/64	9/20/65	M			
Moore	Patrick		Priv	18	63	AL	Laborer	Vol	9/23/64		Abs/sick			
Miller	Wilson		Priv	28	66	NC	Farmer	Vol	3/13/65	9/20/65	M			
Merrick	Anthony		Priv	27	73	NC	Farmer	Vol	3/13/65	9/20/65	M			
McCreby	John		Priv	22	70	PA	Musician	Dra	7/14/63	9/20/65	M			
McCoy	Eli		Priv	18	67.5	NC	Farmer	Vol	3/13/65	9/20/65	M			
McCoy	Moses		Priv	17	66	NC	Farmer	Vol	3/13/65		AWOL			
Nicholson	Jacob		Priv	21	67.5	MD	Waiter	Vol	7/29/63	9/20/65	M			
Patterson	Charles		Priv	22	63.5	Can	Farmer	Dra	9/29/64		Abs/sick			
Pugh	Matthew		Priv	20	66.5	PA	Barber	Vol	7/10/63		No show			
Ridley	Charles		Priv	22				Vol	7/30/63		M			
Rawes	Henry		Priv	21	63	VA	Farmer	Vol	9/28/64	9/20/65	M			
Rad	George		Priv	22	65.5	KY	Farmer	Vol	9/29/64	9/20/65	M			
Redman	Barney		Priv	20	70	PA	Laborer	Sub	7/30/63	9/20/55	M			
Ray	Augustine	F	Priv	33	63		Laborer	Vol	1/31/65	9/20/55	M			
Robinson	Daniel		Priv					Vol	8/16/63	1/27/64	Dis/Surg			
Robinson	Wm	W	Priv	26	63	PA	Farmer	Vol	7/29/63	9/29/64	MIA	MIA	9/29/64	New Market

COMPANY B (*continued*)

Last Name	First Name	Mid Init	Rank	Age	Hgt (in)	Birth-place	Occupation	Status	Muster-in Date	Separation Date	Separation Manner	Status	Casualty Date	Place
Sands	Israel		Priv	17	66	PA	Waiter	Vol	7/31/63	9/20/65	M			
Sands	Jacob		Priv	16	67	PA	Farmer	Vol	7/31/63	9/20/65	M			
Spencer	James		Priv	37	67	VA	Laborer	Dra	7/10/63	9/20/65	M			
Smith	John		Priv	28	67	Can	Sailor	Vol	9/24/64		Abs/sick			
Simmons	Peter		Priv					Vol	11/10/64	9/20/65	M			
Swartz	Henry		Priv	24	67	PA	Laborer	Dra	7/17/63	9/29/64	Died/W	Died/W	9/29/64	
Shinn	Amos	M	Priv	28	67.5	PA	Farmer	Vol	7/28/63	9/29/64	K	K	9/29/64	New Market
Simpess	Isaac		Priv	22	64	MD	Farmer	Vol	7/29/63	9/29/64	K	K	9/29/64	New Market
Stewart	Chas	H	Priv	26	67	DE	Laborer	Dra	7/16/63	9/29/64	MIA	MIA	9/29/64	
Thompson	Isaac		Priv	26	64	PA	Blacksmith	Dra	7/16/63	9/20/65	M			
Tibbs	William		Priv	26	67	VA	Sailor	Vol	9/26/64		Abs/sick			
Terman	Benj	W	Priv	35	64.5	Can	Laborer	Vol	3/28/65	9/20/65	M			
Valentine	Abra'm		Priv	18	65	PA	Farmer	Vol	7/29/63		Abs/sick			
Van Clief	Emanuel		Priv	26	64	NJ	Laborer	Vol	2/1/65	9/20/65	M			
Welch	Robert		Priv	23	65.5	MD	Waiter	Sub	7/31/63	9/20/65	M			
Washington	Geo		Priv	20	69	MD	Laborer	Vol	9/27/64	9/20/65	M			
Wright	Henry		Priv					Vol	11/16/64	9/20/65	M			
Williams	Edward	T	Priv	33	61	ME	Laborer	Vol	10/6/64	6/29/65	Dis/SpOr			
White	Stephen		Priv	23		MD	Farmer	Vol	7/15/63	9/27/64	Died/W	Died/W	9/27/64	Wlmngtn NC
White	Paul		Priv	27	65	Can	Sailor	Vol	10/3/64	4/4/65	Died	Died	4/4/65	Sgr Lf Hll
Williams	Charles		Priv	22	65.5	Can	Laborer	Vol	9/27/64	2/11/65	K	K	2/11/65	
Williams	Thomas		Priv	35	67.5	MO	Laborer	Vol	9/12/64	10/27/64	Des			
Wright	William		Priv	26	65	NC	Farmer	Vol	3/13/65	4/12/65	Des			
Wright	Benjamin		Priv	18	62	NC	Farmer	Vol	3/13/65	4/12/65	Des			
Wright	Jacob		Priv	18	69	NC	Farmer	Vol	3/13/65	4/12/65	Des			
Wilson	Joseph		Priv	22	69	NC	Laborer	Vol	3/13/65	4/3/65	Des			
Young	John		Priv					Vol	10/29/64	9/20/65	M			

SIXTH REGIMENT OF THE UNITED STATES COLORED INFANTRY, COMPANY C

Last Name	First Name	Mid Init	Rank	Age	Hgt (in)	Birth-place	Occupation	Status	Muster-in Date	Separation Date	Separation Manner	Status	Casualty Date	Place
Dill	Daniel	M	Capt					Vol	9/15/63		M			
Jackman	Enoch	F	Lt1					Vol	9/26/63	11/23/64	Dis			

Last Name	First Name	Mid Init	Rank	Age	Hgt (in)	Birth-place	Occupation	Status	Muster-in Date	Separation Date	Separation Manner	Status	Casualty Date	Place
Kellogg	Norton	P	Lt1					Vol	11/25/64	9/20/65	Dis			
Chamberlain	M	J	Lt2					Vol	8/22/63					
Osborne	Frank	A	Lt2					Vol	11/2/63					
Hinckley	Ephraim		Lt2					Vol		4/20/65	Dis/SO			
Lawrence	James		Lt2					Vol	7/3/65		M			
Webster	George		Sgt1	29	67	PA	Shoemaker	Dra	7/14/63		AWOL			
Ellet	George	H	Sgt1	31	69	PA	Barber	Vol	8/7/63	9/29/64	K	K	9/29/64	New Market
Cole	Archy		Sgt	37	70.5	MD	Laborer	Sub	7/28/63		M			
Julius	John	D	Sgt	17	67	PA	Farmer	Vol	8/3/63		M			
Brown	Edward		Sgt	27	68	PA	Farmer	Vol	8/7/63		M			
Butler	William		Sgt	23	67	PA	Teamster	Vol	8/3/63	5/29/65	Dis/Surg			
Sterling	William		Sgt	25	64.5	PA	Cooper	Dra	7/13/63	9/12/64	Died	Died	9/12/64	Phila
Lewis	Abraham		Corp	29	74	PA	Miner	Dra	7/14/63		Abs/sick			
Smith	Henderson		Corp	20	72	PA	Farmer	Dra	7/14/63		Abs/lv			
Gover	Richard		Corp	28	65	PA	Farmer	Vol	8/7/63		M			
Brown	Joseph		Corp	19	68.5	PA	Farmer	Vol	8/5/63		Abs/sick			
Walker	Henry		Corp	37	65	PA	Farmer	Vol	8/7/63		M			
Thomas	Alexander		Corp	21	69.5	PA	Laborer	Vol	8/7/63		M			
Stump	Gideon		Corp	26	68.5	Can	Sailor	Vol	9/15/64		M			
Spencer	James		Corp	21	66	NC	Laborer	Sub	8/1/63		M			
Kane	James	A	Corp	30	68	PA	Steward	Dra	7/31/63	10/19/64	Ded	Died	10/19/64	
Skeere	Henry	J	Corp	37	70	MD	Farmer	Vol	8/5/53	9/29/64	K	K	9/29/64	New Market
Wheeler	Joseph		Musn	20	66	PA	Farmer	Dra	7/14/63		M			
Smith	Lewis		Musn	16	64.5	PA		Vol	8/3/53		M			
Atkins	James		Priv	42	63	VA	Laborer	Vol	12/14/64		M			
Ash	Rentz		Priv					Vol	3/13/65	4/26/65	Des			
Becket	Alfred		Priv	21	65.5			Vol	8/4/63		M			
Brisco	John		Priv	30	62	MD	Farmer	Vol	8/7/63		M			
Black	James		Priv	22	69.5	MD	Farmer	Vol	8/1/63		M			
Bonks	Jones		Priv	22	66	PA	Laborer	Dra	7/14/53		M			
Burges	Jeremiah		Priv	25	67	PA	Farmer	Dra	7/14/53		M			
Butcher	Eli		Priv	23	64	PA	Laborer	Dra	7/14/53		M			

COMPANY C (continued)

Last Name	First Name	Mid Init	Rank	Age	Hgt (in)	Birth-place	Occupation	Status	Muster-in Date	Separation Date	Separation Manner	Status	Casualty Date	Place
Brody	Andrew		Priv					Vol	3/13/65		M			
Boulder	Andrew		Priv					Vol	8/7/63	1/4/64	Dis/CM			
Bannister	William	H	Priv	29	70.5	MI	Sailor	Vol	10/6/64	6/23/65	Dis			
Boyder	Manus		Priv					Vol	3/13/65	4/26/65	Des			
Brown	Peter		Priv					Vol	3/13/65	4/26/65	Des			
Cork	Lewis		Priv	18	67	PA	Farmer	Vol	8/7/63		M			
Corson	William		Priv	35	72	DE	Farmer	Vol	8/7/63		M			
Congo	Charles		Priv	32	65	DE	Waiter	Vol	10/17/64		M			
Champlin	John		Priv	40	65	Can	Laborer	Vol	3/22/65		M			
Carter	Alexander		Priv	35	67	Can	Farmer	Vol	3/22/65		M			
Cane	Andrew	M	Priv	21	66	PA	Farmer	Dra	7/14/63	4/28/64	Dis/Surg			
Curry	Eli		Priv	30	66	PA	Miner	Dra	7/14/63	6/19/65	Dis/Surg			
Cook	William	H	Priv	18	64.5	VA	Laborer	Vol	8/7/63	3/23/65	Died	Died	3/23/65	Cox Brdg NC
Cole	Joseph		Priv	24				Vol	8/4/63	8/15/63	Des			
Dempster	Alexander		Priv	25	68	PA	Laborer	Dra	7/14/63		Abs/sick			
Elzey	William	P	Priv	30	66	PA	Farmer	Vol	8/7/63		M			
Edwards	William		Priv	25	63	VA	Farmer	Vol	8/3/63	4/15/64	Died	Died	4/15/64	
Fullum	Joseph		Priv	20	73	PA	Farmer	Vol	7/14/63		Abs/sick			
Fronk	William	G	Priv	23	69	NY	Farmer	Vol	9/13/64		Abs/sick			
Freeman	Arnold		Priv	38	62	VA	Laborer	Vol	9/26/64		M			
Freeman	George		Priv	21	68	DE	Laborer	Vol	12/31/64		M			
Freeman	John		Priv	32	66	NJ	Laborer	Sub	8/7/63	8/15/63	Des			
Farr	Alexander		Priv					Vol	3/13/65	8/26/65	Des			
Gover	William		Priv	17	68	PA	Farmer	Vol	8/7/63		M			
Green	Emanuel		Priv	27	69.5	DE	Laborer	Sub	8/5/63		M			
Grayson	Wesley		Priv	20	66		Laborer	Dra	7/14/63	1/18/64	Died	Died	1/18/64	Yorktown VA
Gadsly	John		Priv	25	67.5	PA	Barber	Dra	7/15/63	1/15/64	Died	Died	1/15/64	Ft Monroe
Garrett	Thomas	H	Priv	35	70	PA	Miner	Dra	7/14/63	7/23/65	Died	Died	7/23/65	
Holland	Thomas		Priv	28	63	PA	Laborer	Sub	8/3/63		M			
Howard	George		Priv	17	63	PA	Laborer	Vol	4/25/64		M			
Holland	Lemuel		Priv					Dra	12/3/64		M			

Last Name	First Name	Mid Init	Rank	Age	Hgt (in)	Birth-place	Occupation	Status	Muster-in Date	Separation Date	Separation Manner	Status	Casualty Date	Place
Holden	John		Priv	22	63	Can	Tanner	Vol	9/14/64		M			
Harris	Edward		Priv	20	64	VT	Laborer	Vol	1/3/65		M			
Hill	Ishmael		Priv					Vol	3/13/65		Abs/sick			
Hunt	Israel		Priv					Vol	8/7/63	6/7/65	Dis/Surg			
Hawkins	Thomas	R	Pr/SM	23	64.5	OH	Plasterer	Sub	8/4/63			W	9/29/64	New Market
Ingraham	Samuel		Priv					Vol	3/13/65	8/26/65	Des			
Jenkins	George		Priv	28	66	PA	Farmer	Dra	7/14/63		M			
Johnson	James		Priv	20	66	PA	Porter	Dra	7/14/63	6/19/65	Dis			
Johnson	Clayton		Priv	35	64	NJ	Laborer	Sub	7/3/63	6/28/65	Died	Died	6/28/65	Gldsbro NC
Johnson	Joseph		Priv	22	65.5	NJ	Farmer	Vol	8/7/63	1/31/65	Des			
Johnson	Henry		Priv	22	68	NY	Laborer	Vol	1/3/65	2/5/65	Des			
Johnson	Oliver		Priv					Vol		6/10/65	Des			
Kemp	Jefferson		Priv	26	70.5	GA	Blacksmith	Vol	1/5/65	6/7/65	M			
Knight	Jeremiah		Priv	34	68	PA	Gardener	Dra	7/14/63	6/7/65	Dis/Surg			
Lomox	Elisha		Priv	22	70	PA	Farmer	Vol	8/7/63		M			
Lewis	Charles		Priv	31	67.5	MD	Farmer	Vol	8/7/64	6/21/65	Dis			
Maloney	Wesley		Priv	32	62.5	PA	Driver	Dra	7/15/63		M			
Miller	James		Priv	24	71	PA	Farmer	Dra	7/14/63		M			
Mathews	Jeremiah		Priv	19	62	VA	Laborer	Dra	12/1/64		AWOL			
Moore	William		Priv	23	66.5	Can	Laborer	Vol	9/28/64		M			
Morble	James		Priv					Vol	3/13/65		M			
Madison	James		Priv	19	68	NC	Laborer	Vol	10/7/64	7/15/65	Died	Died	7/15/65	Smthvil NC
Money	Joseph	S	Priv	32	64	NJ	Laborer	Sub	8/5/63	10/24/64	Died	Died	10/24/64	Ft Monroe
McKeon	Sandy		Priv					Vol	3/13/65		AWOL			
McGowan	George		Priv					Vol	3/13/65	8/26/65	Des			
Nelson	David		Priv	31	66	NY	Laborer	Vol	8/7/63		M			
Nelson	Josiah		Priv	17	65.5	NY	Waiter	Vol	8/7/63		Abs/sick			
Oates	Simon		Priv					Vol	3/13/65	4/26/65	Des			
Price	Marshall		Priv	29	69	PA	Farmer	Vol	8/7/63		M			
Parker	Henry		Priv	31	67	MD	Laborer	Vol	8/7/63		Abs/sick			
Pence	William		Priv	25	66	PA	Porter	Dra	7/15/63	9/29/64	K	K	9/29/64	New Market
Robinson	William		Priv	21	64.5	VA	Laborer	Vol	4/25/64		M			

COMPANY C (*continued*)

Last Name	First Name	Mid Init	Rank	Age	Hgt (in)	Birth-place	Occupation	Status	Muster-in Date	Separation Date	Manner	Status	Casualty Date	Place
Richards	Alfred		Priv					Vol	9/24/64		M			
Ralph	Nathaniel		Priv	20	66	PA	Laborer	Dra	7/15/63		M			
Richardson	Robert		Priv					Sub	8/5/63	1/13/64	Dis/Surg			
Reeder	James	E	Priv	21	68	MD	Laborer	Sub	8/6/63	6/7/65	Dis/Surg			
Robinson	Robert		Priv	27	68.5	SC	Laborer	Vol	9/13/64	6/18/65	Dis			
Robinson	Alexander		Priv	22	72	PA	Teamster	Vol	8/7/63	10/19/64	Died	Died	10/19/64	Ft Monroe
Stryker	Fred	B	Priv	20	63.5	NJ	Laborer	Sub	8/6/63		M			
Sullivan	William	H	Priv	18	65	DE	Farmer	Vol	8/5/63		M			
Stokely	Isaac		Priv	40	69	MD	Laborer	Vol	9/28/64		M			
Stevens	Isaac		Priv	36	64	NY	Watchman	Vol	12/30/64		M			
Scott	John		Priv	23	65	NY	Laborer	Vol	1/3/65		M			
Shinn	George	W	Priv	33	70	PA	Laborer	Dra	7/14/64		Abs/sick			
Slyder	Jacob		Priv	17	68	PA	Farmer	Vol	8/3/63	2/11/65	Died	Died	2/11/65	Ft Monroe
Strange	Albert		Priv	21	66	OH	Laborer	Sub	8/8/63	2/28/65	Des			
Span	William		Priv					Vol	3/13/65	4/26/65	Des			
Stokes	Patrick		Priv	21	68	NC	Laborer	Vol	3/13/65	4/26/65	Des			
Stokes	John		Priv	25	66	NC	Laborer	Vol	3/13/65	4/26/65	Des			
Thomas	George	W	Priv	24	65	DE	Laborer	Sub	8/3/63		M			
Thompson	William		Priv	39	70	Can	Laborer	Vol	9/30/64		Abs/sick			
Tallman	William		Priv	23	65	PA	Barber	Vol	3/21/65		M			
Thornton	Samuel	F	Priv	22	69	PA	Laborer	Sub	7/31/63	10/19/64	Died	Died	10/19/64	Ft Monroe
Thompson	Robert	R	Priv	21				Vol	8/4/63	8/15/63	Des			
Wheeler	Henry		Priv	37	68	NC	Laborer	Vol	9/29/64		M			
Wilmon	James		Priv	20	63	Can	Laborer	Vol	10/6/64		Abs/sick			
Williams	John		Priv					Vol	10/7/64		M			
Williams	James		Priv	19	66	VA	Laborer	Vol	3/13/65		M			
Wallace	William	H	Priv	29	67	PA	Shoemaker	Dra	7/14/63	11/17/63	Dis/Surg			
Wallace	John		Priv	25	63.5	PA	Coachman	Vol	8/7/63	6/27/65	Dis			
Wheeler	Isaiah		Priv	27	73	PA	Miner	Dra	7/14/63	6/26/65	Dis			
West	John		Priv	33	67	PA	Farmer	Dra	7/14/63	9/29/64	K	K	9/29/64	New Market
Williams	Edward		Priv	37	68	PA	Laborer	Vol	8/7/63	10/23/64	Died	Died	10/23/64	Ft Monroe
White	James		Priv	21				Vol	8/4/63	8/15/63	Des			

Last Name	First Name	Mid Init	Rank	Age	Hgt (in)	Birth-place	Occupation	Status	Muster-in Date	Separation Date	Manner	Status	Casualty Date	Place
Westbrook	Wiley		Priv	21	65	NC	Laborer	Vol	3/13/65	4/26/65	Des			
Wilson	Duncan		Priv	18	63	NC	Laborer	Vol	3/13/65	4/26/65	Des			
Young	Isaac		Priv					Vol	8/7/63		Abs/sick			
Yokely	Joseph		Priv					Vol	3/27/65		Abs/arr			
Gilman	William		Priv	49	67.5	MD	Laborer	Vol	8/7/63		M			

SIXTH REGIMENT OF THE UNITED STATES COLORED INFANTRY, COMPANY D

Last Name	First Name	Mid Init	Rank	Age	Hgt (in)	Birth-place	Occupation	Status	Muster-in Date	Separation Date	Manner	Status	Casualty Date	Place
McMurray	John		Capt					Vol	9/24/63	9/20/65	M			
Heath	George	E	Lt1					Vol	8/24/63	1/26/65	Dis/SO	W	9/29/64	New Market
Johnson	John	B	Lt1					Vol	10/5/63	9/20/65	M			
McCrea	Thomas	P	Lt2					Vol	3/3/65	9/20/65	M	W	9/29/64	New Market
Parker	Miles		Sgt1	25	70	PA	Laborer	Vol	8/12/63	9/20/65	M			
Faussett	Francis		Sgt					Vol	8/10/63	9/20/65	M			
Biles	Robert		Sgt	20	67	NJ	Laborer	Vol	8/12/63	9/20/65	M			
Jones	Alexander		Sgt	25	70	PA	Laborer	Dra	7/15/63	9/20/65	M			
Campbell	Moses		Sgt	23	70	MD	Laborer	Vol	8/10/63	9/20/65	M			
Maloney	Ephraim		Sgt	25	65	PA	Laborer	Dra	7/15/63	1/15/65	Dis/Surg			
Servant	Richard		Sgt	24	66	VA	Laborer	Vol	8/10/63	11/6/64	Died/W	Died/W	11/6/64	Prtsmth VA
Johnson	George		Sgt	25	70		Laborer	Sub	7/15/63	10/10/63	Des			
Scott	Joseph		Corp	18	66	NJ	Laborer	Vol	8/10/63	9/20/65	M			
Jackson	Lawrence		Corp	20	72	NC	Laborer	Sub	7/15/63	9/20/65	M			
Bruce	Andrew		Corp	30	62	VA	Laborer	Sub	7/16/63	9/20/65	M			
Richmond	John		Corp	22	71	PA	Laborer	Vol	8/10/63	9/20/65	M			
Miller	John		Corp	17	69	PA	Laborer	Sub	8/13/63	9/20/65	M			
Ballet	William	H	Priv	24	64.5	PA	Laborer	Vol	8/10/63	9/20/65	M			
Hamilton	Mark		Priv	34	68	PA	Laborer	Vol	8/13/63	9/20/65	M			
Roberts	Frank		Corp	20	68	MD	Laborer	Vol	7/10/63	9/20/65	M			
Walker	Jeremiah		Corp	25	70	VA	Laborer	Vol	8/10/63	9/29/64	K	K	9/29/64	New Market
Lucas	William		Corp	23	71	DC	Servant	Vol	8/10/63	9/29/64	K	K	9/29/64	New Market
Bryant	Richard		Corp	23	68	PA		Vol	8/10/63	9/29/64	K	K	9/29/64	New Market

COMPANY D *(continued)*

Last Name	First Name	Mid Init	Rank	Age	Hgt (in)	Birth-place	Occupation	Status	Muster-in Date	Separation Date	Separation Manner	Status	Casualty Date	Place
Law	William		Musn	21	71	PA	Laborer	Sub	8/10/63	10/29/64	Died	Died	10/29/64	Ft Monroe
Simmons	Workman		Musn	35	69.5	PA	Waiter	Dra	7/14/63	9/20/65	M			
Mason	John		Musn	18	64	MD	Laborer	Dra	9/13/64	9/20/65	M			
Gould	David		Musn					Vol	8/13/63	8/8/64	Died	Died	8/8/64	
Smith	Isaac		Priv	26	63	PA	Barber	Dra	7/10/63	12/15/64	Des			
Allen	Josiah		Priv	23	68	PA	Laborer	Dra	7/15/63	9/20/65	M			
Boggs	James		Priv	35	71	PA	Laborer	Sub	7/15/63	9/20/65	M			
Brown	Moses		Priv	29	73	VA	Laborer	Dra	7/15/63	9/20/65	M			
Brown	Joseph		Priv	21	72	PA	Laborer	Dra	7/16/63	9/20/65	M			
Bryant	Joseph		Priv	20	72	PA	Laborer	Dra	7/14/63	12/1/63	Dis			
Brown	Charles		Priv	23	72	PA	Laborer	Dra	7/17/63	10/26/64	Died	Died	10/26/64	Ft Monroe
Crawford	Samuel	E	Priv	29	66	PA	Laborer	Dra	7/15/63	9/20/65	M			
Clark	Robert		Priv	21	67	MD	Laborer	Sub	7/17/63	9/20/65	M			
Chaplin	Levi	R	Priv	21	67	PA	Barber	Sub	8/14/63		Det serv			
Cole	Philip		Priv	23	70	PA	Laborer	Sub	7/17/63	9/20/65	M			
Cooper	William		Priv	23	65	WInd	Sailor	Sub	1/6/65		Abs/sick			
Cribb	William		Priv	40	70	PA	Laborer	Dra	7/17/63	1/5/65	Died	Died	1/5/65	
Ceaser	Hubbard		Priv	38	64.5	NJ	Laborer	Sub	7/17/63	3/16/65	Died	Died	3/16/65	
Cherry	Alphonso		Priv	18	62	PA	Laborer	Vol	8/10/63	4/15/65	Des			
Ditcher	Samuel		Priv	20	66	PA	Laborer	Sub	7/16/63		Abs/sick			
Dorsey	Perry		Priv	26	66	PA	Laborer	Dra	7/16/63	9/20/65	M			
Dorman	Francis		Priv	48	65	MD	Laborer	Sub	11/1/64	9/20/65	M			
Dugget	Thomas	C	Priv	21	67.5	PA	Laborer	Dra	10/21/64		Abs/arr			
Dunmore	Edward		Priv	25	68	VA	Laborer	Dra	7/16/63	8/6/64	Died	Died	8/6/64	Wlmngtn NC
Diggs	John		Priv	38	67	MD	Laborer	Dra	11/10/64	5/29/65	Died	Died	5/29/65	New Market
Danks	Nathaniel		Priv	25	68	PA	Laborer	Dra	7/16/63	9/29/64	MIA	MIA	9/29/64	
Duffey	Richard		Priv	32	68	PA	Laborer	Vol	8/10/63	8/11/63	Des			
Dickson	Robert		Priv	22	60	NC	Laborer	Vol	3/13/65	4/15/65	Des			
Dickson	John		Priv	25	60	NC	Laborer	Vol	3/13/65	6/20/65	Des			
Edwards	Henry		Priv	27	64.5	MD	Laborer	Sub	10/21/63	2/14/65	Died	Died	2/14/65	Ft Frshr NC
Foster	Jesse	P	Priv					Sub	7/17/63		Det serv			

Last Name	First Name	Mid Init	Rank	Age	Hgt (in)	Birth-place	Occupation	Status	Muster-in Date	Separation Date	Separation Manner	Status	Casualty Date	Place
Frenchman	John		Priv					Sub	12/30/64	8/23/65	Abs/sick			
Freeman	Charles		Priv					Vol	1/3/65		Abs/sick			
Ferrill	James		Priv					Dra	7/16/63		Dis			
Framer	Major		Priv	44	68	MD	Laborer	Dra	11/10/64	7/15/65	Died	Died	7/15/65	Smthvll NC
Gordon	Joseph		Priv	20		VA	Laborer	Dra	11/12/64	9/20/65	M			
Green	Joseph		Priv					Sub	10/22/64	9/20/65	M			
Goodwin	George		Priv					Sub	8/13/63	3/19/64	Died	Died	3/19/64	Yrktwn VA
Gibson	Charles	H	Priv					Sub	8/14/63	9/29/64	K	K	9/29/64	New Market
Goings	Allen		Priv					Sub	10/21/64	4/15/65	Des			
Howard	James		Priv	24	67	PA	Laborer	Vol	8/10/63	9/20/65	M			
Harris	Benjamin		Priv	34	66	PA	Laborer	Dra	7/17/63	9/20/65	M			
Hilton	Joseph		Priv	30	66	PA	Laborer	Dra	7/16/63	9/20/65	M			
Hill	Peter		Priv	22	65.5	VA	Laborer	Sub	10/29/64	9/20/65	M			
Holmes	Martin		Priv	25	70.5	MD	Laborer	Dra	10/21/64		Abs/sick			
Howard	Wesley		Priv	36	65	MD	Laborer	Dra	11/10/64	9/20/65	M			
Hughes	Thomas		Priv	22	66.75	VA	Laborer	Sub	12/25/64	9/20/65	M			
Hubbard	Charles		Priv	30	68	PA	Tradesman	Vol	8/10/63	9/29/64	K	K	9/29/64	New Market
Harris	Charles		Priv	27	68		Laborer	Sub	8/14/63	9/29/64	K	K	9/29/64	New Market
Hall	Thomas		Priv	23	70.5	MD	Laborer	Dra	10/10/64	4/21/65	Died	Died	4/21/65	Wlmngtn NC
Hammond	Jacob		Priv	22	69	PA	Laborer	Vol	10/10/63	8/21/65	Died	Died	8/21/65	Wlmngtn NC
Harris	Isaac		Priv	35	66	NC	Laborer	Vol	3/13/65	4/15/65	Des			
Innis	William		Priv	30	60	MD	Laborer	Dra	11/12/64	9/20/65	M			
Jackson	Andrew		Priv	26	66	MD	Laborer	Sub	11/12/64	9/20/65	M			
Jackson	John	W	Priv	23	66	VA	Laborer	Dra	11/4/64	9/20/65	M			
Johnson	Richard		Priv	44	63.5	MD	Laborer	Sub	11/10/64	9/20/65	M			
Johnson	William	L	Priv	20	69	PA	Laborer	Sub	7/27/63	1/24/64	Dis			
Jones	Noah		Priv	35	66	VA	Laborer	Dra	7/17/63	9/29/64	K	K	9/29/64	New Market
Johnson	Charles		Priv	22	67	MD	Laborer	Sub	8/14/63	9/29/64	K	K	9/29/64	New Market
Johnson	Samuel	W	Priv	21	67	PA	Laborer	Sub	7/17/63	10/27/64	Died	Died	10/27/64	Ft Monroe
Kenney	William		Priv	22	67		Laborer	Sub	8/14/63	9/29/64	K	K	9/29/64	New Market
Keyser	Thomas		Priv	20	65	NY	Laborer	Sub	7/19/63	9/29/64	K	K	9/29/64	New Market
Lett	Malin		Priv	23	66	PA	Laborer	Dra	7/16/63	9/20/65	M			

COMPANY D (*continued*)

Last Name	First Name	Mid Init	Rank	Age	Hgt (in)	Birth-place	Occupation	Status	Muster-in Date	Separation Date	Manner	Status	Casualty Date	Place
Lewis	Martin	D	Priv	21	63	NY	Servant	Vol	4/10/65	9/20/65	M			
Mitchell	Andrew		Priv	23	68	MD	Laborer	Dra	7/17/63	9/20/65	M			
Miller	William		Priv	20	68	PA	Laborer	Sub	7/15/63	9/20/65	M			
Martin	Richard		Priv	24	67	PA	Laborer	Dra	7/16/63	9/20/65	M			
Mason	Benjamin		Priv	20	66	MD	Laborer	Sub	11/2/64	9/20/65	M			
Mathews	William		Priv	27	66.5	MD	Laborer	Sub	10/29/64	9/20/65	M			
Miles	Henry		Priv	18	65.5	MD	Laborer	Dra	11/2/64	9/20/65	M			
Major	George		Priv	28	64	PA	Laborer	Sub	9/29/64	6/23/65	Dis/SO			
Moody	Samuel		Priv	24	68		Laborer	Sub	8/12/63	9/4/63	Died	Died	9/4/63	Phila
Malone	Moses		Priv	19	67	GA	Laborer	Dra	11/4/64	8/3/65	Des			
Ogle	Henry		Priv	25	65	MD	Laborer	Dra	11/2/64	9/20/65	M			
Powell	George		Priv	19	66	PA	Laborer	Vol	8/10/63	9/20/65	M			
Perkins	Henry		Priv	20	67	PA	Laborer	Sub	7/16/63	9/20/65	Abs/sick			
Pearl	Joseph		Priv	25	65.3	PA	Laborer	Dra	7/16/63	9/20/65	M			
Parker	James		Priv	23	68.75	Jam	Barber	Sub	12/23/64	9/20/65	Abs/sick			
Patterson	Emanuel		Priv	23	68	PA	Laborer	Dra	7/16/63	9/29/64	K	K	9/29/64	New Market
Parker	Joseph		Priv	42	67	MD	Carpenter	Sub	9/24/64	9/11/65	Died	Died	9/11/65	Wlmngtn NC
Perrill	Albert		Priv	20	68	PA	Laborer	Dra	7/16/63	10/5/63	Des			
Redman	William	H	Priv	20	66	VA	Laborer	Sub	7/17/63	9/20/65	M			
Richardson	Beverly		Priv	30	72	VA	Laborer	Dra	7/16/63	9/20/65	M			
Richmond	James		Priv	26	64.5	PA	Laborer	Sub	8/14/63	6/18/65	Dis/SO			
Richmond	Peter		Priv	28	66	PA	Laborer	Sub	7/17/63	12/5/64	Died	Died	12/5/64	
Russell	Lloyd		Priv	22	67	VA	Laborer	Dra	9/28/64	7/10/65	Died	Died	7/10/65	
Shaw	William		Priv	20	60	NC	Laborer	Vol	3/13/65	9/20/65	M			
Shaw	George		Priv	18	65	NC	Laborer	Vol	3/13/65	9/20/65	Abs/sick			
Shaw	Archer		Priv	21	66	NC	Laborer	Vol	3/13/65	9/20/65	M			
Scott	Henry		Priv	18	65	VA	Laborer	Vol	8/11/63	9/20/65	M			
Smith	William		Priv	23	71	PA	Laborer	Dra	8/4/63	9/20/65	M			
Somers	James	A	Priv	43	65.5	DE	Laborer	Sub	9/28/64		Abs/sick			
Settles	Winfield		Priv	19	66	VA	Laborer	Sub	11/1/64	9/20/65	M			
Simpson	John		Priv	24	66	VA	Laborer	Sub	10/21/64	9/20/65	M			

Last Name	First Name	Mid Init	Rank	Age	Hgt (in)	Birth-place	Occupation	Status	Muster-in Date	Separation Date	Manner	Status	Casualty Date	Place
Smith	Alfred		Priv	34	69	VA	Laborer	Sub	11/5/64	9/20/65	M			
Stanley	Charles		Priv	19	65	MD	Laborer	Sub	9/29/64	9/20/65	M			
Sandy	John		Priv	19	67	VA	Laborer	Vol	8/10/63	4/1/65	Dis/Surg			
Sawyer	Charles		Priv	19	66	VA	Laborer	Vol	8/10/63		Died	Died		
Sperlock	Harvey		Priv	20	74	VA	Laborer	Sub	9/24/64	5/25/65	Died	Died	5/25/65	Raleigh NC
Shepard	Eli		Priv	21	68	TN	Laborer	Sub	8/8/63	12/19/64	Des			
Sempler	Jerry		Priv	19	65.75	VA	Laborer	Sub	11/10/64	4/15/65	Des			
Taylor	Thomas		Priv	26	63.25	VA	Laborer	Dra	11/2/64	9/20/65	M			
Thomas	Oliver		Priv	21	71.5	MD	Laborer	Sub	10/31/64	9/20/65	M			
Thomas	John		Priv	19	63	MD	Laborer	Dra	10/29/64	9/20/65	M			
Tucker	William		Priv	32	69.75	MD	Laborer	Sub	11/12/64	9/20/65	M			
Taylor	John		Priv	22	67	Can	Laborer	Vol	4/6/65	8/13/65	Died	Died	8/13/65	
Williams	Robert		Priv	22	66	MD	Laborer	Vol	8/10/63		Abs/sick			
West	John		Priv	21	71	PA	Laborer	Dra	7/16/63	9/20/65	M			
Wyatt	John		Priv	26	67	WInd	Sailor	Vol	10/7/64		AWOL			
Wesley	James		Priv	21	67	PA	Laborer	Sub	7/10/63	9/20/65	M			
White	Andrew		Priv	21	63	PA	Servant	Dra	8/14/63	6/30/64	Died/W	Died/W	6/30/64	
Wheeler	Jesse		Priv	25	64	NC	Machinist	Vol	8/10/63	6/16/64	Died/W	Died/W	6/16/64	Petersburg

SIXTH REGIMENT OF THE UNITED STATES COLORED INFANTRY, COMPANY E

Last Name	First Name	Mid Init	Rank	Age	Hgt (in)	Birth-place	Occupation	Status	Muster-in Date	Separation Date	Manner	Status	Casualty Date	Place
Harkness	Edson	J	Capt					Vol	9/30/63	9/20/65	M			
Glass	William	A	Lt1					Vol	6/26/61	5/15/64	Died	Died	5/15/64	Mnsfld PA
Hammond	W	R	Lt2					Vol	8/22/63					
Ellis	Marshall	D	Lt2					Vol	4/21/65	9/20/65	M			
Johnson	Thomas	C	Sgt1					Vol	8/14/63	9/20/65	M			
Strange	William		Sgt	28	69	MD	Laborer	Dra	7/14/63		Abs/sick			
Johnson	Jeremiah		Sgt	28				Vol	8/21/63	9/20/65	M			
Phares	Joseph	R	Sgt	21	63.5	PA	Miner	Dra	8/14/63					
Scott	Thomas		Sgt	26	66.5	PA	Cook	Dra	7/9/63	9/26/64	K	K	9/26/64	New Market
McClintock	Robert		Sgt	44	63.5	PA	Farmer	Dra	7/14/63	8/4/64	Died	Died	8/4/64	
St. Clair	William		Sgt	35				Vol	8/22/63	10/13/63	Des			
Diton	John		Corp	19	67	PA	Laborer	Sub	8/18/63	9/20/65	M			

COMPANY E (*continued*)

Last Name	First Name	Mid Init	Rank	Age	Hgt (in)	Birth-place	Occupation	Status	Muster-in Date	Separation Date	Separation Manner	Status	Casualty Date	Place
Boyce	Samuel		Corp	19	63.5	NJ	Laborer	Sub	7/24/63	9/20/65	M			
Smith	Dury	C	Corp	29	67	VA	Engineer	Dra	7/14/63	9/20/65	M			
Richards	Benjamin		Corp	34	67.5	PF	Farmer	Dra	7/9/63	6/23/65	Dis/SO			
Augustus	Charles	H	Corp	20	69	DE	Laborer	Vol	8/14/63	10/14/64	Died/W	Died/W	10/14/64	New Market
Mitchell	James		Corp	19	65	VA	Laborer	Sub	8/21/63	8/21/65	Died	Died	8/21/65	Wlmngtn NC
Cole	James		Musn	16				Vol	8/19/63	9/20/65	M			
Crozier	Alfred		Musn	18	62.75	PA	Laborer	Vol	8/22/63	9/20/65	M			
Adkins	John		Priv	24	66	NY		Vol	9/7/64	9/20/65	M			
Adkins	William		Priv	37	68	VA	Barber	Vol	9/7/64	9/20/65	M			
Addison	Richard	F	Priv	24	62.5	VA	Waiter	Vol	8/17/63	9/29/64	K	K	9/29/64	New Market
Armstrong	Harrison		Priv	23	66.5	PA	Farmer	Dra	7/14/63	11/12/64	Died	Died	11/12/64	
Anderson	Thomas		Priv	20	69	PA	Farmer	Vol	8/18/63	10/3/64	W/drnd	W/drowned	10/3/64	DtchGp/JmsR
Bell	Coleman		Priv	23	66.5	NY	Laborer	Vol	9/7/64	9/20/65	M			
Brown	Isaac		Priv	38	66.25	WInd	Sailor	Vol	9/10/64	9/20/65	M			
Brockway	Charles		Priv	30	66	PA	Farmer	Sub	8/21/63		Abs/sick			
Barks	James	O	Priv	20	72.5	PA	Farmer	Sub	8/20/63		Abs/sick			
Brunswick	Thomas		Priv	19	69	IN	Cook	Vol	8/19/63	9/20/65	M			
Bolden	Jeremiah		Priv	22	66	PA	Miner	Vol	8/13/63	9/20/65	M			
Book	George		Priv	20	66.75	PA	Laborer	Sub	8/17/63	5/26/65	Dis/Surg			
Bacon	William		Priv	29	67	PA	Farmer	Dra	7/17/63	6/29/65	Died	Died	6/29/65	Smthvll NC
Bennett	Lewis	A	Priv	35	69	NY	Farmer	Vol	9/6/64	5/18/65	Died	Died	5/18/65	Wlmngtn NC
Brister	Levi		Priv	20	63.5	PA	Farmer	Vol	8/19/63	7/21/65	Died	Died	7/21/65	Wlmngtn NC
Crable	James		Priv	23	68	PA	Laborer	Dra	7/9/63	11/21/64	Died	Died	11/21/64	Yorktown
Coons	James		Priv	21	65			Vol	8/19/63	7/1/65	Died	Died	7/1/65	Ft Monroe
Campbell	Pauldo		Priv	15	65	NC	Farmer	Vol	3/13/65	4/2/65	Died	Died	4/2/65	FsnsSta NC
Chappell	Leander		Priv	34	64	VA	Engineer	Vol	9/9/64	9/10/65	Died	Died	9/10/65	Wlmngtn NC
Carter	George		Priv	24	64.5	LA	Waiter	Vol	8/19/63	12/29/64	Des			
Dye	Thomas	W	Priv	25	67	PA	Boatman	Sub	8/18/63	9/20/65	Det serv			
Davis	William	H	Priv	43	66.5	Can	Waiter	Vol	9/14/64		M			
Davis	Benjamin		Priv	28	62	PA	Barber	Dra	8/15/63	9/29/64	Cap/died	Cap/died	9/29/64	New Market
Dunn	Miller		Priv	18		NJ	Farmer	Vol	8/18/63	10/4/63	Died	Died	10/4/63	Phila

Last Name	First Name	Mid Init	Rank	Age	Hgt (in)	Birth-place	Occupation	Status	Muster-in Date	Separation Date	Separation Manner	Status	Casualty Date	Place
Dickson	David		Priv	21	60	NC	Farmer	Vol	3/13/65	5/9/65	Des			
Dickson	Edward		Priv	31	69	NC	Farmer	Vol	3/13/65	6/3/65	Des			
Ellett	William		Priv	20	63	VA	Farmer	Vol	9/17/64	9/20/65	M			
Fernandes	Andreas		Priv	20	63	WInd	Sailor	Vol	9/16/64	9/20/65	M			
Fells	Allen		Priv					Dra	7/14/63		Abs/sick			
Firman	Josiah		Priv	24		PA	Farmer	Vol	8/19/63		M			
Firman	Alfredo		Priv	30	68	PA	Farmer	Vol	8/19/63	9/20/65	M			
Firman	Charles		Priv	22		PA	Farmer	Vol	8/19/64	8/2/65	Died	Died	8/2/65	Wlmngtn NC
Griffin	William		Priv	18	70	PA	Boatman	Vol	9/13/64	9/20/65	M			
Graves	Albert		Priv	24	68	NY	Waiter	Vol	9/13/64	9/20/65	M			
Gray	John		Priv	19	65	NJ	Laborer	Sub	8/15/63		Abs/sick			
Griffin	David		Priv	21	67	VA	Laborer	Vol	4/26/64	9/20/65	M			
Gould	Joseph		Priv	20				Vol	8/19/63	8/24/64	Died	Died	8/24/64	
Hill	Lewis	H	Priv	18	68	VA	Laborer	Vol	8/24/64	9/20/65	M			
Hill	Alexander		Priv	23	66.5	DC	Engineer	Vol	9/15/64	9/20/65	M			
Henry	William		Priv	18	68	PA	Waiter	Vol	8/20/63	9/20/65	M			
Hall	George		Priv					Vol	8/22/63	9/20/65	M			
Haslet	Jacob	S	Priv	21	63			Vol	8/14/63	9/20/65	M			
Harrison	William		Priv	21	67	TN	Laborer	Dra	7/14/63	9/20/65	M			
Hollins	Charles	H	Priv					Sub	8/18/63	9/29/64	K	K	9/29/64	New Market
Hurley	Samuel		Priv	18	63	NJ	Laborer	Vol	8/18/63	7/4/64	Died	Died	7/4/64	Cty Pnt VA
Hughes	Ellis		Priv	28	69	NY	Barber	Vol	9/7/64	10/12/64	Died/W	Died/W	10/12/64	Pt Rcks VA
Hagerman	Theodore		Priv	28	59.5	NJ	Laborer	Dra	8/17/63	8/31/63	Des			
Jenkins	Charles	G	Priv					Vol	9/10/64	9/20/65	M			
Johnson	Henry	1st	Priv					Vol	9/14/64	9/20/65	M			
Johnson	James	2nd	Priv					Sub	8/6/63	9/20/65	M			
Johnson	James		Priv					Vol	9/15/64	9/20/65	M			
Johnson	William		Priv					Vol	8/22/63	9/20/65	M			
Johnson	Josiah		Priv					Dra	10/26/64	9/20/65	M			
James	Josiah		Priv					Dra	10/14/64	9/20/65	M			
Jones	Richard	M	Priv	21				Vol	8/14/63	9/16/63	Died	Died	9/16/63	Phila
Jackson	John		Priv	31	67	PA	Farmer	Sub	8/20/63	11/20/64	Died	Died	11/20/64	

COMPANY E (*continued*)

Last Name	First Name	Mid Init	Rank	Age	Hgt (in)	Birthplace	Occupation	Status	Muster-in Date	Separation Date	Separation Manner	Status	Casualty Date	Place
Jackson	Andrew		Priv	35				Vol	8/22/63	9/5/63	Des			
Landrum	Jeremiah		Priv	24	64	PA	Farmer	Dra	7/14/63	9/7/65	Died	Died	9/7/65	
Lawton	Randall		Priv	33	67	NC	Farmer	Vol	3/13/63	4/2/65	Des			
Little	Newton		Priv	18				Vol	8/17/63		Not/Mstr			
Marsh	Peter		Priv	24	64	PA	Laborer	Dra	8/16/63	9/20/65	M			
Murray	Benjamin		Priv	25	65	MD		Dra	8/24/63	9/20/65	M			
Mathews	Michael		Priv	25	65	MD	Laborer	Sub	7/28/63	9/20/65	M			
Miles	Henry		Priv	18	67	MD	Farmer	Sub	11/2/64	9/20/65	M			
Melontur	Moses		Priv	30				Vol	8/22/63	9/20/65	M			
Murdock	John	W	Priv	25				Vol	8/22/63		Abs/sick			
Manloff	Charles		Priv	24	69.5	CT	Laborer	Sub	8/11/63	1/27/64	Dis/Surg			
Mitchell	John	H	Priv	23	68.375	DE	Farmer	Sub	8/19/63	8/30/65	Died	Died	8/30/65	Wlmngtn NC
McDonnell	Isaac		Priv	30	67.5	NC	Farmer	Vol	3/13/65	5/12/65	Des			
McCoy	Archer		Priv	19	66	NC	Farmer	Vol	3/2/65	5/9/65	Des			
Nicholas	Cornelius		Priv	19	65	VA	Laborer	Sub	8/28/63	9/20/65	M			
Ogden	Harrison		Priv	38	67	PA	Farmer	Dra	7/16/63	11/20/63	Dis/Surg			
Pierce	Jonathon		Priv	26	71	PA	Laborer	Sub	8/18/63	9/20/65	M			
Patterson	Joseph		Priv	18	69.5	PA	Farmer	Vol	8/20/63	9/20/65	M			
Porter	Richard		Priv	25	63	VA	Boatman	Vol	9/15/64	9/20/65	M			
Queen	Nace		Priv	36	68	MD	Laborer	Dra	11/10/64	9/20/65	M			
Ringle	Benjamin		Priv	34	67.5	MD	Laborer	Dra	8/11/63		Furl			
Redding	William		Priv	19	66	VA	Laborer	Sub	11/12/64	9/20/65	M			
Ruff	Jacob		Priv	32	67	VA	Laborer	Sub	11/15/64	9/20/65	M			
Redding	Frank		Priv	20	64	NJ	Farmer	Sub	8/18/63	6/23/64	Died	Died	6/23/64	Prtsmth VA
Sherwood	Frederick		Priv	20	65.75	VA	Waiter	Vol	9/12/64	9/20/65	M			
Snowden	Henry		Priv	20	70.5	PA	Farmer	Vol	8/20/63	9/20/65	M			
Smallwood	William		Priv	19	66.5	PA	Barber	Vol	8/22/63	9/20/65	M			
Sedwick	Raisin		Priv	23	71	MD	Laborer	Dra	11/18/64		Abs/sick			
Simmons	Calvin		Priv	19	62.5	NC	Farmer	Vol	3/13/65	11/20/63	Dis/Surg			
Stewart	Thomas		Priv					Vol	8/19/63	7/18/65	Dis/Surg			
Scott	George		Priv	30	64	VA	Cook	Sub	10/22/64	7/18/65	Died	Died	7/18/65	Smthvll NC

Last Name	First Name	Mid Init	Rank	Age	Hgt (in)	Birth-place	Occupation	Status	Muster-in Date	Separation Date	Separation Manner	Status	Casualty Date	Place
Sellers	Calvin		Priv	20	63	NC	Farmer	Vol	3/13/65	4/5/65	Des			
Thomas	Adam		Priv	19	66	NJ	Farmer	Vol	9/6/64	9/20/65	M			
Tiddle	Newton		Priv					Vol	8/17/63		Abs/sick			
Tann	Reuben	R	Priv	22	68	IL	Farmer	Vol	8/19/63	9/20/65	M			
Tillman	Daniel		Priv	20	65	MD	Labcrer	Dra	7/14/63	9/20/65	M			
Turner	John		Priv	45	61.5	PA	Porter	Sub	8/4/63	12/1/64	Dis/Surg			
Tunison	Henry		Priv	21	63.5	NJ	Labcrer	Sub	8/17/63	6/7/65	Dis/Surg			
Vroom	George		Priv	19	67.5	NJ	Farmer	Dra	8/15/63	9/20/65	M			
Wood	George		Priv	20	62.5	Can	Tobacconist	Vol	9/14/64	9/20/65	M			
Wilson	Charles		Priv	22	68	NY	Farmer	Vol	9/17/64	9/20/65	M			
Williams	Benjamin		Priv	31	69	MD	Labcrer	Dra	11/10/64		Abs/sick			
Williams	Charles		Priv	23	67	VA	Labcrer	Sub	10/4/64	9/20/65	M			
Wright	Henry		Priv	30				Dra	7/14/63	11/17/63	Dis/Surg			
Williamson	Alfred		Priv					Sub	8/15/63	1/27/65	Dis/Surg			
Wilson	John	H	Priv	23				Vol	8/15/63	6/21/64	Died	Died	6/21/64	Hampton VA
Wilson	Robert		Priv	41	69	VA	Labcrer	Dra	11/19/64	5/26/65	Died	Died	5/26/65	Wlmngtn NC
Williams	Peter		Priv	34				Sub	8/8/63	10/13/63	Des			
Wright	Simon		Priv	20	64	NC	Farmer	Vol	3/13/65	4/12/65	Des			
Wright	Thomas		Priv	20	61.5	NC	Farmer	Vol	3/13/65	4/12/65	Des			
Wright	John		Priv	18	65.5	NC	Farmer	Vol	3/7/65	5/9/65	Des			
White	Ether		Priv	28	67	NC	Farmer	Vol	3/7/65	4/22/65	Des			
Wooden	James		Priv	30	63	NC	Labcrer	Vol	3/2/65	5/9/65	Des			
Walls	James		Pr/Crp	22	66.5	PA	Farmer	Sub	7/14/63	9/20/65	M			
Johns	William		Pr/Crp					Sub	8/19/63	9/20/65	M			
Augustus	John	R	Pr/Crp	20	65.5	PA	Farmer	Scb	8/15/63		Abs/lve			
Brown	Horace		Pr/Crp	21	65.75	NJ	Farmer	Sub	8/22/63	9/20/65	M			

SIXTH REGIMENT OF THE UNITED STATES COLORED INFANTRY, COMPANY F

Last Name	First Name	Mid Init	Rank	Age	Hgt (in)	Birth-place	Occupation	Status	Muster-in Date	Separation Date	Separation Manner	Status	Casualty Date	Place
Hotchkiss	Newton	J	Capt					Vol	9/23/63	1/21/65	Died/W	Died/W	1/21/65	Sgr Lf Hll
Buckman	Aaron	N	Capt					Vol	9/15/63	9/20/65	M			
Healey	Daniel	K	Lt1					Vol	10/5/63		Abs/sick	W	2/11/65	Sgr Lf Hll
Roberts	William	F	Lt2					Vol	12/15/64	9/19/65	Died	Died	9/19/65	Wilmington

COMPANY F (continued)

Last Name	First Name	Mid Init	Rank	Age	Hgt (in)	Birth-place	Occupation	Status	Muster-in Date	Separation Date	Separation Manner	Status	Casualty Date	Place
Proctor	Jeremiah		Sgt1	28	69	PA	Laborer	Sub	8/25/63	9/20/65	M			
Kelly	Alexander		Sgt	23	63	PA	Miner	Sub	8/24/63	9/20/65	M			
Lee	Benjamin	H	Sgt	21	68			Vol	8/26/63	9/20/65	M			
Porter	George		Corp	18	68	PA	Laborer	Sub	8/26/63	9/20/65	M			
Skenk	Peter		Corp	29	67	NJ	Laborer	Sub	8/20/63	9/20/65	M			
Webster	Alfred		Sgt	32	65.5	PA	Farmer	Dra	7/18/63	7/26/65	Died	Died	7/26/65	
Peters	William		Corp	39	61	PA	Laborer	Dra	7/20/63	9/20/65	M			
Lee	Charles	W	Corp	35	67			Vol	8/26/63	9/20/65	M			
Brown	Charles		Corp	29	67	PA	Farmer	Sub	8/26/63	9/20/65	M			
Rias	John	D	Priv	30	69	DE	Laborer	Vol	8/25/63	9/20/65	M			
Spencer	John		Priv	25	66	MD	Laborer	Dra	8/12/63	9/20/65	M			
Crippen	James	B	Priv	21	61	PA	Laborer	Sub	8/12/63	9/20/65	M			
Graves	Robert		Priv	22	69	DE	Laborer	Dra	8/12/63	9/20/65	M			
Rowland	Solomon		Priv	22	60	PA	Carter	Dra	8/12/63	9/20/65	M			
Cummings	Edward		Corp	22	71	DE	Laborer	Dra	8/12/63	2/11/65	K	K	2/11/65	Sgr Lf Hll
Draper	Charles		Musn	22	62	DE	Laborer	Sub	8/12/63	9/20/65	M			
Chase	Elijah		Musn					Vol	3/3/65	9/20/65	M			
Augustus	Clarkson		Priv	21	63.5	PA	Farmer	Sub	8/24/63	1/28/65	Died	Died	1/28/65	
Baptist	Jesse		Priv	32	72.25	PA	Brickman	Dra	7/20/63	9/20/65	M			
Baker	Richard		Priv	51	72.5	PA	Farmer	Sub	8/22/63	9/20/65	Abs/sick			
Bryant	John		Priv	21	63.25	PA	Driver	Dra	7/20/63	9/20/65	M			
Brent	Thomas		Priv	20	62	VA	Laborer	Sub	11/20/64	9/20/65	M			
Brown	William		Priv	19	65	MD	Baker	Sub	11/26/64	9/20/65	M			
Brooks	Walter		Priv	23	69.75	PA	Laborer	Sub	11/30/64	9/20/65	M			
Bayard	Samuel		Priv	24	67	DE	Laborer	Dra	8/12/63	6/15/64	K	K	6/15/64	Petersburg
Brogart	John		Priv					Vol	7/20/63					
Caldwell	Hezekiah		Priv	26	60	DE	Farmer	Dra	8/12/63	9/20/65	M			
Carey	Stephen		Priv	23	67.25	PA	Farmer	Sub	7/16/63	9/20/65	M			
Catlin	Ephraim		Priv	20	61.75	PA	Farmer	Dra	7/14/63	9/20/65	M			
Chew	Richard	H	Priv	36	70	NY	Laborer	Sub	8/15/63	9/20/65	M			
Clinton	James		Priv	20	61.5	DE	Laborer	Dra	8/12/63	9/20/65	M			

Last Name	First Name	Mid Init	Rank	Age	Hgt (in)	Brth-Place	Occupation	Status	Muster-in Date	Separation Date	Manner	Status	Casualty Date	Place
Carter	Henry		Priv	25	65	VA	Laborer	Sub	11/22/64	9/20/65	M			
Carroll	Henry		Priv	40	66	MD	Laborer	Dra	11/28/64	9/20/65	M			
Cook	Edward		Priv	18	66			Vol	8/25/63	8/23/64	Died	Died	8/23/64	
Curry	James		Priv	20	67.5	PA	Laborer	Sub	7/16/63	10/15/64	Died/W	Died/W	10/15/64	
Davis	John		Priv	23	64.5	NJ	Laborer	Sub	8/26/63		Abs/sick			
Dernby	John		Priv	33	68	DE	Laborer	Dra	8/12/63	9/20/65	M			
Dean	Amos		Priv	36	63.5	VA	Laborer	Dra	11/12/64	9/20/65	M			
Dolson	John	H	Priv	44	67	MD	Laborer	Dra	11/22/64	9/20/65	M			
Dien	Lewis		Priv					Sub	8/22/63	4/18/65	Dis/Surg			
Dawson	Andrew		Priv	22	66	KY	Laborer	Vol	8/24/63	6/28/64	Died	Died	6/28/64	
Denny	William		Priv	23	64			Vol	8/23/63	3/11/65	K	K	3/11/65	Petersburg
Diggs	John		Priv	29	65.25	MD	Farmer	Sub	8/26/63	9/20/65	Died	Died		
Ebbs	Lewis		Priv	19	63	MD	Laborer	Sub	11/26/64	9/20/65	M			
Ford	James		Priv	19	65	PA	Laborer	Sub	11/29/64		Abs/sick			
Flowers	Robert		Priv	42	70	PA	Laborer	Sub	8/27/63	9/20/65	M			
Frisby	Moses		Priv	22	68	NJ	Farmer	Dra	8/15/63		Not/Mstr			
Green	John		Priv	35	68	PA	Laborer	Sub	7/20/63	9/20/65	M			
Gardiner	Samuel		Priv					Sub	11/21/63	9/20/65	M			
Griffith	Francis	J	Priv	20	65.5	PA	Laborer	Sub	8/19/63	7/26/65	Dis/Surg			
Guilford	Daniel		Priv	25	68	GA	Laborer	Sub	7/22/63	8/13/65	Dis/Surg			
Grant	Alfred		Priv	33	69	VA		Vol	8/25/63					
Green	George	W	Priv	20	65	VA	Laborer	Dra	8/16/63	9/29/64	K	K	9/29/64	New Market
Gibbs	Absalom		Priv	21	66	DE	Laborer	Dra	7/28/63	3/12/65	Died/W	Died/W	3/12/65	
Hendel	Henry		Priv			DE		Dra	11/22/64	9/20/65	M			
Hunter	Henry		Priv					Dra	11/21/64	9/20/65	M			
Hitchins	Lewis		Priv	27	65.5	DE	Laborer	Sub	8/28/63	9/20/65	M			
Hamilton	Thomas	W	Priv	23	68	VA	Farmer	Sub	8/22/63	9/29/64	K	K	9/29/64	New Market
Johnson	George		Priv	27	60	DE	Farmer	Sub	8/26/63	9/20/65	M			
Johnson	Isaac	S	Priv	18	68			Sub	8/26/63	9/20/65	M			
Johnson	George	W	Priv					Vol	3/10/64	9/20/65	M			
Jones	John	T	Priv	19	66			Dra	8/24/63	9/20/65	M			
Jones	Thomas		Priv					Dra	11/30/64	9/20/65	M			

COMPANY F (continued)

Last Name	First Name	Mid Init	Rank	Age	Hgt (in)	Birth-place	Occupation	Status	Muster-in Date	Separation Date	Separation Manner	Status	Casualty Date	Place
Jones	Adolphus		Priv					Sub	11/22/64	9/20/65	M			
Jackson	David		Priv					Sub	11/20/64	9/20/65	M			
Johnson	Washington		Priv	26	70			Vol	8/26/63	6/12/65	Dis/Surg			
Johnson	Moses		Priv	20	70			Vol	8/26/63	8/29/64	Drwnd	Drowned	8/29/64	James Riv
James	John		Priv	21	64	VA	Laborer	Sub	8/21/63	9/29/64	K	K	9/29/64	New Market
Johnson	George	S	Priv	21	71.75			Dra	8/12/63	9/29/64	K	K	9/29/64	New Market
Keener	Isaac		Priv	28	62			Vol	8/25/63	6/7/65	Dis/Surg			
Mills	Lewis		Priv	35	64			Vol	8/26/63	9/20/65	M			
Murray	James	E	Priv	18	65			Vol	8/25/63	9/20/65	M			
Myers	Alexander		Priv	21	64	PA	Laborer	Sub	8/28/63	9/20/65	M			
Mathews	Thomas		Priv					Sub	11/26/64	9/20/65	M			
Miller	John		Priv					Vol	3/4/65	9/20/65	M			
Madison	Alexander		Priv	19	69	PA	Farmer	Vol	8/26/63	7/27/64	Dis/Surg			
Morgan	Joshua		Priv	21	68.5	PA	Farmer	Sub	8/25/63	6/15/64	K	K	6/15/64	Petersburg
Nelson	George		Priv					Dra	11/30/64	9/20/65	M			
Pinkney	Moses	S	Priv	21	63.5	PA	Laborer	Sub	8/25/63	9/20/65	M			
Powell	Thomas		Priv	24	71	PA	Farmer	Sub	7/16/63		Abs/sick			
Proctor	Samuel		Priv	21	71.25	PA	Laborer	Dra	7/16/63	4/5/65	Died	Died	4/5/65	Ft Monroe
Perry	Timothy		Priv					Sub	8/15/63		Not/Mstr			
Rider	Joseph		Priv	25	63	DE		Dra	8/12/63	9/20/65	M			
Rider	Charles		Priv	22	63	DE		Sub	8/26/63	9/20/65	M			
Richardson	Jackson		Priv				Laborer	Sub	11/21/64		Abs/sick			
Robinson	Charles		Priv					Vol	3/17/65	9/20/65	M			
Rollins	Samuel		Priv	33	66	MD	Laborer	Dra	8/12/63	1/3/65	Died	Died	1/3/65	
Richmond	John		Priv	27	66.5	PA		Dra	8/15/63	7/2/65	Died	Died	7/2/65	
Steveson	Peter	W H	Priv					Vol	4/4/65	9/20/65	M			
Smith	John		Priv	24	64	PA	Laborer	Dra	8/18/63	9/20/65	M			
Smith	John		Priv	19	63	PA	Laborer	Sub	7/20/63	9/20/65	M			
Smith	Finley		Priv					Sub	11/30/64		Abs/sick			
Stevenson	Richardson		Priv	21	62	DE	Laborer	Sub	8/21/63	9/20/65	M			
Scott	William		Priv	28	66	PA	Laborer	Sub	8/25/63	9/29/64	K	K	9/29/64	New Market

Last Name	First Name	Mid Init	Rank	Age	Hgt (in)	Birth-place	Occupation	Status	Muster-in Date	Sep. Date	Sep. Manner	Status	Casualty Date	Place
Smith	John		Priv	27	65.5	PA	Laborer	Dra	7/22/63	10/12/64	Died/W	Died/W	10/12/64	
Smiley	Henry		Priv					Sub	11/19/64	7/23/65	Died	Died	7/23/65	
Thompson	James		Priv	23	70	NJ	Farmer	Vol	8/25/63	9/20/65	M			
Todd	William		Priv	21	61.5	DE	Laborer	Dra	8/12/63	9/20/65	M			
Tibbs	George		Priv					Sub	11/26/64	9/20/65	M			
Toles	George		Priv					Sub	11/26/64	9/20/65	M			
Thomson	William		Priv	25	65.5	NJ	Farmer	Sub	11/22/64	9/20/65	M			
Turner	Daniel		Priv					Dra	11/28/64	9/20/65	M			
Valentine	Edward		Priv	20	65	MD	Waiter	Sub	7/26/63	7/30/64	K	K	7/30/64	Petersburg
Wesley	Spencer	P	Priv	18	68.5	PA	Laborer	Sub	8/11/63	9/20/65	M			
Wilson	Wilson	E	Priv	20	64.5	PA	Farmer	Sub	8/27/63		Abs/sick			
White	Arthur		Priv					Dra	11/23/64		Abs/sick			
White	John		Priv					Sub	11/30/64	9/20/65	M			
Ward	John		Priv					Sub	11/26/64	9/20/65	M			
West	Jeremiah		Priv					Vol	3/17/65	9/20/65	M			
Worley	Aaron	C	Priv	32	70			Vol	8/26/62		Abs/sick			
White	Dennis		Priv	21	65			Vol	8/29/62	9/20/65	M			
Whitney	John		Priv	21	67			Vol	8/26/63	9/5/64	Died	Died	9/5/64	
Woods	Preston		Priv	21	67	TN	Laborer	Dra	7/14/63		Died	Died		Ft Monroe
Green	William		Priv					Vol	8/26/63	9/20/65	M			

SIXTH REGIMENT OF THE UNITED STATES COLORED INFANTRY, COMPANY G

Last Name	First Name	Mid Init	Rank	Age	Hgt (in)	Birth-place	Occupation	Status	Muster-in Date	Sep. Date	Sep. Manner	Status	Casualty Date	Place
Herbert	Henry		Capt					Vol	9/24/63	5/15/65	Died	Died	5/15/65	Gldsbr NC
Chamberlain	Myron	M	Lt1					Vol	8/23/63	9/20/65	M			
Kingsbury	Alonzo	C	Lt1					Vol	10/5/63	9/14/64	Died/acc	Died/acc	9/14/64	Dtch Gp VA
Grow		W	Lt1					Vol	10/5/63					
Pratt	Eber	C	Lt2					Vol	9/2/63	9/29/64	Died/W	Died/W	9/29/64	NMkt/Ft Mon
Phillips	Lionel	D	Lt2					Vol	1/7/65					
Wideman	Albert		Lt2					Vol	9/5/65					
Elsburg	James	H	Sgt1	29	68	PA	Shoemaker	Vol	9/14/63	9/20/65	Dis			
Johnson	Thomas		Sgt	21	68.5			Vol	9/14/63	9/20/65	Abs/arr			
Lucas	Henry	R	Sgt	21	70	PA	Laborer	Sub	7/16/63	9/20/65	M			

COMPANY G (*continued*)

Last Name	First Name	Mid Init	Rank	Age	Hgt (in)	Birth-place	Occupation	Status	Muster-in Date	Separation Date	Manner	Status	Casualty Date	Place
Waters	William		Sgt	20	64.5	NJ	Barber	Dra	9/3/63	9/20/65	M			
Taylor	Joseph		Sgt	20	65	PA	Blacksmith	Sub	7/18/63	9/20/65	M			
Miles	Giles		Corp	22	62	VA	Farmer	Sub	8/29/63	9/20/65	M			
Walker	John	R	Corp	27	64	DE	Laborer	Dra	8/12/63		Abs/fur			
Jones	William		Corp	29	65	MD	Butler	Dra	9/1/63	9/20/65	M			
Albert	Oliver		Corp	19	72	PA	Farmer	Vol	9/14/63	9/20/65	M			
Clay	Henry		Corp	20	66	GA	Farmer	Sub	9/3/63	9/20/65	M			
Williams	John		Corp	20	64	VA	Waiter	Sub	9/3/63	9/20/65	M			
Jacobs	Samuel		Corp	18	64.5	PA	Farmer	Vol	9/14/63	9/20/65	M			
Berry	Charles	W	Corp					Vol	9/14/63	9/29/64	K	K	9/29/64	New Market
Wright	Archibald		Corp					Sub	8/29/63	9/29/64	K	K	9/29/64	New Market
Robinson	George		Corp	28	70	PA	Laborer	Dra	8/29/63	10/15/63	Des			
Anderson	Samuel		Corp	23	66	DE	Laborer	Sub	9/2/63	9/20/65	M			
Alexander	Charles	L	Priv	19	66.5	DE	Laborer	Sub	9/2/63	9/20/65	M			
Boyer	William	H H	Priv	19	73	PA	Farmer	Sub	9/1/63		Abs/sick			
Black	James		Priv	19	66	DE	Laborer	Dra	7/16/63	9/20/65	M			
Brown	Joseph		Priv	28	66.5	PA	Laborer	Sub	8/29/63	9/20/65	M			
Bolden	George		Priv	23	66	DE	Laborer	Dra	8/12/63	9/20/65	M			
Bronson	Aquilla		Priv	18	66	OH	Farmer	Vol	9/14/63	9/20/65	M			
Brooks	Charles		Priv	19	62.5	VA	Farmer	Vol	2/21/65	9/20/65	M			
Brooks	John	A	Priv	35	67	MD	Laborer	Dra	8/29/63	11/9/63	Dis/Surg			
Black	Edwin	J	Priv	24	68	PA	Farmer	Dra	7/16/63	4/29/65	Dis/Surg			
Beckett	John		Priv					Dra	7/30/63	9/29/64	K	K	9/29/64	New Market
Bradley	Lewis	C A	Priv	29	66	PA	Miner	Dra	7/16/63	2/15/65	Died	Died	2/15/65	Ft Fshr NC
Chambers	Thomas		Priv	20	67	DE	Laborer	Sub	9/1/63	9/20/65	M			
Clarkson	George		Priv	23	67	DE	Laborer	Dra	8/12/63	9/20/65	M			
Coy	George	W	Priv	26	64.5	PA	Laborer	Dra	7/14/63		Abs/sick			
Cooper	Isaac		Priv	21	66.5	MD	Laborer	Vol	8/12/63	9/9/65	Died	Died	9/9/65	Wlmngtn NC
Davis	Edward		Priv	26	68	PA	Seaman	Vol	12/30/64	9/20/65	M			
Davis	Robert		Priv	34	67.5	DE	Farmer	Sub	8/2/63		Abs/wnd			
Dorsey	Thomas		Priv	32	69.5	MD	Barber	Dra	8/29/63		Abs/hosp	W		Dtch Gp VA

Last Name	First Name	Mid Init	Rank	Age	Hgt (in)	Birth-place	Occupation	Status	Muster-in Date	Separation Date	Manner	Status	Casualty Date	Place
Dennis	Joseph		Priv	19	68	VA	Farmer	Vol	2/23/65	9/20/65	M			
Derry	John		Priv	20	64	PA	Farmer	Sub	7/17/63	9/20/65	M			
Derry	Moses		Priv	30	66.5	PA	Laborer	Sub	9/1/63	9/29/64	Died/W	Died/W	9/29/64	NMkt/Ft Mon
DeLeige	Hartwick		Priv	36	64.5	PA	Laborer	Sub	7/24/63	8/3/65	Died	Died	8/3/65	Wlmngtn NC
Fisher	Thomas		Priv	28	69	MD	Laborer	Sub	9/1/63	9/20/65	M			
Graham	John	H	Priv	23	65.5	VA	Laborer	Dra	7/16/63	9/20/65	M			
Gross	Henson		Priv	21	65.5	DE	Laborer	Dra	8/12/63	9/20/65	M			
Green	George	D	Priv	20	65	VA	Laborer	Dra	7/16/63	11/10/64	Died	Died	11/10/64	Ft Monroe
Hatfield	John		Priv	23	68.5	DE	Laborer	Dra	8/12/63	9/20/65	M			
Harris	Abraham		Priv	24	68.5	DE	Laborer	Dra	8/12/63	9/20/65	M			
Hill	Thomas		Priv	23	67	VA	Laborer	Sub	11/25/64	9/20/65	M			
Heynes	George		Priv	24	64	MD	Laborer	Dra	11/17/64	9/20/65	M			
Heyson	John		Priv	22	67	MD	Laborer	Dra	9/19/64	9/20/65	M			
Holland	James		Priv	40	68	DE	Laborer	Dra	11/22/64	9/20/65	M			
Henson	Jonathon		Priv	34	61	PA	Laborer	Dra	7/18/63	9/29/64	Died/W	Died/W	9/29/64	New Market
Hopkins	Benjamin		Priv	44	61	MD	Laborer	Dra	11/25/63	6/7/65	Died	Died	6/7/65	Gldsbr NC
Hopkins	James		Priv	32	67	MD	Teamster	Dra	8/29/63	7/26/65	Died	Drowned	7/26/65	Wlmngtn NC
Humphrey	William	V	Priv					Vol	9/14/63	10/9/63	Des			
Johnson	Richard	M	Priv	21	63	MD	Farmer	Dra	7/16/63	9/20/65	M			
Johnson	Richard		Priv	25	63	MD	Farmer	Sub	9/1/63		Abs/arr			
Johnson	Benjamin		Priv	32	69	MD	Farmer	Dra	9/20/64	9/20/65	M			
Johnson	Samuel	N	Priv	18	66	MD	Farmer	Vol	11/30/64	9/20/65	M			
Johnson	Henry		Priv	28	70	MD	Laborer	Dra	11/26/64	9/20/65	M			
Johnson	William		Priv	21	64	DE	Laborer	Dra	11/15/64		Abs/sick			
Jones	William		Priv	39	65	VA	Laborer	Sub	11/21/64		Abs/sick			
Johnson	Daniel		Priv	35	69	PA	Farmer	Dra	7/14/63	5/24/65	Dis/GO			
Johnson	Matthew	B	Priv	19	67	PA	Laborer	Vol	9/14/63	9/20/64	Des			
Kumard	Frederick		Priv					Dra	11/20/64	9/20/65	M			
Laws	Daniel		Priv	20	70	DE	Laborer	Sub	9/2/63	3/15/65	Died	Died	3/15/65	Wlmngtn NC
Lewis	Alexander		Priv	25	62	PA	Farmer	Sub	9/3/63	3/16/65	Des			
Miller	Charles		Priv	22	64.5	PA	Laborer	Dra	8/12/63	9/20/65	M			
Morgan	John		Priv	43	70	VA	Laborer	Sub	8/27/63	9/20/65	M			

COMPANY G (continued)

Last Name	First Name	Mid Init	Rank	Age	Hgt (in)	Birth-place	Occupation	Status	Muster-in Date	Separation Date	Separation Manner	Status	Casualty Date	Place
Massey	Thomas		Priv	26	67.5	DE	Laborer	Sub	8/31/63	9/20/65	M			
Masson	James		Priv	23	73	MD	Laborer	Dra	9/20/64	9/20/65	M			
Murray	Lewis		Priv	25	64	MD	Laborer	Sub	11/23/64	9/20/65	M			
Mann	Benjamin		Priv	23	68	PA	Sailor	Sub	8/31/63	3/5/64	Died	Died	3/5/64	Yorktown
Murdoch	George		Priv	19	64.5	MD	Laborer	Sub	11/17/64	9/5/65	Died	Died	9/5/65	Pt Rcks VA
Manning	George		Priv	30	67	PA	Laborer	Sub	11/18/64	9/5/65	Died	Died		Wlmngtn NC
Morgan	Joshua	A	Priv	20	66	PA	Laborer	Sub	8/29/63	10/2/63	Des			
Noble	Perry		Priv	21	72	VA	Laborer	Dra	7/16/63	9/20/65	M			
Nicholson	Shanock		Priv	44	74.5	MD	Farmer	Dra	11/20/64	9/20/65	M			
Norris	John	A	Priv	40		VA	Laborer	Vol	9/14/63	9/29/64	K	K	9/29/64	New Market
Orrick	James		Priv	23	66	VA	Laborer	Vol	9/14/63	9/20/65	M			
Pierce	Alfred	P	Priv	33	65	PA	Driver	Sub	7/29/63	9/20/65	M			
Phillips	Benjamin	F	Priv	27	66	PA	Barber	Vol	9/14/63	9/20/65	M			
Parker	James		Priv	28	71.75	MD	Farmer	Dra	11/28/64		Abs/sick			
Pumell	Henry		Priv	34		MD	Farmer	Dra	9/20/64	9/20/65	M			
Pepenger	George	W	Priv	32	63	VA	Laborer	Sub	11/26/64	9/20/65	M			
Pierce	George		Priv	23	65	MD	Laborer	Dra	11/20/64	9/20/65	M			
Phillips	Moses		Priv	44	69.25	MD	Laborer	Dra	11/20/64	9/20/65	M			
Potts	Zion		Priv	35	68	MD	Laborer	Dra	11/20/64	9/20/65	M			
Parker	William	H	Priv	21	67.5	PA	Waiter	Dra	9/2/63	10/2/63	Des			
Queen	Joseph	N	Priv	20	64.5	VA	Laborer	Sub	11/18/64	9/20/65	M			
Rickett	Joshua		Priv	25	64.5	PA	Laborer	Dra	8/12/63	9/20/65	M			
Riley	Richard		Priv	18				Vol	9/14/63		Abs/sick			
Readcamp	George		Priv	43	63	MD	Laborer	Vol	9/25/64	9/20/65	M			
Ross	Franklin		Priv	25	72	MD	Laborer	Dra	9/20/64	9/20/65	M			
Raisins	Benjamin		Priv	37	67	MD	Laborer	Dra	9/20/64	9/20/65	M			
Riley	Beverly		Priv	19	65	VA	Farmer	Vol	9/14/63	4/14/65	Dis/Surg			
Russell	Robert		Priv	21	66.25	MD	Laborer	Sub	7/16/63	9/8/65	Died	Died	9/8/65	Wlmngtn NC
Smallwood	Daniel		Priv	20	60	MD	Farmer	Vol	9/14/63	9/20/65	M			
Smith	Henry		Priv	22	70	PA	Farmer	Dra	5/16/63	9/20/65	M			
Smith	James		Priv	26	62.5	VA	Laborer	Sub	9/21/63	9/20/65	M			

Last Name	First Name	Mid Init	Rank	Age	Hgt (in)	Birth-place	Occupation	Status	Muster-in Date	Separation Date	Separation Manner	Status	Casualty Date	Place
Simms	Charles		Priv	26	67.5	VA	Laborer	Dra	8/29/63	9/20/65	M			
Saulsbury	James		Priv	29	62.5	DE	Laborer	Sub	8/31/63	9/20/65	M			
Simpkins	William		Priv	22	70	VA	Laborer	Sub	11/17/64	9/20/65	M			
Scott	Lawrence		Priv	18	70.5	VA	Laborer	Sub	11/28/64	9/20/65	M			
Scott	Perry		Priv	39	69	MD	Laborer	Dra	11/20/64	9/20/65	M			
Simpson	James		Priv	34	68	PA	Laborer	Dra	7/16/63	6/26/65	Dis/GO			
Sterling	Gilbert		Priv	23	63	PA	Laborer	Dra	7/16/63	9/4/64	Died	Died	9/4/64	Pt Rcks VA
Steward	John		Priv	32	70	PA	Laborer	Dra	7/20/63	11/12/64	Died	Died	11/12/64	Ft Monroe
Stringer	John		Priv	31	66	VA	Farmer	Dra	7/16/63	2/22/65	Died/W	Died/W	2/22/65	Wlmngtn NC
Smith	Joseph		Priv	21	64.5	WInd	Seaman	Sub	1/3/65	5/11/65	Des			
Thorp	Stephen		Priv	24	64	DE	Laborer	Sub	9/24/63	9/20/65	M			
Turner	John		Priv	24	68.5	DE	Laborer	Dra	8/12/63	9/20/65	M			
Umphrey	Joseph	M	Priv	25	70	PA	Farmer	Vol	9/14/63	10/9/63	Des			
Wedge	George		Priv					Sub	8/27/63	9/20/65	M			
Wright	Alexander		Priv					Dra	8/12/63	6/15/64	K	K	6/15/64	Petersburg
Wilson	Anthony		Priv					Sub	9/2/63	7/10/64	Died/W	Died/W	7/10/64	Petersburg

SIXTH REGIMENT OF THE UNITED STATES COLORED INFANTRY, COMPANY H

Last Name	First Name	Mid Init	Rank	Age	Hgt (in)	Birth-place	Occupation	Status	Muster-in Date	Separation Date	Separation Manner	Status	Casualty Date	Place
Sheldon	George	W	Capt					Vol	10/8/63	9/29/64	K	K	9/29/64	New Market
Edgerton	Nathan	H	Capt					Vol	9/16/63	9/20/65	M	W	9/29/64	New Market
Landon	LaFayette		Lt1					Vol	10/5/63	9/29/64	Died/W	Died/W	9/29/64	New Market
Verplanck	Robert	N	Lt2					Vol	10/5/63	7/7/65	Rsgnd			
Blair	David		Sgt1	18	67.5	PA	Waiter	Vol	9/14/63	9/20/65	M			
Davis	Hector		Sgt	24	71	MD	Sailor	Vol	9/7/63	9/20/65	M			
Moore	Thomas		Sgt	21	65	VA	Farmer	Vol	9/4/63	9/20/65	M			
Palmer	Addison		Sgt	16	64	PA	Waiter	Vol	9/5/63	9/20/65	M			
Burrett	James		Sgt	25	69	PA	Barber	Sub	9/7/63	5/15/64	Dis/Surg			
Darrak	Solomon		Sgt	27	68	PA	Laborer	Sub	8/22/63	7/15/65	Dis/Surg			
Hall	William	H	Sgt	31	71	MD	Laborer	Dra	8/7/63	1/19/65	Dis/Surg			
Colder	John	W	Sgt	20	63	PA	Barber	Vol	9/14/63	7/24/65	Died	Died	7/24/65	Smthvll NC
Grant	Wilson		Sgt	24	65	VA	Fireman	Dra	7/10/63	10/1/64	Died/W	Died/W	10/1/64	Ft Monroe
Truman	Charles		Corp	21	65	PA	Laborer	Dra	7/16/63	9/20/65	M			

COMPANY H (*continued*)

Last Name	First Name	Mid Init	Rank	Age	Hgt (in)	Birth-place	Occupation	Status	Muster-in Date	Separation Date	Separation Manner	Status	Casualty Date	Place
Spriddle	Robert		Corp	21	65	MD	Laborer	Vol	9/14/63	9/20/65	M			
Thomas	John	H	Corp	21	63	VA	Servant	Sub	8/2/63	9/20/65	M			
Dawson	David	W	Corp	42	73	VA	Laborer	Vol	4/26/64	9/20/65	M			
Freeman	Philip		Corp	19	64	PA	Laborer	Vol	9/14/63	9/20/65	M			
Walker	Charles		Corp					Vol	9/27/64	9/20/65	M			
Perkins	Ephraim		Corp	17	66	PA	Farmer	Vol	9/5/63	9/20/65	M			
Clark	John	H	Corp	29	68.5	PA	Barber	Vol	9/14/63	9/20/65	M			
Elsbury	Isaiah		Corp	22	65	PA	Coachman	Vol	9/14/63	11/12/63	Dis/Surg			
Webster	Robert		Corp	20	70	PA	Laborer	Vol	9/14/63	9/29/64	K	K	9/29/64	New Market
Armistead	Richard	P	Corp	41	66	VA	Barber	Vol	9/7/63	2/26/64	Missing		2/26/64	
Smith	John		Corp					Sub	8/24/63	2/26/64	Missing		2/26/64	
Piner	Joseph		Corp	21	64	PA	Laborer	Sub	8/29/63	2/9/65	Des			
Bell	Samuel		Corp	21	68.5	PA	Barber	Dra	7/13/63	9/20/65	M			
Parker	Robert	G	Corp	18	63	PA	Typeman	Vol	9/7/63	9/20/65	M			
Abrams	Jacob		Priv	20	67	PA	Laborer	Dra	7/1/63	9/20/65	Abs/sick			
Allison	Francis		Priv	19	65	MA	Laborer	Vol	9/7/63	9/20/65	M			
Aston	Thomas		Priv	25	66	PA	Barber	Dra	7/13/63	9/20/65	M			
Anderson	Frank		Priv					Dra	9/17/64	9/20/65	M			
Ayers	Augustus		Priv					Vol	9/27/64	6/24/65	Dis/Surg			
Bates	Alfred		Priv	20	63	NJ	Teamster	Sub	9/7/63	9/20/65	M			
Binn	Joseph		Priv	24	67.5	NJ	Laborer	Sub	9/5/63		Abs/sick			
Binn	William		Priv	17	65	NJ	Farmer	Vol	9/14/63	9/20/65	M			
Brown	Benjamin		Priv	20	65	PA	Laborer	Dra	8/22/63	9/20/65	M			
Brown	Thomas		Priv	23	66	MD	Laborer	Dra	8/29/63	9/20/65	M			
Brown	John		Priv					Vol	1/24/65	9/20/65	M			
Barnett	Walter		Priv					Dra	10/19/64	9/20/65	M			
Bazier	Patterson		Priv					Dra	7/16/63	6/20/65	Dis/Surg			
Barrett	William	H	Priv	25	68	PA	Farmer	Dra	7/18/63	5/29/65	Dis/Surg			
Brown	Edward		Priv	21	67.5	NC	Laborer	Sub	8/21/63	12/15/64	Dis/Surg			
Brice	John		Priv	14	62	PA	Farmer	Vol	9/14/63	6/26/64	K	K	6/26/64	Ptrsbrg VA
Brice	Peter	L	Priv	21	72	PA	Farmer	Vol	9/14/63	9/29/64	K	K	9/29/64	New Market

Last Name	First Name	Mid Init	Rank	Age	Hgt (in)	Birth-place	Occupation	Status	Muster-in Date	Separation Date	Separation Manner	Status	Casualty Date	Place
Clark	Alexander		Priv	38	62	PA	Miner	Dra	7/16/63	9/20/65	M			
Colley	Ellwood		Priv	18	66	PA	Miner	Vol	9/7/63	9/20/65	M			
Colley	Abram		Priv	20	67	NJ	Farmer	Vol	9/7/63		Abs/sick			
Crummell	Samuel		Priv	29	62	NJ	Farmer	Vol	9/7/63	9/20/65	M			
Carey	James		Priv					Dra	10/12/64	9/20/65	M			
Clark	Stephen		Priv					Dra	10/15/64	9/20/65	M			
Clayton	Newton		Priv					Sub	11/11/64	9/20/65	M			
Cookman	Charles		Priv					Sub	11/16/64	9/20/65	M			
Coleman	George		Priv					Dra	10/20/64	9/20/65	M			
Crawford	William		Priv					Dra	11/15/64	9/20/65	M			
Criswell	David		Priv	28	69	PA	Laborer	Vol	9/7/63	9/29/64	K	K	9/29/64	New Market
Ditcher	George		Priv	19	71	PA	Laborer	Vol	9/14/63	9/20/65	M			
Douglass	Jacob		Priv	23	67	MD	Laborer	Vol	9/14/63	1/5/64	Dis/Surg			
Dorse	John		Priv					Sub	11/4/63	6/22/65	Died	Died	6/22/65	Wlmngtn NC
Edmonds	Samuel		Priv					Sub	11/4/64	9/20/65	M			
Enty	Peter	B	Priv	21	66	PA	Laborer	Dra	7/18/63	11/23/64	Died	Died	11/23/64	Wlmngtn NC
Enty	Peter	F	Priv	29	67.5	PA	Laborer	Vol	9/14/64	7/7/65	Died	Died	7/7/65	Wlmngtn NC
Fields	Isaac		Priv					Dra	5/13/64	9/20/65	M			
Fields	Bryson		Priv					Sub	10/25/64	9/20/65	M			
Franklin	Jarrett		Priv					Dra	5/3/64	9/20/65	M			
Gates	George		Priv					Dra	11/17/64		Abs/arr			
Gross	Eli		Priv	28	68	MD	Butcher	Vol	9/14/63	9/20/65	M			
Golden	Charles		Priv	20	67	PA	Laborer	Sub	9/2/63	7/10/64	K	K	7/10/64	Petersburg
Hubbard	Leroy	P	Priv	32	68	KY	Barber	Vol	9/7/63	9/20/65	M			
Hughes	William		Priv	22		VA	Farmer	Dra	9/2/63		Abs/sick			
Hooper	Cyrus		Priv					Vol	9/28/64	9/20/65	M			
Holland	Stephen		Priv					Dra	11/17/64	9/20/65	M			
Howard	Benjamin		Priv					Dra	11/25/64	9/20/65	M			
Henry	Leander		Priv					Sub	10/12/64	9/20/65	M			
Heintzleman	Chas		Priv					Dra	11/15/64	9/20/65	M			
Holland	George		Priv					Dra	11/19/64	9/20/65	M			
Imes	Benjamin		Priv	20	73	MD	Waiter	Dra	7/8/63	1/28/64	Dis/Surg			

COMPANY H (*continued*)

Last Name	First Name	Mid Init	Rank	Age	Hgt (in)	Birth-place	Occupation	Status	Muster-in Date	Separation Date	Separation Manner	Status	Casualty Date	Place
Johnson	John		Priv	20	63	DE	Laborer	Dra	10/19/64	9/20/65	M			
Johnson	Peter		Priv	21	64	PA	Laborer	Sub	9/25/63	9/20/65	Abs/sick			
Jones	Jacob		Priv					Sub	9/28/63	9/20/65	M			
Jones	Isaac		Priv					Vol	9/28/63	9/20/65	M			
Jefferson	John		Priv					Vol	2/4/65	9/20/65	M			
Jefferson	James		Priv	21	66	PA		Dra	7/21/63		Abs/sick			
Johnson	Charles		Priv	21	69	PA	Laborer	Sub	9/4/63	5/22/64	Dis/Surg			
Jenkins	John		Priv	20	67	PA	Laborer	Dra	7/16/63	6/22/64	Died	Died	6/22/64	Petersburg
James	Charles	H	Priv					Vol	9/22/64	1/16/65	Died	Died	1/16/65	Moorfld WV
Johnson	Samuel	I	Priv					Sub	9/4/63	9/13/63	Des			
Johnson	Shadwick		Priv	21	69	PA	Laborer	Sub	9/9/63	9/13/63	Des			
Keith	Wilson		Priv					Vol	1/24/65	9/20/65	M			
Lovett	Josiah		Priv	25	71	PA	Laborer	Dra	7/18/63	9/20/65	M			
Laboo	Levi		Priv	26	66.5	PA	Laborer	Sub	8/10/63	9/20/65	M			
Lewis	John		Priv					Sub	12/27/64	9/20/65	Abs/DtSrv			
Lucas	Edward		Priv	21	67	VA	Farmer	Sub	7/16/63	11/9/63	Dis/Surg			
Lloyd	Edward		Priv	35	61	PA	Laborer	Sub	9/7/63	1/28/64	Dis/Surg			
Morgan	Henry		Priv	33	68	PA	Barber	Dra	8/29/63	9/20/65	M			
Morris	Hyland		Priv	18	64	NJ	Laborer	Vol	9/8/63	9/20/65	M			
Murphy	Robert	M	Priv	25	68	PA	Miner	Vol	9/4/63	9/20/65	M			
Naylor	Thomas		Priv	24	68	VA	Miner	Dra	7/10/63	1/5/65	Dis/Surg			
Palmer	George		Priv	17	67	PA	Laborer	Vol	9/4/63	9/20/65	M			
Perkins	George		Priv	18	65	PA	Wagonier	Vol	9/5/63	9/20/65	M			
Perry	Major		Priv	26	67	NJ	Laborer	Dra	8/21/63	9/20/65	M			
Pennington	Sam'l		Priv	22	68	NJ	Laborer	Vol	9/7/63	6/15/64	Died	Died	6/15/64	Ft Monroe
Poters	Jason		Priv	23	66	VA	Laborer	Sub	9/3/63	1/7/65	Died	Died	1/7/65	Pt Rcks VA
Pryor	Charley		Priv	32	66	PA	Laborer	Sub	8/22/63	9/29/64	K	K	9/29/64	New Market
Roberts	Jacob		Priv	18	68.5	PA	Farmer	Vol	9/14/63	9/20/65	M			
Rolland	George		Priv	22	58.5	PA	Laborer	Sub	9/8/63	5/17/65	Dis/Surg			
Scott	Jackson		Priv	27	62.5	PA	Blacksmith	Sub	8/14/63	9/20/65	M			
Smith	James		Priv	24	64	MD	Shoemaker	Dra	8/9/63	9/20/65	Abs/sick			

Last Name	First Name	Mid Init	Rank	Age	Hgt (in)	Birth-place	Occupation	Status	Muster-in Date	Separation Date	Separation Manner	Status	Casualty Date	Place
Semple	John		Priv	21	66	DE	Laborer	Vol	4/20/64	9/20/65	M			
Steel	John	A	Priv	19	65	PA	Farmer	Vol	9/16/63	10/27/64	Died/W	Died/W	10/27/64	
Till	Anthony		Priv					Sub	9/27/64	9/20/65	M			
Tyler	Henry		Priv					Sub	11/4/64	9/20/65	M			
Thomas	Henry		Priv					Vol	2/10/65		Abs/sick			
Thompson	Daniel		Priv	17	66.5	PA		Vol	9/14/63	5/15/64	Dis/Surg			
Taylor	Charles		Priv	17	67.5	PA	Barber	Vol	9/14/63	6/9/64	K	K	6/9/64	Petersburg
Viney	Franklin		Priv	25	64	PA	Coachman	Vol	9/7/63	9/20/65	M			
Webster	Reason		Priv	18	64	PA	Laborer	Vol	9/4/63	9/20/65	M			
Wade	William		Priv					Dra	10/21/64	9/20/65	M			
Wallace	Morris		Priv					Sub	10/27/64	9/20/65	M			
Webb	James		Priv					Dra	10/19/64	9/20/65	M			
Williams	Samuel		Priv					Dra	10/31/64	9/20/65	M			
Williams	James	E	Priv					Sub	11/14/64	9/20/65	M			
Wilson	John		Priv	17	65	PA	Boatman	Sub	9/7/63	3/25/65	Des			

SIXTH REGIMENT OF THE UNITED STATES COLORED INFANTRY, COMPANY I

Last Name	First Name	Mid Init	Rank	Age	Hgt (in)	Birth-place	Occupation	Status	Muster-in Date	Separation Date	Separation Manner	Status	Casualty Date	Place
Weinman	Philip		Capt					Vol	10/5/63	2/27/66	Died	Died	2/27/66	Ft Macon
Devereux	John	F	Capt					Vol	1/1/65	9/20/65	M			
Landon	LaFayette		Lt1					Vol	10/5/63		Trnsfrd			
Grow	Alonzo	W	Lt1					Vol	10/5/63	9/20/65	M			
McEvoy	William	H	Lt2					Vol	3/30/64	11/9/64	Died/W	Died/W	11/9/64	New Market
Ballou	Wayland		Lt2					Vol	2/9/65	9/20/65	M			
Terry	Charles	L	Sgt1	20	83	VA	Barber	Dra	9/10/63	9/20/65	M			
Maxfield	William		Sgt	30	64	DE	Laborer	Dra	8/12/63	9/20/65	M			
Collons	Simon	C	Sgt	26	64	PA	Barber	Dra	8/13/63	9/20/65	M			
Fisher	George		Sgt	31	66	DE	Laborer	Dra	7/22/63	9/20/65	M			
Robinson	Edward		Sgt	23	67.5	DE	Laborer	Dra	8/12/63	9/20/65	M			
Deets	Charles	H	Sgt	25	67	PA	Boatman	Dra	9/10/63	11/7/63	Died	Died	11/7/63	Yrktwn VA
Williams	George		Corp	22	66.5	DE	Laborer	Dra	8/12/63	9/20/65	M			
Anderson	Elias		Corp	20	65	PA	Laborer	Dra	9/10/63	9/20/65	M			
Peters	Charles		Corp	20	62.5	DE	Laborer	Dra	8/12/63	9/20/65	M			
Davis	Lewis		Corp	22	69	DE	Laborer	Dra	8/12/63	9/20/65	M			

COMPANY I (*continued*)

Last Name	First Name	Mid Init	Rank	Age	Hgt (in)	Birth-place	Occupation	Status	Muster-in Date	Separation Date	Separation Manner	Status	Casualty Date	Place
Barton	John		Corp	22	63.5	G.B.	Waiter	Sub	1/6/65	9/20/65	M			
Richardson	Henry		Corp	29	67.625	PA	Laborer	Sub	9/9/63	9/20/65	M			
Richardson	George		Corp	25	64	PA	Tailor	Sub	9/3/63	9/20/65	M			
Palmer	James	C	Corp	24	61.75	PA	Laborer	Sub	9/10/63	5/26/65	Dis/Surg			
Worrace	Alfred		Musn	19	65	NJ	Waiter	Vol	9/11/63	9/20/65	M			
Anderson	Robert		Priv	38	60	VA	Laborer	Dra	11/24/64	9/20/65	M			
Allen	George		Priv	30	65.5	MD	Laborer	Dra	11/23/64	9/20/65	M			
Anderson	Wm	H	Priv	24	61	NJ	Farmer	Sub	9/10/63	2/3/65	Died	Died		Ft Fshr NC
Butler	Robert		Priv	21	63	VA	Laborer	Sub	9/11/63	9/20/65	M			
Boyer	Joseph		Priv	20	63	DE	Laborer	Dra	8/12/63	9/20/65	M			
Boulden	James		Priv	21	65.5	DE	Laborer	Dra	8/12/63	9/20/65	M			
Boulden	Elijah		Priv	19	64.5	PA	Laborer	Vol	9/11/63	9/20/65	M			
Brown	Wilson		Priv	22	65	NY	Laborer	Vol	10/22/64	9/20/65	M			
Bostick	Isaac		Priv	24	70	DE	Laborer	Dra	8/13/63	4/15/65	Dis/Surg			
Badger	William		Priv	42	67	DE	Laborer	Dra	8/12/63		Dis/Surg			
Brown	John		Priv	28	70	PA	Sailor	Vol	11/11/64	4/1/65	Des			
Blackstone	Henry		Priv	23	68	DE	Laborer	Sub	9/9/63	9/29/64	K	K	9/29/64	New Market
Brisco	William		Priv	23	64	DE	Laborer	Vol	9/11/63	9/29/64	K	K	9/29/64	New Market
Cooper	Ebenezer		Priv					Vol		9/20/65	M			
Cromady	John		Priv	17	63	NC		Vol	3/14/65	9/20/65	M			
Cromady	Peter		Priv	18	61.5	NC		Vol	3/14/65	9/20/65	M			
Cromady	James		Priv	18	65	NC		Vol	3/14/65	9/20/65	M			
Cooper	George		Priv	22	71.75	NJ	Laborer	Sub	9/11/63	4/19/65	Dis/Surg			
Clark	Alexander		Priv	23	66	DE	Laborer	Dra	8/12/63	9/29/64	K	K	9/29/64	New Market
Couders	William		Priv	21	65	DE	Laborer	Vol	9/11/63	12/7/64	Died	Died	12/7/64	
Draper	Alexander		Priv	24	66.5	DE	Farmer	Vol	9/11/63	9/20/65	M			
Davis	Henry		Priv	25	71	DE	Laborer	Dra	8/12/63	9/20/65	M			
Dayton	James		Priv	24	70	DE	Laborer	Dra	8/12/63	5/30/65	Dis/GO			
Duckery	John		Priv	36	67	DE	Laborer	Dra	8/12/63	11/18/63	Dis/Surg			
Duncan	George		Priv	19	67	NJ	Laborer	Vol	9/11/63	2/1/64	Died	Died	2/1/64	YrktwnVA
Empson	William		Priv	28	61	DE	Laborer	Vol	8/13/63	10/2/64	Died/W	Died/W	10/2/64	Ft Monroe
Frisbee	James		Priv	25	67	DE	Laborer	Sub	9/18/63	8/25/65	Died	Died	8/25/65	Wlmngtn NC

Last Name	First Name	Mid Init	Rank	Age	Hg. (in)	Birth-Place	Occupation	Status	Muster-in Date	Separation Date	Separation Manner	Status	Casualty Date	Place
Guy	William		Priv	31	65.5	DE	Laborer	Sub	9/4/63	9/20/65	M			
Goldsbury	Alexander		Priv	25	63	MD	Laborer	Dra	8/13/63	9/20/65	M			
Griffin	Hiram		Priv	27	67	Can	Laborer	Vol	10/15/64	9/20/65	M			
Henderson	George		Priv	20	66	PA	Waterman	Sub	8/12/63	9/20/65	M			
Harris	George		Priv	21	67.75	NJ	Tobacconist	Sub	9/11/63		Abs/sick			
Harris	Wm	D	Priv	20	63	DE	Driver	Dra	9/1/63	9/20/65	M			
Hampton	Edward		Priv	21	64.75	NJ	Farmer	Sub	9/7/63	9/20/65	M			
Hicks	James		Priv	21	66	PA	Laborer	Dra	8/12/63	6/6/65	Dis/GO			
Hale	William		Priv	20	66.5	DE	Laborer	Dra	8/12/63	1/28/65	Dis/Surg			
Jones	Benjamin		Priv	33	65	TN	Laborer	Vol	10/11/64	9/20/65	M			
Johnson	Robert		Priv	32	69	PA	Farmer	Sub	9/10/63		Abs/W	W		
Johnson	Moses		Priv	22	65	PA	Farmer	Vol	9/10/63	9/20/65	M			
Johnson	George		Priv	19	62.5	VA	Laborer	Dra	11/11/64	9/20/65	M			
Jones	Charles	W	Priv	22	63	PA	Barber	Dra	7/29/63	1/8/64	Dis/GCM			
Jackson	John		Priv	29	66	DE	Laborer	Dra	8/12/63	11/18/63	Dis/Surg			
Justice	Levy		Priv	25	68	DE	Laborer	Sub	8/12/63	5/15/65	Ds/GO			
Justice	George		Priv	26	64.5	PA	Laborer	Dra	7/24/63	5/24/65	Died	Died	5/24/65	Raleigh
Jones	James		Priv	21	63	VA	Drayman	Dra	7/28/63	6/15/64	Died/W	Died/W	6/15/64	
Johnson	Henry	G	Priv	24	69	NY	Waiter	Vol	10/9/64	3/15/65	Des			
Johnson	Adolphus		Priv	20	63.5	DE	Laborer	Sub	9/18/63	12/25/64	Des			
Long	Robert		Priv	23	67	PA	Laborer	Dra	7/24/63	9/20/65	M			
Lewis	Solomon		Priv	20	66.5	DE	Laborer	Dra	8/12/63		Abs/sick			
Lloyd	Samuel		Priv	25	69	DE	Laborer	Dra	8/12/63	12/7/64	Died	Died	12/7/64	Pt Rcks VA
Lovett	Benjamin		Priv	20	65	NC	Farmer	Vol	12/11/64	3/15/65	Died	Died	3/15/65	
Moore	Robert		Priv	34	68	DE	Laborer	Dra	8/12/63	9/20/65	M			
Morris	David		Priv	20	62.5	DE	Laborer	Dra	8/12/63	9/20/65	M			
Martin	Thomas		Priv	30	68	Can	Laborer	Vol	10/11/64	9/20/65	M			
McEntire	Patrick		Priv	17	69	NC	Laborer	Vol	3/14/65	9/20/65	M			
O'Brian	James		Priv	20	71	NY	Laborer	Vol	12/3/64	9/20/65	M			
Price	John		Priv	31	65.5	DE	Laborer	Sub	9/8/63	1/6/65	Dis/GO			
Patterson	Hartshorn		Priv	32	66	PA	Laborer	Dra	8/13/63	5/28/65	Dis/Surg			
Porter	George		Priv	20	65.5	MD	Laborer	Dra	8/12/63	6/12/65	Dis/GO			

COMPANY I (*continued*)

Last Name	First Name	Mid Init	Rank	Age	Hgt (in)	Birth-place	Occupation	Status	Muster-in Date	Separation Date	Separation Manner	Status	Casualty Date	Place
Pryor	Emory		Priv	26	63	DE	Farmer	Vol	9/11/63	7/15/65	Died	Died	7/15/65	Wlmngtn NC
Rhodes	Perry		Priv	20	69	MD	Laborer	Dra	8/13/63	9/20/65	M	K	9/29/64	New Market
Robinson	James		Priv	24	63	PA	Laborer	Sub	9/3/63	9/29/64	K	K	8/2/64	Petersburg
Robinson	Henry		Priv	28	65	PA	Barber	Dra	8/14/63	8/2/64	K	Died	9/3/64	Ft Monroe
Rogers	Alexander		Priv	21	66	DE	Laborer	Dra	8/13/63	9/3/64	Died			
Shorter	George	M	Priv	30	66.5	PA	Laborer	Dra	8/14/63	9/20/65	M			
Smith	Daniel	W	Priv	22	65	PA	Laborer	Dra	8/13/63		Abs/sick			
Smith	James		Priv	20	67.5	DE	Laborer	Sub	9/8/63	9/20/65	M			
Smith	William		Priv	19	66.5	NY	Laborer	Vol	12/5/64	9/20/65	M			
Spencer	Wilson		Priv	35	64	DE	Laborer	Dra	8/14/63	9/20/65	M			
Simmons	George		Priv	24	66	NC	Cook	Vol	10/29/64	9/20/65	M			
Singer	Joseph		Priv	20	-67.5	MD	Laborer	Sub	9/8/63		Abs/sick			
Snowden	Wm	H	Priv	32	71	MD	Laborer	Dra	11/25/64	9/20/65	M			
Stookley	Noah		Priv	36	70	MD	Laborer	Dra	9/20/64	9/20/65	M			
Somerville	Joseph		Priv	30	68.25	MD	Laborer	Dra	11/25/64	9/20/65	M			
Scott	Isaac		Priv	19	66	SC	Laborer	Vol	10/29/64	9/20/65	M			
Scott	Henry		Priv	24	70	MD	Laborer	Vol	10/6/64	9/20/65	M			
Sampson	Charles		Priv	22	69	MD	Laborer	Dra	8/12/63	5/23/65	Dis/Surg			
Simmons	Wm	T	Priv	19	63	DE	Farmer	Dra	8/12/63	12/14/64	Dis/Surg			
Scott	Caleb		Priv	21	67.5	DE	Laborer	Dra	8/12/63	7/8/64	Died	Died	7/8/64	PtRcks VA
Smith	William	2d	Priv	21	67.5	VA	Laborer	Dra	11/12/64	6/18/65	Des			
Taylor	Lewis		Priv	27	67.5	MD	Laborer	Dra	8/12/63	9/20/65	M			
Taylor	Thomas		Priv	33	67	MD	Laborer	Dra	9/20/64	9/20/65	M			
Truitt	Caleb		Priv	24	67.5	DE	Laborer	Dra	8/12/63		Abs/sick			
Tippett	Samuel		Priv	24	65	DE	Laborer	Dra	8/10/63					
Turner	Thomas		Priv	28	65	DE	Laborer	Dra	9/25/64	9/20/65	M			
Tyddings	Wm	J	Priv	40	69	MD	Blacksmith	Dra	9/20/64	9/20/65	M			
Thomas	Thomas		Priv	28	67.75	MD	Laborer	Dra	9/20/64	9/20/65	M			
Thomas	Daniel		Priv	43	67.5	MD	Laborer	Dra	9/24/64	5/10/65	Died	Died	5/10/65	
Williams	William		Priv	21	72	DE	Laborer	Dra	8/12/63	9/20/65	M			
Williams	Isaac		Priv	21	60	DE	Laborer	Dra	8/11/63	9/20/65	M			

Last Name	First Name	Mid Init	Rank	Age	Hgt (in)	Birth-place	Occupation	Status	Muster-in Date	Separation Date	Manner	Status	Casualty Date	Place
Warner	Daniel		Priv	23	69	MD	Laborer	Dra	9/24/64	9/20/65	M			
Wallace	Joseph		Priv	27	67	MD	Laborer	Dra	9/29/64	9/20/65	M			
Webb	Asbury		Priv	35	67.5	MD	Laborer	Dra	9/19/64	9/20/65	M			
West	Frank		Priv	18	63	VA	Laborer	Sub	3/23/64		Abs/sick			
Wright	James		Priv	34	63.5	NC	Laborer	Dra	3/28/64		Abs/sick			
Williams	Caleb		Priv	20	64	DE	Laborer	Sub	3/22/64	9/20/65	M			
Wilson	Hezekiah		Priv	33	68.75	DE	Shoemaker	Dra	6/25/63	9/20/65	M			
Watson	William		Priv	31	69	DE	Farmer	Vol	9/10/63		Promoted			
Willson	George		Priv	18	66	FA	Laborer	Vol	6/23/63	12/25/64	Des			
Wright	Adam		Priv				Laborer	Vol	3/14/64	6/1/65	Des			
Young	Anthony		Priv	32	65.5	DE	Laborer	Dra	8/12/63	7/14/64	Died	Died	7/14/64	Pt Rcks VA

SIXTH REGIMENT OF THE UNITED STATES COLORED INFANTRY, COMPANY K

Last Name	First Name	Mid Init	Rank	Age	Hgt (in)	Birth-place	Occupation	Status	Muster-in Date	Separation Date	Manner	Status	Casualty Date	Place
Riley	Girard	P	Capt					Vol	10/6/63	9/20/65	M			
Woodward	James		Lt1					Vol	10/6/63	8/10/67	Dis			
Lovewell	Baron	P	Lt1					Vol	10/6/63	9/20/65	M			
Golding	Joseph	H	Lt2					Vol	10/5/63		Det ser			
Campbell	Abraham		Sgt1	22	67	MD	Barber	Dra	7/9/63	9/20/65	M			
Hazzard	Wm	H	Sgt1	25	70	DE	Laborer	Dra	8/13/63	12/30/64	Died/W	Died/W	12/30/64	Pt Rcks VA
Garner	Charles		Sgt	19	65	PA	Laborer	Sub	9/8/63	9/20/65	M			
Henry	James		Sgt	37	71.5	PA	Farmer	Dra	9/11/63	9/20/65	M			
Pattern	Charles		Sgt	21	63	DE	Farmer	Dra	8/13/63	9/20/65	M			
Keith	Martin		Sgt	32	70	PA	Laborer	Dra	9/11/63	11/4/64	Died	Died	11/4/64	Ft Monroe
Ramer	Edward		Corp	18	67	NC	Laborer	Sub	9/10/63	9/20/65	Abs/hsp	W	9/29/64	
Henry	Alexander		Corp	30	60	DE	Laborer	Dra	8/13/63	9/20/65	M			
Bowen	David		Corp	28	72	MD	Hackman	Dra	8/7/63	9/20/65	M			
Stevely	Richard	M	Corp	21	69	NC	Farmer	Vol	3/15/65	9/20/65	M			
Johnson	Henry		Corp	25	73	DE	Laborer	Sub	9/10/63	9/20/65	M			
Green	Alexander		Corp	26	68	PA	Laborer	Dra	8/13/63	9/20/65	M			
Harris	Thomas		Corp	24	70	DE	Laborer	Dra	8/13/63	9/20/65	M			
Sebell	John		Corp	19	69.5	VA	Laborer	Sub	12/6/64	9/20/65	M			
Campbell	James		Corp	21	67	PA	Laborer	Sub	7/16/63		Dis			

COMPANY K (*continued*)

Last Name	First Name	Mid Init	Rank	Age	Hgt (in)	Birth-place	Occupation	Status	Muster-in Date	Separation Date	Manner	Status	Casualty Date	Place
Doran	Harrison		Corp	25	66	PA	Laborer	Vol	9/12/63		Dis	Died		
Miller	Wesley		Corp	36	64	PA	Laborer	Dra	8/13/63		Died	Died		
Williams	William		Corp						8/13/63	1/19/65	Died	Died/W	1/19/65	Ft Monroe
Berry	Vincent		Corp	31	67.5	DE	Farmer	Dra	8/13/63	9/2/64	Died/W		9/2/64	
Loper	John		Musn					Dra	8/13/63	9/20/65	M			
Meads	David		Musn	15		PA	Laborer	Vol	9/12/63		Abs/sick			
Adams	John		Priv	23	63.5	S.I.	Sailor	Sub	1/3/63	9/20/65	M			
Boo	David		Priv	25	68	DE	Farmer	Dra	8/13/63	9/20/65	M			
Briskey	John		Priv	30	67	MD	Laborer	Dra	12/7/64	9/20/65	M			
Bailey	Lewis		Priv	26	65	MD	Laborer	Dra	12/7/64	9/20/65	M			
Brent	Elsie		Priv	37	64.5	VA	Laborer	Dra	12/6/64	9/20/65	M			
Brown	Charles		Priv	22	63.5	VA	Laborer	Sub	12/1/64	9/20/65	M			
Buckner	Humph'y		Priv	30	64.5	VA	Laborer	Sub	12/6/64		Abs/sick			
Berry	Charles		Priv	21	68	DE	Farmer	Dra	8/13/63	9/20/65	M			
Brister	William		Priv	25	68	DE	Laborer	Dra	8/18/63		Dis			
Borton	Harrison		Priv	23	68	DE	Laborer	Dra	9/11/63	3/21/65	Died	Died	3/21/65	Wlmngtn NC
Brown	Salvador	H	Priv	26	67	PA	Mechanic	Sub	12/7/64	10/8/63	Des			
Crump	William		Priv	22	64	VA	Laborer	Dra	12/8/64	9/20/65	M			
Compton	William		Priv	20	64	MD	Laborer	Dra	8/13/63	9/20/65	M			
Cork	Hezekiah		Priv	20	69	DE	Laborer	Dra	12/8/64	9/20/65	M			
Cobb	Samuel		Priv	28	68.5	VA	Laborer	Sub	8/13/63		Abs/sick			
Cortin	David		Priv	20	66	DE	Laborer	Dra	8/13/63	6/11/65	Dis/Surg			
Cooper	Alfred		Priv	35	65	DE	Farmer	Dra	8/13/63		Dis			
Cannon	John	H	Priv	25	70	DE	Laborer	Dra	9/10/63		Dis			
Davis	Peter		Priv	21	65	DE	Laborer	Sub	12/8/64	9/20/65	M			
Day	Nathaniel		Priv	40	65.5	MD	Laborer	Dra	12/7/64	9/20/65	M			
Dorson	Isaac		Priv	41	65	VA	Laborer	Sub	1/3/63	9/20/65	M			
Douglass	John		Priv	21	62	Can	Sailor	Sub	9/11/63	9/20/65	M			
Dorsey	James		Priv	20	69	PA	Laborer	Sub	8/13/63	6/15/65	Died	Died	6/15/65	City Pt VA
Emory	William		Priv	30	68	DE	Laborer	Dra	3/11/65		Abs/sick			
Emory	Samuel		Priv	35	65	DE	Laborer	Dra		3/11/65	Died	Died	3/11/65	Wlmngtn NC

Last Name	First Name	Mid Init	Rank	Age	Hgt (in)	Birth-place	Occupation	Status	Muster-in Date	Separation Date	Separation Manner	Status	Casualty Date	Place
Emory	James		Priv	21	65	DE	Farmer	Dra	8/13/63	2/7/65	Died	Died	2/7/65	Pt Rcks VA
Fisher	Benjamin		Priv	36	70	DE	Labcrer	Dra	8/13/63	5/29/65	Died	Died	5/29/65	Wlmngtn NC
Green	William		Priv	20	69	DE	Labcrer	Dra	8/13/63	9/20/65	M			
Gales	Isaac		Priv	24	70	DE	Labcrer	Dra	8/13/63	9/20/65	M			
Gettis	James		Priv	22	66	DE	Labcrer	Dra	8/13/63	9/20/65	M			
Gaunt	Paul		Priv	20	66	MD	Labcrer	Sub	12/3/64	9/20/65	M			
Gales	Joseph		Priv	28	70	DE	Laborer	Dra	8/13/64	1/19/65	K	K	1/19/65	Sgr Lf Hl NC
Goodman	Cater		Priv	24	65.5	NC	Laborer	Sub	12/7/64	5/10/65	Died	Died	5/10/65	Ft Monroe
Howard	John		Priv	24	66	DE	Laborer	Dra	8/13/63	9/20/65	M			
Hall	John	B	Priv	25	66	DE	Laborer	Dra	8/13/63	9/20/65	M			
Hubbardson	Isaac		Priv	24	69	DE	Laborer	Dra	8/13/63		Ats/sick			
Henderson	George		Priv	21	67	PA	Laborer	Dra	9/11/63	9/20/65	M			
Holt	Benjamin		Priv	24	65	DE	Laborer	Sub	9/10/63	9/20/65	M			
Hubbard	Isaac		Priv	26	72	MD	Farmer	Sub	9/10/63	9/20/65	M			
Hanson	George		Priv	30	67	PA	Laborer	Dra	12/7/64	9/20/65	M			
Hawkins	John		Priv	21	63	MD	Laborer	Dra	9/26/64	9/20/65	M			
Hawkins	James		Priv	24	63	Eng	Sailor	Sub	1/2/64	9/20/65	M			
Henry	Joseph		Priv	24	70	DE	Laborer	Dra	8/13/63		Dis			
Hamilton	Perry		Priv	21	70	DE	Laborer	Dra	8/13/63		Died	Died		Ft Monroe
Johnson	John	H	Priv	20	66	DE	Laborer	Sub	9/10/63	9/20/65	M			
Johnson	Franklin		Priv	20	67	PA	Farmer	Dra	8/13/63	9/20/65	M			
Jackson	Lewis		Priv	21	66	VA	Laborer	Sub	12/1/64	8/10/65	Died	Died	8/10/65	Wlmngtn NC
Kee	Henry	C	Priv	38	65	DE	Laborer	Dra	8/13/63	9/20/65	Abs/sick			
Loat	James		Priv	20	62	DE	Laborer	Dra	8/13/63	9/20/65	M			
Lockeman	Perry		Priv	23	65	DE	Laborer	Dra	8/13/63	9/20/65	M			
Lewis	James		Priv	24	67	DE	Laborer	Dra	8/13/63	9/20/65	M			
Lewis	Charles		Priv	22	65	DE	Laborer	Sub	9/19/63	9/20/65	M			
Lee	Isaac		Priv	30	65	DE	Laborer	Dra	8/13/63	6/16/65	Dis/Surg			
Lewis	William	H	Priv	19	67	VA	Laborer	Vol	10/8/63	9/29/64	K	K	9/29/64	New Market
Manuel	Franklin		Priv	18	66	PA	Laborer	Vol	10/8/63	9/20/65	M			
Madden	Wesley		Priv	21	65	DE	Laborer	Dra	8/12/63		Abs/sick			
Manbool	James		Priv	25	70	DE	Laborer	Dra	8/13/63	9/20/65	M			

COMPANY K (*continued*)

Last Name	First Name	Mid Init	Rank	Age	Hgt (in)	Birth-place	Occupation	Status	Muster-in Date	Separation Date	Separation Manner	Status	Casualty Date	Place
Maxwell	Lewis		Priv	25	70	DE	Farmer	Dra	8/13/63	9/20/65	M	W	9/29/64	New Market
Mills	Edward		Priv	35	65	PA	Laborer	Dra	8/13/63	9/20/65	Abs/hsp			
Motley	William		Priv	20	68.5	VA	Laborer	Sub	12/1/64	9/20/65	M			
Molten	Robert		Priv	18	66	VA	Laborer	Sub	12/7/64	9/20/65	M			
Mattie	Isaac		Priv	25	65	DE	Laborer	Sub	9/10/63		Dis			
Morris	Charles		Priv	25	68	DE	Farmer	Dra	8/13/63		Dis			
Mifflin	Charles		Priv	28	60	PA	Farmer	Sub	9/11/63	6/5/65	Dis/GO			
Potter	James		Priv	30	68	DE	Laborer	Sub	9/11/63	9/20/65	M			
Pernell	Isaac		Priv	22	67	DE	Laborer	Sub	9/11/63		Abs/hsp	W	9/29/64	New Market
Pierce	Noah		Priv	34	69	DE	Farmer	Dra	8/13/63	9/20/65	M			
Pine	John	E	Priv	20	65	VA	Chimney Swp	Sub	9/13/63	9/20/65	M			
Payne	Thomas		Priv	25	64.5	VA	Laborer	Dra	12/1/64	9/20/65	M			
Rias	Joseph		Priv	35	65	DE	Laborer	Sub	9/12/63	9/20/65	M			
Richardson	Isaac		Priv	20	68	DE	Laborer	Sub	9/9/63		Dis			
Robertson	Isaac		Priv	26	66	PA	Laborer	Sub	9/11/63	7/26/65	Dis/Surg			
Short	John		Priv	29	65	PA	Ship Carpntr	Sub	9/11/63	9/20/65	M			
Snowden	Wm	E	Priv	22	68	MD	Laborer	Sub	9/10/63	9/20/65	M			
Stewart	Frederick		Priv	21	67	VA	Laborer	Sub	12/6/64	9/20/65	M			
Smith	William		Priv	21	67.5	VA	Laborer	Vol	11/2/64	9/20/65	M			
Simpson	Thomas		Priv	20	65	NC	Laborer	Vol	3/13/65	9/20/65	M			
Starkey	Jacob		Priv	38	69	DE	Laborer	Dra	8/13/63	6/26/65	Dis/GO			
Simpson	Robert		Priv	25	66	NC	Laborer	Vol	3/12/65	4/20/65	Des			
Smith	Henry		Priv	30	70	MO	Laborer	Sub	12/2/64		Dis			
Tucker	Aaron		Priv	20	63	MD	Laborer	Dra	12/8/64	9/20/65	M			
Tucker	David		Priv	30	64.5	VA	Laborer	Sub	12/3/64	9/20/65	M			
Thompson	Joseph		Priv	20	65.5	Can	Boatman	Sub	1/3/65	9/20/65	M			
Till	John		Priv	23	65	DE	Laborer	Dra	8/12/63	6/26/65	Dis/GO			
Thomas	Alfred		Priv	19	64.5	MD	Laborer	Dra	12/6/64	8/12/65	Died	Died	8/12/65	Wlmngtn NC
Thomas	William		Priv	32	67.5	DE	Laborer	Sub	9/12/63		Des			
Williams	Elijah		Priv	26	64	DE	Laborer	Dra	9/13/63	9/20/65	M			
Williams	Charles		Priv	28	68	DE	Laborer	Sub	9/9/63	9/20/65	M			

Last Name	First Name	Mid Init	Rank	Age	Hgt (in)	Birth-place	Occupation	Status	Muster-in Date	Separation Date	Separation Manner	Status	Casualty Date	Place
White	James		Priv					Sub	9/12/63	9/20/65	M			
Wright	James	A	Priv					Vol	11/23/64	9/20/65	M			
Washington	Sam'l		Priv					Sub	12/5/64	9/20/65	M			
Walker	John	H	Priv					Vol	3/18/65	9/20/65	M			
Williams	Jacob		Priv					Dra	8/13/63	9/20/65	M			
Ward	William	H	Priv	25	64	DE	Laborer	Dra	8/12/63		Dis			
Williams	Richard		Priv	27	69	DE	Laborer	Dra	8/13/63	5/16/65	Dis/Surg			
Weams	Thomas		Priv					Sub	12/3/64	6/26/65	Died	Died	6/26/65	Wlmngtn NC
Williams	Jose'h	H	Priv					Sub	9/11/63		Died	Died		
Watters	Albert		Priv					Sub	9/11/63	9/29/64	K	K	9/29/64	New Market
Wilson	James		Priv					Sub	1/7/65	7/18/65	Des			

SIXTH REGIMENT OF THE UNITED STATES COLORED INFANTRY, UNASSIGNED MEN

Last Name	First Name	Mid Init	Rank	Age	Hgt (in)	Birth-place	Occupation	Status	Muster-in Date	Separation Date	Separation Manner	Status	Casualty Date	Place
Laws	James		Priv					Vol	4/4/65	6/15/65	Dis/GO			
Phillips	Albert		Priv					Vol	3/15/65	9/20/65	Dis/GO			

NOTES

CHAPTER 1 — BACKGROUND

1. Roy P. Basler, ed., *The Collected Works of Abraham Lincoln*, 9 vols. (New Brunswick, N.J.: Rutgers University Press, 1953–1955) V, 357; Dudley T. Cornish, *The Sable Arm: Negro Troops in the Union Army* (New York: Longmans Green and Co., 1956) from *The New York Tribune*, Aug. 5, 1862, V, 50–51, from *The New York Times*, Aug. 6, 1862.

2. James M. McPherson, *The Negro's Civil War: How American Negroes Felt and Acted During the War for the Union* (New York: Vintage Books, 1965), 19–20.

3. Ibid., 20–21.

4. Ibid., 22; and William Wells Brown, *The Negro in the American Rebellion: His Heroism and His Fidelity* (New York: Lee & Shepard, 1867, Reprint, New York: Johnson Reprint Corporation, 1968), 100–108.

5. Ibid., 22; and Cornish, 6, quoting from Horace Greeley, *The American Conflict: A History of the Great Rebellion in the United States of America*, 2 vols. (Hartford: O. D. Case & Co., 1866), II, 514, 515.

6. Cornish, 6–7, quoting from Frederick Phisterer, Comp., *New York in the War of the Rebellion, 1861–1865*, Third Edition, 5 vols. (Albany: J. B. Lyon Co. 1912), I, 22.

7. Brown, 54.

8. William Lloyd Garrison to Aaron M. Powell, May 14, 1861, *Miscellaneous Manuscripts Collection*, Library, Swarthmore College.

9. McPherson, 17–17, quoting *Douglass' Monthly*, III (May 1861), 450.

10. Basler, V, 48–49.

11. Ibid., V, 342–43.

12. Francis B. Carpenter, *Six Months in the White House With President Lincoln* (New York: Hurd & Houghton, 1866), 13.

13. Joseph T. Glatthaar, *Forged in Battle: The Civil War Alliance of Black Soldiers and White Officers* (New York: The Free Press, Collier Macmillan, 1990), 7.

14. Basler, VI, 28–30.

15. Carpenter, 22.

16. Cornish, 95–96.

17. Ibid., 32, from *The War of the Rebellion: A Compilation of the Official Records of the Union and Confederate Armies*, Four Series, 70 vols. in 128 vols. (Washington: Government Printing Office, 1880–1891), 1 ser., VI, 264 (hereafter cited as OR).

18. For a history of the First South Carolina Regiment see Thomas Wentwork Higginson, *Army Life in a Black Regiment* (Boston: Beacon Press, 1962).

19. Cornish, 66, citing OR, 3 ser., II, 436–37.

20. Ibid., 69–73.

CHAPTER 2—RECRUITMENT

1. Luis F. Emilio, *A Brave Black Regiment: History of the Fifty–Fourth Regiment of Massachusetts Volunteer Infantry* (Boston: Boston Book Company, 1894), 9.
2. Emilio, 9.
3. Frank H. Taylor, *Philadelphia in the Civil War 1861–1865* (Philadelphia: Published by the City, 1913), 187, from *The Philadelphia Inquirer*, June 26, 1863.
4. Ibid., 9–11.
5. Ibid., 10.
6. Ibid., 12.
7. Ibid., 26.
8. McPherson, 255, quoting *Douglass' Monthly*, IV (Feb. 1862), 593.
9. Ibid.
10. Russell F. Weigley, "The Border City in Civil War 1854–1865," 387, in Philadelphia, *A 300-Year History*, Russell F. Weigley, ed., Nicholas B. Wainwright, Edwin Wolf II, assoc. eds., Joseph E. Illick, Thomas Wendel, editorial consultants (A Barre Foundation Book, New York, London: W. W. Norton Company, Inc., 1982).
11. Ibid., 389–90.
12. Ibid., 390.
13. Ibid.
14. William Dusinberre, *Civil War Issues in Philadelphia, 1856–1865* (Philadelphia: University of Pennsylvania Press, 1965), 161.
15. George W. Fahnestock Diary, June 6, 1863, The Historical Society of Pennsylvania, Philadelphia.
16. Sam to Father, May 17, 1863, Evans Family Papers, Ohio Historical Society, quoted in Glatthaar, 31.
17. Maxwell Whiteman, *Gentlemen in Crisis: The First Century of The Union League of Philadelphia 1862–1962* (Philadelphia: The Union League of Philadelphia, 1975), 46.
18. Ibid.
19. Whiteman, 46; Stewart Sifakis, *Who Was Who in The Civil War* (New York: Facts on File Publications, 1988), 618.
20. Ibid., 49.
21. *The* (Philadelphia) *Age*, April 1, 3, 9, 10, 1863, passim; Whiteman, 49.
22. *The Age*, Aug. 11, 1863, 1.
23. Taylor, 243, 351.
24. Harry C. Silcox, "Nineteenth Century Philadelphia Black Militant: Octavius V. Catto (1839–1871)," *Pennsylvania History*, XLIV, 1 (Jan. 1977), 59.
25. Ibid.
26. Ibid.
27. (Philadelphia) *Public Ledger*, June 18, 1863, 1.
28. Taylor, 188, 243.
29. Silcox, 59.
30. *Public Ledger*, June 19, 1863, 1 ; Silcox, 59; Frederick M. Binder, "Pennsylvania Negro Regiments in the Civil War," *The Journal of Negro History*, XXXVII (Oct. 1952), 386.
31. Ibid., June 19, 1863, 1.
32. Ibid., June 20, 1863, 1.
33. *The* (Philadelphia) *Press*, June 25, 1863, 2.
34. *The Press*, June 25, 1863, 2; Binder, 388.
35. Taylor, 188.
36. *The Press*, June 25, 1863, 2.
37. Ibid.
38. Ibid.

39. Whiteman, 47.
40. Taylor, op. cit., Military Map of Philadelphia, following page 360.
41. *The Press*, June 25, 1863, 2.
42. Dusinberre, 151–90; Whiteman, 49; Charles L. Blockson, "A History of the Black Man in Montgomery County," *The Bulletin of The Historical Society of Montgomery County*, XVIII (Spring, 1973), 345; Jeffry D. Wert "Camp William Penn and the Black Soldier", *Pennsylvania History*, XXXXVI, 4 (Oct. 1979), 340.
43. Wert, 340; Whiteman, 49.
44. Fahnestock Diary, June 30; Weigley, 363, 411.
45. Weigley, 411.
46. Whiteman, 47.
47. Wert, 341, from Philip S. Foner, *The Life and Writings of Frederick Douglass*, 5 vols. (New York: International Publishers, 1950–52), III, 366.
48. Whiteman, 46, Report of the Supervisory Committee for Recruiting Colored Regiments, Abraham Barker Collection, Historical Society of Pennsylvania.
49. Taylor 188; William A. Gladstone, *Men of Color* (Gettysburg, Pennsylvania: Thomas Publications, 1993), 108, 109.
50. Gladstone, *Men of Color*, 110, 111.
51. Ibid., 111.

CHAPTER 3 – CAMP WILLIAM PENN

1. Mark M. Boatner III, *The Civil War Dictionary* (New York: David McKay Company Inc., 1959), 883.
2. Wert, 342.
3. *The Philadelphia Inquirer*, Oct. 12, 1863, 8.
4. John McMurray, *Recollections of a Colored Troop* (Brookville, Pennsylvania: privately printed, 1916), 4.
5. Ibid.
6. Ibid.
7. Ibid.
8. *The Philadelphia Inquirer*, Sept. 2, 1863, 8.
9. Wert, 342.
10. McMurray, 5.
11. Wert, 342; *The Philadelphia Inquirer*, July 20, 1863, 8.
12. Ibid., Sept. 2, 1863, 8.
13. Ibid., Sept. 16, 1863, 8.
14. Ibid., Sept. 2, 1863, 8.
15. Wert, 345.
16. RG 94 Orders, vol. 4, 6th Regiment U.S. Colored Troops, Cos. A–K, National Archives (hereafter cited as NA).
17. *The Philadelphia Inquirer*, Aug. 22, 1863, 8.
18. Jeremiah Asher to Edward D. Townsend, Nov. 18, 1864, RG 94, Office of the Adjutant General, U.S. Colored Troops, Regimental Papers, Box 13, NA.
19. *The Philadelphia Inquirer*, Aug. 5, 1863, 8.
20. RG 94 Orders, U.S. Colored Troops, 6th Infantry, Co. D, vol. 4, Adjutant General's Office, NA.
21. Ibid.
22. Ibid.
23. Samuel P. Bates, History of Pennsylvania Volunteers, 1861–5, 5 vols. (Harrisburg: B. Singerly, State Printer, 1869–1871), V, 152.
24. RG 94 Orders 6th Infantry, Co. D, vol. 4, Adjutant General's Office, NA.
25. Bates, V, 153.

26. RG 94 U.S. Colored Troops—Orders, 6th Infantry, Co. H, vol. 4, Adjutant General's Office, NA.

27. Bates, V, 161.

28. Ibid., 159.

29. Cornish, 181–196; Glatthaar, 169–76.

30. Gladstone, *Men of Color*, 97.

31. Patricia Faust, ed., *Historical Times Illustrated Encyclopedia of the Civil War* (New York: Harper and Row, 1986), 72–73.

32. Gladstone, *Men of Color*, 67; Frederick M. Binder, "Pennsylvania Negro Regiments in the Civil War," *The Journal of Negro History*, XXXVII (Oct. 1952), 393.

33. Philip S. Foner, "The Battle to End Discrimination Against Negroes on Philadelphia Streetcars" Part I, *Pennsylvania History*, XL, 3 (July 1973), 268.

34. William Still, *A Brief Narrative of the Struggle For the Rights of the Colored People of Philadelphia in the City Railway Cars* (Philadelphia: Merrihew, 1867), 7–9.

35. McPherson, 256 (From Thirteenth Annual Report of the Philadelphia Female Anti-Slavery Society, 1864, 23–24)

36. For a more thorough study of this struggle see Report of the Committee Appointed for the Purpose of Securing to the Colored People in Philadelphia the Right to the Use of the Street Cars (Philadelphia, 1867); Still, *A Brief Narrative*; Foner, "The Battle to End Discrimination", Part I, *Pennsylvania History*, XL, 3 (July 1973), 261–90; Part III, Ibid., XL, 4 (October 1973), 355–79.

37. *The Philadelphia Inquirer*, Sept. 2, 1863, 8.

38. Ibid.

39. Ibid.

40. Wagner to Foster, Feb. 20, 1865, RG 94, Camp William Penn Letters, NA.

41. *The Philadelphia Inquirer*, Aug. 10, 1863, 8.

42. Ibid., Aug. 11, 1863, 8.

43. *Public Ledger*, Aug. 10, 1863, 1; *The Philadelphia Inquirer*, Aug. 10, 1863, 8.

44. *The Philadelphia Inquirer*, Aug. 11, 1863. 8.

45. Ibid., Aug. 10, 1863, 8, Aug. 11, 1863, 8; *Public Ledger*, Aug. 10, 1863, 1.

46. *Public Ledger*, Aug. 10, 1863, 1.

47. *Inquirer*, Aug. 10, 1863, 8.

48. Ibid., Nov. 19, 1863, 4.

49. Ibid., Nov. 19, 1863, 4.

50. *Public Ledger*, Aug. 10, 1863, 1.

51. *The Philadelphia Inquirer*, Aug. 10, 1863, 8.

52. Ibid., Aug. 10, 1863, 8.

53. *Public Ledger*, Aug. 10, 1863, 1.

54. *The Age*, Aug. 11, 1863, 8.

55. *The Philadelphia Inquirer*, Aug. 11, 1863, 8.

56. *Public Ledger*, Aug. 11, 1863, 8.

57. Wert, 344.

58. Bates, V, 949.

59. Theodore W. Bean, *History of Montgomery County, Pennsylvania*, 2 vols. (Philadelphia: Everts & Peck, 1884), I, 547.

60. Ibid, I, 541.

61. *The Philadelphia Inquirer*, Nov. 19, 1863, 4.

62. Bates, V: 949; Individual Service Record, Charles Ridley, RG 94, National Archives.

63. Individual Service Record, Charles Ridley, RG 94, National Archives.

64. *The Philadelphia Inquirer*, Aug. 31, 1863, 8; Richard A. Sauers, *Advance the Colors: Pennsylvania Civil War Battle Flags* (Harrisburg: Capitol Preservation Committee, 1987), 46.

65. *The Philadelphia Inquirer*, Aug. 31, and Sept. 1, 1863, 8.
66. Ibid.
67. Sauers, 46–47; Gladstone, *Men of Color*, 155 for photograph of flag, see appendix.
68. *The Philadelphia Inquirer*, Sept. 1, 1863, 8.
69. Julie Winch, *Philadelphia's Black Elite: Activism, Accommodation, and the Struggle for Autonomy, 1787–1848* (Philadelphia: Temple University Press, 1988), 156–57.
70. *The Philadelphia Inquirer*, Sept. 1, 1863, 8.
71. Ibid.
72. Ibid.
73. Ibid.
74. Sauers, 46; *The Philadelphia Inquirer*, Sept. 1, 1863, 8; Sept. 21, 1863, 8.
75. Ibid., Sept.21, 1863, 8.
76. Ibid., Sept. 12, 1863, 8.
77. Ibid.
78. Ibid., Sept. 16, 1863, 8.
79. Ibid., Sept. 12, 1863, 8.
80. Ibid., Sept. 16, 1863, 8.
81. Ibid., Sept. 25, 1863, 8.
82. Ibid.
83. Ibid.
84. Ibid.
85. *The* (Philadelphia) *Press*, Oct. 5, 1863, 4.
86. George P. Lathrop to Thomas Webster, March 23, 1882, Abraham Barker Collection, The Historical Society of Pennsylvania.
87. *The Press*, Oct. 5, 1863, 4.
88. Ibid.
89. *Public Ledger*, Oct. 5, 1863, 1.
90. See Map 1 in appendix, based on *The Press*, Oct. 5, 1863, 4.
91. *The Press*, Oct. 5, 1863, 4.
92. Ibid.
93. Whitman, 52; Lathrop to Webster.
94. *The* (Philadelphia) *Daily Age*, Jan. 14, 1865, 2; Thomas Wester to Hon. Edwin M. Stanton, July 30, 1863, quoted in Ira Berlin, Joseph P. Reidy, and Leslie S. Rowland, eds., *Freedom: A Documentary History of Emancipation, 1861–1867* (2 ser., series II, *The Black Military Experience*, New York: Cambridge University Press) 1982, 97.
95. Ibid.; Sauers, 46; Binder, 398 (Binder and Sauers write that the flag incident occurred during the October parade of the 6th Regiment, but base their conclusion on the January 14, 1865, newspaper account that identifies neither the date nor the unit involved. Webster's letter dated July 30, 1863, however, describes a remarkably similar event. More likely the incident occurred at that earlier time during July recruiting.)
96. Ibid.
97. *The Press*; Oct. 5, 1863, 4.
98. *The Daily Age*, Jan. 14, 1865, 2.

CHAPTER 4 — THE MEN

1. Muster Rolls.
2. Obituaries, *The* (San Francisco) *Daily Evening Post*, April 6, 1878, *The San Francisco Sunday Chronicle*, April 7, 1878, and Biographical Information Page, Harrisburg Civil War Round Table Collection, Captain John W. Ames Folder, U.S. Army Military History Institute, Carlisle Barracks, Pennsylvania.

3. Bates, 943; McMurray, 6–7, Muster Rolls.
4. Glatthaar, 17.
5. McMurray, 8.
6. Glatthaar, 17.
7. Basler, VI, 401.
8. Edwin S. Redkey, "Black Chaplains in the Civil War," *Civil War History*, XXXIII, 4 (Dec. 1987), 332; Gladstone, *Men of Color*, 50.
9. Jeremiah Asher, *Incidents in the Life of the Rev. J. Asher* (London: Charles Gilpin, 1850) copy in Charles L. Blockson African American Collection, Temple University, original volume in Fisk University; Taylor, 188; Gladstone, *Men of Color*, 109, 110, 111.
10. Ira Berlin, Joseph P. Reidy, and Leslie S. Rowland, eds., *Freedome: A Documentary History of Emancipation, 1861–1867*, series II, vol. 1, *The Black Military Experience* (New York: Cambridge University Press, 1982), 359; see also John W. Blassingame, "Negro Chaplains in the Civil War," *Negro History Bulletin*, XXVII, 1 (Oct. 1963), 23–24.
11. John W. Ames to Charles W. Foster, Dec. 3, 1863, U.S. Colored Troops Regimental Papers, Office of Adjutant General, RG 94, National Archives.
12. Ibid., Charles W. Foster to John W. Ames, Dec. 7, 1863.
13. Muster Rolls; Faust, 731.
14. Muster Rolls.
15. Ibid.
16. Ibid.
17. Ibid.
18. Ibid.
19. Ibid., see table 8 and graph 26.
20. Muster Rolls.
21. Ibid.
22. Ibid., McMurray, 8; for an examination of the relationship between Congressman Stevens and Mrs. Smith see Fawn M. Brodie, *Thaddeus Stevens: Scourge of the South* (New York: W. W. Norton & Co. Inc., 1959), 86–93.
23. Ibid., 10.
24. Ibid., 9–10.
25. McMurray, 76.
26. Ibid.
27. Ibid., 76–77; Muster Rolls.
28. McMurray, 22.
29. Ibid.
30. Ibid.

CHAPTER 5 – THEY ALSO SERVE

1. Records of Movements and Activities of Volunteer Organizations (hereafter cited as M and A), 6th U.S. Colored Infantry, Companies G and K, Oct. 1863, RG 94, NA.
2. Horace Montgomery, "A Union Officer's Recollections of the Negro as a Soldier," *Pennsylvania History*, XXVIII (April 1961), 160; *Inquirer*, Oct. 12, 1863, 8.
3. McMurray, 5.
4. McMurray, 5, 10; M and A, Cos. G and K, Oct. 1863.
5. McMurray, 10.
6. Orders, 6th U.S. Colored Infantry, Oct. 27, 1863, RG 94, NA.
7. McMurray, 10; Sauers, 50.
8. Montgomery, 161.
9. McMurray, 5, 6, 10; Montgomery, 161–62.

10. Montgomery, 161–62.
11. McMurray, 11.
12. Montgomery, 162.
13. Ibid., 162; *New York Tribune*, Nov. 25, 1863.
14. McMurray, 12.
15. Ibid., 12.
16. Ibid., 12.
17. Ibid., 13.
18. Ibid., 11.
19. M and A, Cos. A, B, and K, Dec. 1863; OR, ser. I, vol. XXIXX, Pt. 1, 975.
20. Idem.
21. OR, ser. I, vol. XXIX, Pt. 1, 974–76.
22. Ibid., 974.
23. Ibid., 976.
24. Ibid., 976.
25. M and A, Cos. A, B, and K, Dec. 1863.
26. Benjamin F. Butler, *Butler's Book* (Boston: A. M. Thayer & Co., 1892), 619–20.
27. Ibid., 620.
28. Ibid., Appendix No 16, General Wistar's Report of Operation, Feb. 9, 1864, Appendix 13.
29. Ibid., Appendix, 13.
30. McMurray, 25.
31. M and A, Co. D, Feb., 1864.
32. Butler, Appendix, 13.
33. Ibid., 619.
34. McMurray, 24.
35. M and A, Co. F, Feb. 1864.
36. McMurray, 24.
37. Ibid., 25.
38. Ibid., Appendix, 13–14.
39. Ibid.
40. McMurray, 25.
41. M and A, Feb. 1864.
42. McMurray, 25.
43. Bates, V, 943.
44. M and A, Cos. B, D, F.
45. Ibid., Cos. A–K.
46. McMurray, 25.
47. Faust, 417.
48. Butler, 621.
49. M and A, Field and Staff and Cos. A–K, March 1864.
50. M and A, Co. K, March 1864.
51. M and A, Co. H, March 1864; Muster Roll, 6th USCI.
52. M and A, March–April 1864.
53. Ibid., March 1864.
54. Ibid., Cos. F and K.
55. Ibid., Cos. A–K.
56. OR, ser. 1, XXXIII, 255.
57. M and A, March 1864.
58. Ibid.

CHAPTER 6 — THE ASSAULT ON PETERSBURG

1. Montgomery, 165; Ulysses S Grant, *Personal Memoirs of US Grant*, 2 vols. (New York: Charles L Webster & Co, 1885) II, 123–32.
2. OR, ser. 1, XXXIII, 1055; Montgomery, 165.
3. Faust, 825.
4. M and A, May 1864.
5. Robert U. Johnson and Clarence C. Buel, *Battles and Leaders of the Civil War* (4 vols., New York: Century, 1884–88), IV, 207 (hereafter cited as B and L).
6. Grant, II, 147–8.
7. Bates, 943–4, 961.
8. Montgomery, 165; B and L, 146; M and A, May 1864.
9. B and L, IV, 146.
10. Grant, II, 148–50.
11. McMurray, 28.
12. Ibid., 29; Montgomery, 166; Bates, 944.
13. McMurray, 31; Bates, 944; Montgomery, 166.
14. McMurray, 31, 33.
15. M and A, May 1864.
16. Ibid., May–June 1864.
17. McMurray, 31.
18. Ibid., 32.
19. Ibid.
20. Ibid.
21. Ibid., 32–33.
22. Ibid., 33; Muster Roll, Co. D.
23. McMurray, 34.
24. M and A, May–June 1864.
25. Grant, II, 285.
26. McMurray, 33–34; Montgomery, 168.
27. Faust, 57.
28. Montgomery, 168.
29. McMurray, 35–36.
30. Ibid., 36; Muster Roll, Co. D.
31. McMurray, 35.
32. Ibid., 34.
33. OR, ser. 1, XL, pt. 1, 722.
34. M and A, Co. B, June 1864.
35. McMurray, 34.
36. Ibid., 35.
37. Ibid.
38. Ibid., 36.
39. Harvey Covell to his wife, June 20, 1864, Harrisburg Civil War Round Table — Steljes Collection, U.S. Army Military History Institute, Carlisle Barracks, Pennsylvania.
40. Ibid.
41. Ibid.
42. Ibid.; OR, ser. 1, vol. LI, pt. 1, 267–69; Joseph T. Wilson, *The Black Phalanx* (Hartford, Connecticut: American Publishing Co., 1890, reprint, New York: Arno Press and The New York Times, 1968), 402; Benjamin Quarles, *The Negro in the Civil War* (New York; Russell & Russell, 1953), 298–300; George W. Williams, *A History of the Negro Troops in the War of the Rebellion, 1861–1865* (New York: Harper & Brothers, 1888, reprint, New York: Negro Universities Press, 1969), 235–42.

43. OR, ser. 1, LI, pt. 1, 267; Wilson, 402–5.
44. McMurray, 37–38.
45. Faust, 1.
46. McMurray, 38.
47. Ibid.
48. Grant, II, 295; B and L, 151.
49. Hondon B. Hargrove, *Black Union Soldiers in the Civil War* (Jefferson, North Carolina and London: McFarland & Company, Inc., 1988), 182.
50. McMurray, 38–39.
51. Noah A. Trudeau, *The Last Citadel: Petersburg, Virginia, June 1864–April 1865* (Boston, Toronto, London: Little, Brown & Company, 1991), 46.
52. B and L, IV 151.
53. Grant, 293–94.
54. Henry Pleasants Jr., and George H. Straley, *Inferno at Petersburg* (Philadelphia: Chilton Company, 1961), 7.
55. B and L, IV, 540.
56. Grant, 296–97.
57. Williams, 242.
58. Ibid.
59. Ibid.
60. Covell letter.
61. McMurray, 39.
62. Ibid., 40.
63. Ibid.
64. Ibid.
65. Ibid., 41.
66. M and A, Co. G, July–Aug. 1864.
67. McMurray, 41; Sauers, 45.
68. McMurray, 42; Bates, 946.
69. McMurray, 41.
70. Ibid., 42.
71. Faust, 190.
72. McMurray, 43.
73. Ibid., 44.
74. Gladstone, *Men of Color*, 167.
75. McMurray, 44.

CHAPTER 7 — DUTCH GAP

1. B and L, IV, 575; "Dutch Gap Canal," article from unidentified source, Jan. 1870, John W. Ames folder, Harrisburg Civil War Round Table Collection, U.S. Army Military History Institute, Carlisle Barracks, Pennsylvania, 30; Faust, 231.
2. M and A, Cos. G & K, July–Aug. 1864; "Dutch Gap Canal," 30; McMurray, 45; Montgomery, 174.
3. Cornish, 185, 258.
4. "Dutch Gap Canal," 31–32.
5. Ibid., 32.
6. Ibid.
7. Ibid., 32–33.
8. Ibid., 33.
9. Ibid., 33, 34.
10. Ibid., 34.

11. Ibid.
12. Horace Porter, *Campaigning With Grant* (New York: The Century Company, 1897), 371; Butler, 748; Montgomery, 174.
13. OR Ser. 1, XLII, pt. 2, 959 and pt. 3, 216–17; Butler, 599–605; McMurray, 46: Montgomery, 174–75; "Dutch Gap Canal, 37; for a discussion of Confederate policy toward captured black troops see Brainerd Dryer, "The Treatment of Colored Troops by the Confederates, 1861–1865," *Journal of Negro History*, XX, July 1935, 273–86; for a thorough study of the Dutch Gap controversy see Richard J. Sommers, *The Dutch Gap Affair: Military Attrocities and Rights of Negro Soldiers,*" Civil War History, XXI, 51–64.
14. McMurray, 46.
15. Sommers, 61–62.
16. Butler, "Dutch Gap Affair", 747.
17. McMurray, 46.
18. "Dutch Gap Canal," 33.
19. McMurray, 46.
20. "Dutch Gap Canal," 33, 35.
21. Ibid., 33.
22. Ibid., 35.
23. Ibid., 36–37.
24. Ibid., 34.
25. Ibid., 35.
26. Ibid., 37–38.
27. R. J. M. Blackett, ed., *Thomas Morris Chester, Black Civil War Correspondent: His dispatches from the Virginia Front* (Baton Rouge and London: Louisiana State Press, 1989), 124.
28. Blackett, 124–25.
29. "Dutch Gap Canal," 36.

CHAPTER 8 — NEW MARKET HEIGHTS

1. Richard J. Sommers, *Richmond Redeemed: The Siege at Petersburg* (Garden City, New York: Doubleday and Company Inc., 1981), 8.
2. Sommers, *Richmond Redeemed*, 21; William W. Gwaltney, "New Market Heights," in *The Civil War Battlefield Guide*, The Conservation Fund, Frances H. Kennedy, ed. (Boston: Houghton Mifflin Company, 1990), 264; McMurray, 53.
3. Butler, 728.
4. Montgomery, 175.
5. McMurray, 51.
6. Montgomery, 175.
7. McMurray, 51.
8. Ibid.
9. McMurray, 51–52; Gwaltney, 264.
10. Gwaltney, 266; Sommers, *Richmond Redeemed*, 31–33; McMurray, 52: Butler, 731; Sauers, 46.
11. McMurray, 52.
12. Ibid., 52, 53.
13. Ibid., 52.
14. Butler, 731; Wilson, 435; Cornish, 280.
15. McMurray, 53; Williams, 254.
16. McMurray, 53.
17. Butler, 732.
18. McMurray, 51, 53.
19. Ibid., 53–54.
20. Sommers, *Richmond Redeemed*, 35; Bates, 946.

CHAPTER 10 — CLOSING THE BOOKS

1. Muster Rolls; Bates, 945–64.
2. Ibid.
3. Edwin S. Redkey, ed., *A Grand Army of Black Men* (Cambridge: Cambridge University Press, 1992), 237.
4. Berlin, 680.
5. Ibid., 772–73.
6. Ibid., 773.
7. Muster Rolls; Bates, 945–64.
8. Ibid.
9. Ibid.
10. McMurray, 93–94.
11. Ibid., 94.
12. Taylor, 190.
13. Muster Rolls; Bates, 945–64.
14. John W. Ames to Thomas Webster, Nov. 2, 1864, Abraham Barker Collection, Historical Society of Pennsylvania.
15. Ibid.
16. Medal of Honor File, Thomas Hawkins, RG 94, National Archives; Sauers, 46.
17. Brown, 379.
18. Ibid., 379–80.

APPENDIX A — PSYCHOLOGICAL WOUNDS

1. Individual Service Record, Thomas Anderson, Sixth U.S. Colored Infantry, National Archives.
2. Ibid.; Bates, 954.
3. Byron Stinson, M.D., "'Battle Fatigue' and How It Was Treated in the Civil War," *Civil War Times, Illustrated*, IV, 7, Nov. 1965, 40.
4. McMurray, 61–62.
5. Dr. Joseph DiIenno, Interview on Aug. 5, 1993.
6. McMurray, 35.
7. DiIenno.
8. McMurray, 54.
9. DiIenno.
10. Ibid.
11. Ibid.
12. Ibid.
13. McMurray, 62.
14. DiIenno.
15. Ibid.
16. Ibid.
17. Ibid.
18. Ibid.
19. Ibid.
20. Ibid.
21. Ibid., McMurray, 62.

BIBLIOGRAPHY

ARCHIVAL SOURCES

Historical Society of Pennsylvania
    Abraham Barker Collection
    George W. Fahnestock
National Archives
Record Group 94
    Adjutant General's Office Miscellaneous File
        ("Colored Troops")
        Camp William Penn Letters
        Descriptive Muster Rolls, Sixth USCT
        Individual Service Records
        Orders, Sixth USCT
        Records of Movements and Activities of Volunteer Organizations,
          Sixth USCT
Swarthmore College
    Quaker Collection; Miscellaneous Manuscripts
United States Army Military History Institute
    Harrisburg Civil War Round Table Collection
    Steljes Collection
University of Texas Archives
    Martin L. Crimmins Collection
        (Transcript in files of National Parks Service,
        Richmond National Battlefield Park)

PUBLISHED PRIMARY SOURCES

Basler, Roy P. *The Collected Works of Abraham Lincoln*, 9 vols. New Brunswick, New Jersey: Rutgers University Press, 1953–1955.

Berlin, Ira; Joseph P. Reidy; and Leslie S. Rowland, eds. *Freedom: A Documentary History of Emancipation, 1861–1867*. Series II, Vol. 1, *The Black Military Experience*. New York: Cambridge University Press, 1982.

Blackett, R. J. M., ed. *Thomas Morris Chester, Black Civil War Correspondent: His Dispatches from the Virginia Front*. Baton Rouge and London: Louisiana State University Press, 1989.

Brown, William Wells. *The Negro in the American Rebellion: His Heroism and His Fidelity*. New York: Lee and Shepard, 1867; reprint ed., Johnson Reprint Corporation, 1968.

Butler, Benjamin F. *Butler's Book*. Boston: A. M. Thayer &Co., 1892.

Carpenter, Francis B. *Six Months in the White House with President Lincoln*. New York: Hurd & Houghton, 1866.

Emilio, Luis F. *A Brave Black Regiment: History of the Fifty-fourth Regiment of Massachusetts Volunteer Infantry*. Boston: Boston Book Company, 1894.

Grant, Ulysses S. *Personal Memoirs of U. S. Grant*, 2 vols. New York: Charles L. Webster & Company, 1885–86.

Greeley, Horace. *The American Conflict: A History of the Great Rebellion in the United States of America*. 2 vols. Hartford: O. S. Case & Co., 1866.

Higginson, Thomas Wentworth. *Army Life in a Black Regiment*. Boston: Beacon Press, 1962.

Johnson, Robert U., and Clarence C. Buel, eds. *Battles and Leaders of the Civil War*. 4 vols. New York: Century, 1884–88.

McMurray, John. *Recollections of a Colored Troop*. Brookville, Pennsylvania: Privately printed, 1916.

McPherson, James M. *The Negro's Civil War: How American Negroes Felt and Acted During the War for the Union*. New York: Vintage Books, 1965.

Porter, Horace. *Campaigning with Grant*. New York: The Century Company, 1897.

Redkey, Edwin S., ed. *A Grand Army of Black Men*. Cambridge: Cambridge University Press, 1992.

Still, William. *A Brief Narrative of the Struggle for the Rights of the Colored People of Philadelphia in the City Railway Cars*. Philadelphia: Merrihew, 1867.

Taylor, Frank H. *Philadelphia in the Civil War, 1861–1865*. Philadelphia: Published by the City, 1913.

Williams, George W. *A History of the Negro Troops in the War of the Rebellion 1861–1865*. New York: Harper & Brothers, 1888; reprint ed., New York: Negro Universities Press, 1969.

Wilson, Joseph T. *The Black Phalanx*. Hartford, Connecticut: American Publishing Co., 1890; reprint ed., New York: Arno Press and *The New York Times*, 1968.

Yearns, W. Buck, and John G. Barrett, eds. *North Carolina Civil War Documentary*. Chapel Hill: University of North Carolina, 1980.

INTERVIEW

DiIenno, Joseph A. M.D. Interview, August 5, 1993. Dr. DiIenno has practiced psychiatry for 25 years. He has taught group process for 20 years and founded the program for Master of Science in Group Process at Hahnemann University. As a psychiatrist in the United States Air Force, he conducted an evaluation of American prisoners of war from the Vietnam Conflict. He also conducted a study of fire supression for the United States Army in 1978.

GOVERNMENT PUBLICATIONS

The War of the Rebellion: A Compilation of the Official Records of the Union and Confederate Armies. Four Series, 70 vols. in 128 vols. Washington: Government Printing Office, 1880–1891.

NEWSPAPERS

Douglass' Monthly, May 1861–February 1862.

The Philadelphia Inquirer, June 26, 1863–November 19, 1863.

The (Philadelphia) *Press*, June 25, 1863–October 5, 1863.

The (Philadelphia) *Public Ledger*, June 18, 1863–October 5, 1863.

The (Philadelphia) *Age*, April 1, 1863–August 11, 1863.

The (Philadelphia) *Daily Age*, January 14, 1865.

SECONDARY SOURCES

Barrett, John G. *The Civil War in North Carolina*. Chapel Hill: University of North Carolina Press, 1963.

Bates, Samuel P. *History of Pennsylvania Volunteers, 1861–5*. 5 vols. Harrisburg: B. Singerly, State Printer, 1869–1871.

Bean, Theodore W., ed. *History of Montgomery County, Pennsylvania*. 2 vols. Philadelphia: Everts & Peck, 1884.

Binder, Frederick M. "Pennsylvania Negro Regiments in the Civil War." *Journal of Negro History*, XXXVII (October 1952).

Black, Lowell Dwight. *The Negro Volunteer Militia Units of the Ohio National Guard, 1770–1954: The Struggle for Military Recognition and Equality*. Manhattan, Kansas: Military Affairs/ Aerospace Historian Publishing, 1976.

Blassingame, John W. "Negro Chaplains in the Civil War." *Negro History Bulletin*. XXVII, 1 (October 1962): 23–24.

Blockson, Charles L. "A History of the Black Man in Montgomery County." *The Bulletin of the Historical Society of Montgomery County*, XVIII (Spring 1973).

Boatner, Mark M. III. *The Civil War Dictionary*. New York: David McKay Company, Inc., 1959.

Brodie, Fawn M. *Thaddeus Stevens: Scourge of the South*. New York: W. W. Norton & Co. Inc., 1959.

Catton, Bruce. *A Stillness at Appomattox*. Garden City, New York: Doubleday & Co. Inc., 1953.

Cornish, Dudly T. *The Sable Arm: Negro Troops in the Union Army*. New York: Longmans Green and Company, 1956; Lawrence, Kansas: University Press of Kansas, 1987.

Dryer, Brainerd. "The Treatment of Colored Troops by the Confederates, 1861–1865." *Journal of Negro History*, XX (July 1935): 273–86.

Dusinberre, William. *Civil War Issues in Philadelphia, 1856–1865*. Philadelphia: University of Pennsylvania Press, 1965.

Faust, Patricia, ed. *Historical Times Illustrated Encyclopedia of the Civil War*. New York: Harper and Row, 1986.

Foner, Philip S. "The Battle to End Discrimination Against Negroes on Philadelphia Streetcars." Part I, *Pennsylvania History*, XL, 3 (July 1973): 261–90; Part II, *Pennsylvania History*, XL, 4 (October 1973): 355–79.

Gladstone, William A. *Men of Color*. Gettysburg, Pennsylvania: Thomas Publications, 1990.

———. *United States Colored Troops*. Gettysburg, Pennsylvania: Thomas Publications, 1990.

Glatthaar, Joseph T. *Forged in Battle: The Civil War Alliance of Black Soldiers and White Officers*. New York: The Free Press, Collier Macmillan, 1990.

Gragg, Rod. *Confederate Goliath: The Battle of Fort Fisher*. New York: Harper Collins, 1991.

Guthrie, James M. *Campfires of the Afro-American*. Philadelphia: Afro-American Pub. Co., 1899; reprint ed., New York: Johnson Reprint Corporation, 1970.

Gwaltney, William W. "New Market Heights." *The Civil War Battlefield Guide*. The Conservation Fund, Frances H. Kennedy, ed. Boston: Houghton Mifflin Co., 1990.

Hargrove, Hondon B. *Black Union Soldiers in the Civil War*. Jefferson, North Carolina and London: McFarland & Co., Inc., 1988.

Miller, William J. *The Training of an Army: Camp Curtin and the North's Civil War*. Shippensburg, Pennsylvania: White Mane Pub. Co. Inc., 1990.

Moebs, Thomas Truxton. *Black Soldiers, Black Sailors, Black Ink: Research Guide on African Americans in U.S. Military History, 1526–1900*. 4 vols. Chesapeake Bay, Virginia: Moebs Publishing, 1994.

Montgomery, Horace. "A Union Officer's Recollections of the Negro as a Soldier." *Pennsylvania History*, XXVIII (April 1961).

Phisterer, Frederick, comp. *New York in the War of the Rebellion, 1861–1865*. 3rd ed. 5 vols. Albany: J. B. Lyon Co., 1912.

Pleasants, Henry Jr., and George H. Straley. *Inferno at Petersburg*. Philadelphia: Chilton Company, 1961.

Polley, J. B. *Hood's Texas Brigade: Its Marches, Its Battles, Its Achievements*. New York: The Neale Pub. Co., 1910; reprint ed., Dayton, Ohio: Morningside Press, 1988.

Quarles, Benjamin. *The Negro in the Civil War*. New York: Russell & Russell, 1953.

Redkey, Edwin S. "Black Chaplains in the Civil War." *Civil War History*. XXXIII, 4 (December 1987).

Reed, Rowena. *Combined Operations in the Civil War*. Annapolis, Maryland: United States Naval Institute, 1978.

Sauers, Richard A. *Advance the Colors: Pennsylvania Civil War Battle Flags*. Harrisburg: Capitol Preservation Committee, 1987.

Sifakis, Stewart. *Who Was Who in the Civil War*. New York: Facts on File Publications, 1988.

Silcox, Harry C. "Nineteenth Century Philadelphia Black Militant: Octavius V. Catto (1839–1871)." *Pennsylvania History*. XLIV, 1 (January 1977).

Sommers, Richard J. "The Dutch Gap Affair: Military Atrocities and Rights of Negro Soldiers." *Civil War History*. XXI: 51–64.

————. *Richmond Redeemed: The Siege at Petersburg*. Garden City, New York: Doubleday & Co., Inc., 1961.

Stinson, Byron, M.D. "'Battle Fatigue' and How It Was Treated in the Civil War." *Civil War Times, Illustrated*. IV, 7 (November 1965): 40–44.

Trudeau, Noah A. *The Last Citadel: Petersburg, Virginia, June 1864–April 1865*. Boston, Toronto, London: Little, Brown & Co., 1991.

————. *Like Men of War: Black Troops in the Civil War 1862–1865*. Boston, Toronto, London: Little, Brown and Co., 1998.

Weigley, Russell F. "The Border City in the Civil War, 1854–1865." *Philadelphia, A 300-Year History*, Russell F. Weigley, ed., Nicholas B. Wainwright,

Edwin Wolf II, assoc. eds., Joseph E. Illick, Thomas Wendel, editorial consultants. A Barre Foundation Book. New York, London: W. W. Norton & Co., Inc., 1982.

Wert, Jeffry D. "Camp William Penn and the Black Soldier." *Pennsylvania History*. XLVI, 4 (October 1979).

Westwood, Howard C. *Black Troops, White Commanders, and Freedmen During the Civil War*. Carbondale and Edwardsville, Illinois: Southern Illinois University Press, 1992.

Whiteman, Maxwell. *Gentlemen in Crisis: The First Century of the Union League of Philadelphia, 1862–1962*. Philadelphia: Published by the Union League of Philadelphia, 1975.

Winch, Julie. *Philadelphia's Black Elite: Activism, Accommodation, and the Struggle for Autonomy, 1787–1848*. Philadelphia: Temple University Press, 1988.

INDEX

A

Abatis, 55, 70, 83
Abbott, Henry L., 83
Abolitionists
  Philadelphia attitudes toward, 6
  violence against, 67. *See also* Garrison,
    William Lloyd
Admiral Dupont (ship), 82
Age, The (Philadelphia)
  opposes emancipation and black troops,
    8, 21
  shooting at Chelten Hills, 21
American Baptist Missionary Convention, 33
American Journal of Medical Sciences, 96
Ames, John W., 34, 40, 42, 43, 52, 54, 93
  battles, 72–73, 77, 84
  at Camp William Penn, 14
  march through Philadelphia, 28–29
  military experience, 32, 81
Anderson, Thomas, 95
Andrew, John A., 5, 27
Annapolis, Md., 87
Antietam, Battle of, 3
Appomattox River, 49, 52
Armistead, Richard P., 46
Army Life in a Black Regiment, 4
Asher, Jeremiah, 11–12, 33, 35, 80, 81, 89

B

Babe, William, 8, 9
Baltimore, Md., 93
Banks, Enoch A., 22
Baptists, 33
Barbers, 36
Barhamsville, Va., 46
Bass, Frederick, 74
Batteries 5–10 (Petersburg, Va.), 55–57

Beath, Robert B., 32, 72, 75
Beaufort, N.C., 82
Beauregard, Pierre G.T., 56
Bentonville, N.C., 88
Bermuda Hundred, Va., 49, 82
Biddle, George, 26
"Big Sam." *See* Johnson, Samuel
Bingham, Lafayette, 7
Black chaplains, 11–12, 33, 35, 80, 81, 89
Black commissioned officers, 4, 17–18
Black noncommissioned officers, 17, 19,
    73–75, 84, 94
Black soldiers
  authorized by Congress, 3
  discrimination against, 10, 17, 57
  during Gettysburg Campaign, 8–9
  Northern attitudes towards, 1, 2, 7
  pay, 17, 61, 90, 91
  physical labor, 35–36, 61
  recruiting in Philadelphia, 5, 7, 8–12
  volunteers, 1–2, 7–9
  white opposition to, 1–2, 5, 7, 9
Blacks
  Northern prejudice against, 1, 2, 6, 7, 9–11
  in Virginia, 41
Blacksmiths, 36
Boernstein, Augustus S., 81–82
Border states, 1, 3–4
Boston, Mass., 1–2
Bottom's Bridge, Va., 43–46
Bounties, 17
Bowers, John, 23
Bowser, David Bustill, 23
Boyd, James, 22
Bragg, Braxton, 83–85
Brewster, Benjamin, 22
Brown, John, 6–7

Bucks County, Pa., 95
Buffalo, N.Y., 13
Burgaw Creek, N.C., 87
Burnside, Ambrose, 59
Burnt Ordinary, Va., 42, 46
Butler, Benjamin F.
    enlisting of Blacks in New Orleans, 4
    Fort Fisher Expedition, 82
    at New Market Heights, 71, 79
    in Virginia, 41, 43, 44, 46, 48–49, 52, 64

C

Cadwalader, George, 27–28, 29
Camp Hamilton (Fort Familton), Va., 47
Camp William Penn, Pa., 13–31, 36, 40, 41,
    50, 91, 92, 93
    daily schedule, 15
    desertion from, 17, 19, 92
    establishment of, 10–11
    shooting incident, 19–22
    visitors to, 14, 18–19, 22, 26–28, 36
Canada, 35
Canal. See Dutch Gap Canal
Cape Fear River, 83, 86
Carter, Richard, 84
Catto, Octavius V., 8, 10, 11
Cavalry (Confederate), 50–51
Cavalry (Union), 44–45, 46, 51
Ceaser, Hubbard, 36–37, 87
Chaffin's Farm. See New Market Heights
Chamberlain, Maro J., 32
Chambersburg, Pa., 8
Champion (transport), 47
Chaplains, 12, 33. See also Asher, Jeremiah
Chapman, Henry, 22
Charles City Courthouse, Va., 42
Chelten Hills (Cheltenham), Pa., 10, 21, 40,
    91. See also Camp William Penn
Cherry, Alphonso, 51–52
Chester, Thomas Morris, 67
Chickahominy River, 43, 45
Christian Commission, 80
Cincinnati, Ohio, 2
City Point, Va., 49, 58, 93
Clark, John H., 17
Clark, Robert, 16
Clergymen. See Chaplains
Combat stress. See mental illness
Confederate Cabinet, 43
Confederate States Armies
    Army of Northern Virginia, 8, 48, 88
    Army of Tennessee, 88
Congress of the United States, 3
Congressional Medal of Honor. See Medal
    of Honor
Conqueror (ship), 40

Conscription, 17, 34, 90
Continental Hotel, Philadelphia, Pa., 29, 94
Couch, Darius N., 9
Covell, Harvey, 54–55
Cox's Bridge, N.C., 87, 88
Crater, Battle of the, 59
Cummings, Edward, 84
Curtin, Andrew G., 7, 8, 11
Curtis, George William, 7

D

Danks, Nathaniel, 41–42, 76
Davis, Edward M., 10
Davis, Jefferson, 43–44
Deep Bottom, Va., 69
Delaware, 26, 35
Democratic Party, 2, 33, 80
Desertion, 17, 19, 91, 92
Devereau, John F., 84
Dickinson, Anna E., 11, 28
Discipline of troops, 16, 86. See also
    punishments
Disease, 66, 80, 82, 89
Douglass, Frederick, 2, 11
Draft. See Conscription
Draftees, 17, 90
Draper, Alonzo G., 75–76
Duncan, Samuel A., 41, 48, 71, 72, 81
Dutch Gap Canal, 61–67, 80

E

Edgerton, Nathan, 73, 75, 94
Education, 14
Elliott, William, 8
Emancipation
    Emancipation Proclamation, 3
    Northern attitudes toward, 1, 2
Emilio, Luis F., 5
Empire City (steamer), 82

F

Fahnestock, George W., 7, 10–11
Faison's Station (Faison's Depot), N.C., 88
Fatigue duty, 35–36, 61
Ferrero, Edward, 59
Field, Edward, 32, 84
Flags, 22–26, 29, 53, 72–75, 79, 93–94
Food, 15–16, 87
Fort Converse. See Redoubt Converse
Fort Fisher, N.C., 81–85
Fort Gilmer, Va., 76
Fort Hamilton (Camp Hamilton), Va., 48
Fort Harrison, Va., 69, 76–79, 80, 82
Fort Magruder, Va., 43, 46
Forten, William D., 11
Fortress Monroe, Va., 40, 47, 48, 82, 93

Foster, Charles W., 34
Foster, Jesse P., 16
Fox, William, 19–20, 21
Frankford Arsenal, Philadelphia, Pa., 6
Fribley, Charles W., 28

G

Garrison, William Lloyd, 2
Getty's Station, Va., 47
Gettysburg Campaign, 8–9, 11
Gillmore, Quincy A., 52
Gipson, David E., 9
Glass, William Λ., 32
Gloucester County, Va., 47
Gloucester Point, Va., 41
Goldsboro, N.C., 86, 87, 89, 93
Gorgas, Josiah, 6
Grand Reviews, 27–28, 88, 89
Grant, Ulysses S.
    at Fort Fisher, 81, 82
    in Virginia, 48, 52, 56, 57, 59, 64, 69
Great Britain, 18, 35
Gregg, John, 74

H

Hallowell, Norwood Penrose, 6
Hampton, Va., 95
Hancock, Winfield S., 52, 57
Hannibal Guards, 1
Harrisburg, Pa., 8–9
Hawkins, Thomas, 73–75, 94
Healy, Daniel, 84
Heath, George E., 50–51
Henry, Alexander, 7, 8, 9, 11
Herbert, Henry, 89
Herman Livingston (transport), 82
Higginson, Thomas Wentworth, 4
Hinks, Edward W., 48, 52, 53, 55, 57
Hoke, Robert F., 83–84, 86
Holt, Dr. J. F., 20
Hotchkiss, Newton J., 84
Hunsicker, Charles, 22
Hunter, David, 4

I

Institute for Colored Youth, 8
Island Creek, N.C., 87

J

Jackman, Enoch, 54
James River, 49, 61, 93, 95
Johnson, John, 71
Johnson, Samuel, 37, 76
Johnston, Joseph E., 88–89
Johnston, William F., 28
Jones, Asa L., 32, 54

K

Kansas, 4
Kelley, William D., 11
Kelly, Alexander, 73–75, 94
Kenansville, N.C., 87
Kiddoo, Joseph B., 32, 55
Kilpatrick, Hugh Judson, 46
King and Queen County, Va, 47

L

Lancaster, Pa., 13
Lane, James E., 4
Law, William, 53
Lee, Robert E., 48, 64, 88
Lincoln, Abraham
    black chaplains, 33
    emancipation, 1, 2 4
    raising black troops, 1, 3–4
    reelection, 80

M

McMurray, John, 32
    at Camp William Penn, 13–14
    Dutch Gap, 55–56
    Fort Fisher Campaign, 82–84
    nervous breakdown, 96–99
    New Market Heights, 69–76
    North Carolina, 87
    Petersburg, 52–54
    Virginia, 42, 49, 50–52
Maryland, 26, 35
Massachusetts, 1–2, 5
Massachusetts Regiments
    54th, 5, 26
    55th, 5, 6, 26
Mattaponi River, 47
Matthews County, Va., 47
Meade, George G., 48
Medal of Honor, 75, 94
Mental Illness, 66–67, 95–99
Meyer, Frederick, 32, 72
Middlesex County, Va., 47
Militia Act of 1862, 3, 4
Moore, Thomas, 8
Mott, Lucretia Coffin, 10

N

Neuse River, 87
New Hampshire Infantry Regiments, 3rd, 89
New Inlet, N.C., 82
New Jersey, 36
New Jersey Infantry Regiments, 3rd, 57
New Kent Courthouse, Va., 45, 46
New Market Heights (Chaffin's Farm), 69–76, 79, 80
New Orleans, La., 4

New York City, N.Y., 2
New York (state), 2
Noncommissioned officers. *See* Officers,
       noncommissioned
Norristown, Pa., 22
North Carolina, 81–89, 92–93
North East River, 86, 87
North East Station, N.C., 86
North Pennsylvania Railroad, 10, 18, 27

O

Occupations. *See* United States Colored
       Infantry, 6th Regiment, occupations
Officers, commissioned
    in black units, 17–18, 93
    political loyalties, 33
    praise of black soldiers, 94
Officers, noncommissioned, 17, 19, 84
Osborne, Frank, 32

P

Paine, Charles J., 69, 81
Panic attack, 97, 98
Parker, Miles, 72
Patterson, Emanuel, 69–70, 72
Pay for black soldiers, 17, 61, 90, 91
Peninsula, The. *See* Yorktown Peninsula
Pennsylvania Anti-Slavery Society, 6, 23
Pennsylvania Hall (Philadelphia), 6
Petersburg, Va., 49, 51–60, 93
    assault June 15, 1864, 52–57
    Battle of the Crater, 59
    Siege of, 69
Philadelphia, Pa.,
    black community in, 6, 8, 9–10, 11, 22, 23
    black volunteers, 5, 7, 8–12
    bounties, 17
    discrimination on streetcars, 6, 18
    during Gettysburg Campaign, 8–9
    flag presented by black community, 22, 23
    pro-Southern attitudes, 6–7
    racism in, 6, 10, 18, 29
    recruiting for 54th Mass., 5
    6th USCI in, 28–31, 93
Piankatank River, 47
Picket duty, 57, 58–60
Pittsburgh, Pa., 1
Point of Rocks, Va., 52, 61, 95
Portsmouth, Va., 47
Post-traumatic stress disorder, 95, 97, 98.
       See also mental illness
Prejudice
    against black soldiers, 1–2, 5, 7, 9, 10, 11
    in the military, 17, 18, 34, 57
    in Philadelphia, 6–7, 10, 18, 29
Price, John, 26
Prisoners of War (Confederate), 43, 64

Prisoners of War (Union)
    black soldiers taken as prisoners, 46, 64,
       74, 75
    in Confederate prison camps, 43, 46
    in North Carolina, 86–87, 89
Psychological Disorders. *See* mental illness
Punishments, 16, 17, 52
Purvis, Robert, 6

Q

Quakers (Society of Friends), 2, 10

R

Railroads, 22
    in North Carolina, 86, 87, 89, 92–93
    North Pennsylvania Railroad, 10, 18, 27
    Richmond and Petersburg Railroad, 49
    U.S. Military Railroad, 93
    Weldon Petersburg Railroad, 49
    York River Railroad, 45
Raleigh, N.C., 88
Rapidan River, 48
Redoubt Converse, Va., 49
Religion, 14, 27, 33, 36, 80–81. *See also*
       Chaplains
Republican Party, 33
Richmond, Va., 43, 46, 48, 49, 61
Ridley, Charles, 19–22
Riley, Girard P., 32
Royce, Clark E., 32
Ruff, Charles F., 9

S

Sandwich Islands, 35
Segregation
    in Philadelphia, 6
    on streetcars, 6
Seward, William H., 3
Seymour, Horatio, 2
Sharpshooters, 49, 82, 84
Sheldon, George W., 76
Sheperd, Eli, 16–17
Shepherd's Landing, Va., 47
Sherman, William T., 88
Slavery, 1, 2–4, 26, 89. *See also* Emancipation
Smith, Isaac, 36
Smith, John, 46
Smith, Lydia Hampton, 36
Smith, William F., 48, 52, 55–57
Smithfield, N.C., 89
South Carolina, 4
South Carolina Regiments, First South
       Carolina (African American), 4
South Washington, N.C., 87
Spear, Samuel P., 44
Spencer rifles, 77, 79
Spring Hill, Va., 49–52, 79

Stannard, George J., 77
Stanton, Edwin M., 4, 7, 34
Stearns, George L., 7, 9, 23
Stevens, Thaddeus, 36
Still, William, 6, 18
Streetcars, discrimination and segregation
    in, 6, 18
Substitutes, 17, 34, 90
Sugar Loaf, N.C., 83–84
Supervisory Committee on Enlistment of
    Colored Troops, 10, 11, 26, 28
    Visiting Committee of, 15–16
Surgeons, 20, 34, 69–70

T

Taylor, Charles M., 17
Terry, Alfred H., 82, 88
Texas Brigade, 71, 74–75
Thomas A. Morgan (transport), 47
Thomas Powell (hospital steamer), 95
Training camp for black troops. *See* Camp
    William Penn
Transports, 40, 46–47, 48–49, 69, 82, 93
Trent's Reach, Va., 61
Turner, Henry M., 34
Twelve Mile Ordinary. *See* Burnt Ordinary, Va.
Tyddings, William J., 36

U

Union League of Philadelphia, 7, 10, 11, 17.
    See also Supervisory Committee
Union Volunteer Refreshment Saloon, 29, 31
United States Armies
    Army of the James, 48, 81
    Army of the Potomac, 48, 52, 57
        II Corps, 52, 57
        IX Corps, 59
        X Corps, 48, 52, 57
        XVIII Corps, 48, 52, 57, 69, 76, 79
        XXV Corps, 82
United States Colored Cavalry, 51–52
United States Colored Infantry Regiments
    1st, 34, 55, 91
    3rd, 13, 29
    4th, 40–41, 48, 50, 55, 69, 89, 91
    5th, 40–41, 48, 50, 55, 69, 91
    8th, 28
    13th, 84
    22nd, 41, 46, 55, 91
    37th, 84
United States Colored Infantry, 6th
        Regiment
    burial duty, 58
    in combat
        North Carolina, 83, 84, 86, 87–88
        Virginia, 49–56, 70–79
    daily schedules, 15, 40

drill, 15, 22, 27, 41
    formation of, 13
    letters, 90–92
    marches
        North Carolina, 83, 86, 87, 88, 89
        Virginia, 41, 42, 43, 44–47, 49
    moral character, 16, 81, 85
    morale, 66–67, 80, 90–92
    North Carolina recruits, 92
    occupations, 35–36, 120–28
    origin and characteristics of, 34–35, 100–
        119
    in Philadelphia, 29–31, 93
    as post-war occupation troops, 89
    work on fortifications, 41, 49, 83
    See also Camp William Penn, conscription,
        draftees, Dutch Gap Canal, flags,
        food, New Market Heights, Peters-
        burg, picket duty, substitutes,
        surgeons

V

Vermont troops, 77, 79

W

Wagner, Louis
    on desertion, 19
    dismisses slaveowner, 26
    flag presentation, 23, 26
    grand review, 27–29
    march through Philadelphia, 29
    military experience, 13
    shooting incident, 20–22
Washington, D.C., 89
Weinmann, Philip, 49, 84
Weitzel, Godfrey, 81
Weldon Petersburg Railroad, 93
West Indies, 35
West Point, Va., 47
Wheeler, Joseph, 88
White, Jacob, 23
Whiting, William H.C., 83–84
Wilderness, Battle of the, 48
Williamsburg, Va., 41, 46
Wilmington, N.C., 81, 83, 86, 87, 89, 92
Wilmington and Weldon Railroad, 86, 87,
        88, 93
Wilson, Henry, 28
Wistar, Isaac J., 41, 42, 43, 44

Y

York, Charles V., 32, 75, 76
York River, 47, 48
Yorktown, Va., 40, 41, 43, 46, 47
Yorktown Peninsula, 40, 41–47
Young Men's Christian Association
        (YMCA) of Philadelphia, 14, 27